ALSO BY ROBERT P. JONES

*Progressive and Religious: How Christian,
Jewish, Muslim, and Buddhist Leaders
Are Moving Beyond the Culture Wars and
Transforming American Public Life*

*Liberalism's Troubled Search for Equality:
Religion and Cultural Bias in the Oregon
Physician-Assisted Suicide Debates*

The End

of

White

Christian

America

Robert P. Jones

Simon & Schuster

New York London Toronto Sydney New Delhi

Simon & Schuster
1230 Avenue of the Americas
New York, NY 10020

First Simon & Schuster hardcover edition July 2016

SIMON & SCHUSTER and colophon are
registered trademarks of Simon & Schuster, Inc.

For information about special discounts for bulk purchases,
please contact Simon & Schuster Special Sales
at 1-866-506-1949 or business@simonandschuster.com.

The Simon & Schuster Speakers Bureau can bring authors to your live event.
For more information or to book an event contact the
Simon & Schuster Speakers Bureau at 1-866-248-3049
or visit our website at www.simonspeakers.com.

Interior design by Ruth Lee-Mui
Illustration by Tim Duffy

Manufactured in the United States of America

1   3   5   7   9   10   8   6   4   2

Library of Congress Cataloging-in-Publication Data

Names: Jones, Robert P. (Robert Patrick), author.
Title: The end of White Christian America / Robert P. Jones.
Description: First Simon & Schuster hardcover edition. | New York : Simon&
Schuster, 2016. | Includes bibliographical references and index.
Identifiers: LCCN 2015041178| ISBN 9781501122293 | ISBN 1501122290 | ISBN
9781501122330 (ebook)
Subjects: LCSH: Religion and politics—United States—History. | United
States—History—Religious aspects—Christianity. | United States—Race
relations—History. | Whites—United States—History.
Classification: LCC BL65.P7 J66 2016 | DDC 200.973—dc23 LC record
available at http://lccn.loc.gov/2015041178

ISBN 978-1-5011-2229-3
ISBN 978-1-5011-2233-0 (ebook)

To my parents,
Pat and Cherry Jones

Contents

An Obituary for White Christian America   1

1. Who Is White Christian America?   5

2. Vital Signs: A Divided and Dying White Christian America   45

3. Politics: The End of the White Christian Strategy   79

4. Family: Gay Marriage and White Christian America   111

5. Race: Desegregating White Christian America   147

6. A Eulogy for White Christian America   197

    Acknowledgments   241

    Appendix   245

    Notes   249

    Index   299

The End

of

White

Christian

America

An Obituary for White Christian America

After a long life spanning nearly two hundred and forty years, White Christian America—a prominent cultural force in the nation's history—has died. WCA first began to exhibit troubling symptoms in the 1960s when white mainline Protestant denominations began to shrink, but showed signs of rallying with the rise of the Christian Right in the 1980s. Following the 2004 presidential election, however, it became clear that WCA's powers were failing. Although examiners have not been able to pinpoint the exact time of death, the best evidence suggests that WCA finally succumbed in the latter part of the first decade of the twenty-first century. The cause of death was determined to be a combination of environmental and internal factors—complications stemming from major demographic changes in the country, along with religious disaffiliation as many of its younger members began to doubt WCA's continued relevance in a shifting cultural environment.

Among WCA's many notable achievements was its service to the nation as a cultural touchstone during most of its life. It provided a shared aesthetic, a historical framework, and a moral vocabulary. WCA's vibrancy was historically one of the most prominent features of American public life. While the common cultural ground it offered did not prevent vehement—or even bloody—conflicts from erupting, the lingua franca of WCA gave them a coherent frame.

As the nation was being born, George Washington invoked WCA in his first inaugural address.[1] And when it was being torn apart during the Civil War, WCA provided biblical themes and principles that called the nation back to its highest ideals. Without WCA, neither Abraham Lincoln's second inaugural address nor Martin Luther King, Jr.'s, "Letter from Birmingham Jail" could have been written, let alone understood. Virtually every American president has drawn from WCA's well, particularly during moments of strife.

During its long life, WCA also produced a dizzying array of institutions, from churches to hospitals, social service organizations, and civic organizations such as the Boy Scouts, Girl Scouts, and the YMCA. Beyond these direct functions, WCA also helped incubate and promote the missions of countless independent nongovernmental organizations that met in its facilities and were staffed with its members. Widespread participation in WCA's lay leadership positions served as an important source of social capital for the nation, instilling in participants skills they carried, not only to other civic organizations, but to democratic governance itself.[2]

But WCA has not been without its critics and controversies. Its reputation was especially marred by its general accommodation to and participation in the institution of slavery up until the Civil War. In the late nineteenth and twentieth centuries, WCA's apathy toward—and in some quarters even staunch defense of—segregation in the American South did little to overturn these negative associations. Its credibility was also damaged when it became mired in partisan politics in the closing decades of the twentieth century. Late in its life, WCA also struggled to adequately address issues such as lesbian, gay, bisexual, and transgender (LGBT) rights, which were of particular importance to its younger members, as well as to younger Americans overall.

WCA is survived by two principal branches of descendants: a mainline Protestant family residing primarily in the Northeast and upper Midwest and an evangelical Protestant family living mostly in the South. Plans for a public memorial service have not been announced.

1

Who Is White Christian America?

White Christian America's
Life in Architecture

As visitors ascend to the observation deck of One World Trade Center in New York City, they face three floor-to-ceiling video panels, arranged to mimic the feel of a glass-walled elevator. While the elevator climbs 102 floors in 47 seconds, they watch, in time-lapse video, the visual history of the landscape from their current vantage point. After a view of the undeveloped marshes of Manhattan Island in the early 1500s, the low-rise gabled buildings of Dutch settlers in New Amsterdam appear in the simulated panoramic view. Ships fan out in the harbor during the British colonial period, and familiar bridges and skyscrapers begin to appear as the city expands to fill the horizon in the nineteenth and twentieth centuries.

Most of the media attention to the video has focused on the haunting four-second appearance of the old World Trade Center, with its identifiable pinstriped architecture, before it vanishes as the timeline moves past 2001. But the video also offers viewers a unique perspective on the Protestant church steeples that historically dominated the city's streetscape. Two church buildings—both associated with the Episcopalian Trinity Parish—remain the most notable features of the Manhattan skyline from its early history, holding on to their status as some of the tallest and most recognizable buildings in New York nearly until the dawn of the twentieth century.

As the elevator approaches the 250-foot mark and the time-lapse reaches 1760, St. Paul's Chapel appears in lower Manhattan, towering over the rest of the city. St. Paul's—which survived both the massive New York fire of 1835 and the September 11 terrorist attacks—is the oldest public building in continuous use in New York City and has served as an important civic and religious space for more than 250 years. Following his 1789 inauguration, for example, George Washington attended prayer services at St. Paul's Chapel and regularly appeared there on Sunday mornings. By 1790, Trinity Church was completed a few blocks south of St. Paul's, on Broadway. When Trinity Church was rebuilt and enlarged in 1846, it became the tallest building in New York. Trinity held this distinction until 1890, when a building erected to house one of Joseph Pulitzer's newspapers surpassed it. With his private office in the building's dome, Pulitzer could look down not only at his newspaper competitors but at the city's church steeples as well.

As the elevator continues its climb and the video reaches the 1930s, high-rises mushroom across the skyline, dwarfing the city's houses of worship. Corporate structures like the Chrysler Building and the Empire State Building become New York's defining steeples. The great Episcopal churches' lacy spires may once have marked the hub of the city's social scene, but churches are now eclipsed architecturally and culturally by commercial centers.[1]

A time-lapse panorama of virtually every major American city would tell a similar story. Today, accustomed as we are to monuments to commerce, it is difficult to imagine church steeples as the most common defining characteristics of civic space. It is even harder to imagine the transformation in social consciousness this architectural revolution ignited. Where church spires once stirred citizens to look upward to the heavens, skyscrapers allowed corporate leaders to look down upon churches from their lofty offices. Instead of market transactions happening under the watchful eye of the church, these exchanges literally take place over its head and beyond its reach.[2]

Training the camera on White Christian America's monuments to its own power reveals similar social transformations. White Christian America's story can be read in the changing uses of three iconic structures: the United Methodist Building in Washington, D.C.; the Interchurch Center on New York City's Upper West Side; and the Crystal Cathedral in Garden Grove, California. These buildings, edifices of the white Protestant Christian hope and power that rose and receded over the course of the twentieth century, represent—respectively—the high-water mark of the first wave of white mainline Protestant denominational optimism in the Roaring Twenties, the second wave of white mainline Protestant ecumenism at midcentury, and the third wave of white evangelical Protestant resurgence in the 1980s.[3]

At each building's opening ceremony, white Protestant leaders spoke in prophetic tones about the indispensable place of Christianity in upholding America's moral and political health. Today, though, all of these buildings have a different purpose from their founders' ambitions. Each edifice has adapted—or even been transformed—to reflect the realities of a swiftly changing country. Indeed, through the life of these buildings, we can see the decline of white Protestant dominance amid the steady diversification of the American religious landscape.

The United Methodist Building (Washington, D.C., 1923):
White Mainline Protestant Optimism

PHOTOGRAPH PROVIDED BY UNITED METHODIST CHURCH GENERAL BOARD OF CHURCH AND SOCIETY. USED WITH PERMISSION.

The United Methodist Building (Washington, D.C., 1923)

In 1922, the Methodist Episcopal Church purchased a muddy lot across the street from the U.S. Capitol. Completed in 1923 and dedicated in 1924, the United Methodist Building was conceived by the nation's largest and most prominent Christian denomination as a "sentinel" for Protestant Christian witness and social reform in the nation's capital.[4] The five-story triangular limestone edifice would become the only nongovernment building on Capitol Hill. It towered over Maryland Avenue, its balconies and plate glass windows facing onto the Capitol's plaza. Its opposite side faced the future site of the U.S. Supreme Court Building, which would not be completed until 1935. With a price tag of $650,000—nearly $9 million in 2015 currency—the building was designed in the style of the Italian Renaissance, with a pillared entry hall, a sweeping staircase, and gleaming marble floors.[5]

It was an expensive and imposing project, a building that was self-consciously constructed, as one prominent Methodist bishop declared, to "make our church visible and multiply its power at this world's center." The famed orator and three-time presidential candidate William Jennings Bryan spoke at the building's opening ceremony.[6] A vivid symbol of the era's Protestant optimism—but also its desire to secure its power—the structure represented a hope that Christian social values would meld with ideals of American government. It was also intended to give Protestants an advantage over a growing Catholic population, and Methodists a preeminent place among their Protestant peers.

The architects of the United Methodist Building believed that they were returning the country's government to its natural state of Christian righteousness. Workers broke ground on the foundation at the pinnacle of a decades-long Protestant crusade against a reviled but powerful foe: alcohol. Cries for the outright prohibition of alcohol began in the mid-nineteenth century, but the temperance movement really took off in the 1870s, when Anglo-Saxon Protestant housewives began to band together against the saloons that dominated their communities. Led by a Methodist woman named Eliza Jane Trimble Thompson—later known as "Mother Thompson"—devout Protestant women would publicly shame bar owners by praying, singing, and reading the Bible just outside the doors of any watering hole they could find.[7] One of Thompson's followers, Frances Willard, founded the Women's Christian Temperance Union in 1874, and by the early nineteenth century Protestant pastors—from Baptists to Episcopalians—were tirelessly working within a well-organized network of churches to promote abstinence from alcoholic beverages. Some congregations even began to require their members to formally renounce drinking before they were admitted into the fold.[8]

It was a moment of unusual unity for white Protestant denominations, which were fighting furiously in the early years of the twentieth century over the extent to which Christianity could be compatible with the past century of scientific innovation. The struggle for temperance provided an important—albeit fragile—common cause where most Protestants could agree that adherence to a particular kind of Christian morality would lead the country down the path of righteousness. The Methodists were at the center of this crusade, even devoting two full-time clergy to the cause. At one rally in 1915, Dr. Clarence True Wilson, a bespectacled Methodist pastor and fierce evangelist for prohibition, declared that one of the "pillars" of Christian civilization was "sobriety of the people."[9] Their work paid off in 1920 when the Eighteenth Amendment, which prohibited the sale, transport, and production of alcohol, was ratified by the states.

That same year, the Methodist Episcopal Church's General Conference endorsed the construction of a new building, to be overseen by its Board of Temperance, Prohibition, and Public Morals. This was to become the United Methodist Building, a structure that the committee hoped would "offer a center for . . . Protestant activities in Washington" and allow Methodist leaders to "watch the currents of government and promote the reforms now throbbing for expression at the convictions of the people."[10]

From the beginning, the United Methodist Building was imagined as a place where Christian faith and American politics could mingle, bolstering the country's commitment to Protestant moral values in an increasingly uncertain world. Pastor Wilson, whose wife helped with the architectural plans, became intimately involved with the day-to-day operation of the building after its doors opened in 1924.[11] Office space on Capitol Hill was in short supply, and Wilson hoped that senators and Supreme Court justices would rent apartments on the floors above the Methodist Church's office space, ensuring that power brokers and Christian leaders would brush shoulders throughout the day.[12]

The feeling that Protestants needed a firm foothold in the heart of American political life was strong enough, even for everyday people in the pews, that it formed the backbone of fundraising appeals. The pledge cards from ordinary Methodists whose donations paid for the building's marble columns were all embossed with the same goal: "to establish a Protestant presence on Capitol Hill."[13] The building was, plainly speaking, a platform for stamping federal legislation with Protestant morality, for leveraging the power of politics to usher in the kingdom of God on earth.

Those who signed the pledges were animated by a sense of proud triumphalism and a palpable expectation that the world could be on the verge of a golden age guided by Protestant Christian values. Prohibition had passed because of nearly a century of Christian agitation, and now the country was on a path to righteousness. Wilson, on his speaking tours in the early years of Prohibition, declared that America was finally returning to its Christian foundation. The public tide against Prohibition began to turn before the ink had dried on the Eighteenth Amendment, but Wilson continued to defend the ban on alcohol as the "greatest moral triumph of Christianity in a century."[14]

But this extravagant building and brash rhetoric also betrayed an undercurrent of anxiety. Why, after all, was it necessary to have an expensive, imposing building on Capitol Hill if Protestant Christianity was truly the country's guiding compass? The truth was, Protestant leaders' power had already begun to wane, even as they cheered Christianity's victory against "demon rum." Just sixteen years earlier, in 1907, Methodist leaders had exercised a more formidable form of informal power. They held a small conference in Washington, D.C., to draft a statement of fundamental moral principles, most of which centered on fair labor practices. U.S. Vice President Charles Fairbanks attended the conference and was so impressed by the document that he invited the five principal drafters to present them to President Theodore Roosevelt over breakfast at the White House.[15]

By the Roaring Twenties, however, Protestant leaders were in a more precarious position. The growth of powerful national corporations gave business leaders unprecedented economic power and access to political leaders. Fractured internally by infighting over issues like the teaching of evolution in public schools, Protestant leaders were also acutely aware of the threat posed by the growing influence of the Catholic Church.

It is perhaps not a coincidence that the United Methodist Building was inaugurated in a period of intense anti-Catholic sentiment. The temperance movement had always been tinged with a strong anti-Catholic flavor. Stereotypes of the drunken, lazy Irish immigrant fed currents of anxiety that uncontrollable aliens were subverting the morally upright, abstinent impulses of American society. Well into the twentieth century, Protestant critics accused the Catholic Church of debasing Christianity, encouraging ignorance and superstition among its members, and stifling religious freedom and democratic citizenship through blind obedience to the pope and his U.S. deputies, local Catholic bishops and priests. But by the 1920s, thanks to rapid population growth, Roman

Catholicism's influence could no longer be ignored—hence the need for an assertive "Protestant presence" in the nation's capital. The building's role as "sentinel" had a double meaning—both to keep a watchful eye on congressional activity and to warn against potential Catholic encroachment.

For the first few years of its existence, the building's caretakers felt that they were on the path to success. There was an abundance of tenants, including a handful of senators, and thanks to the rental income, the building was turning a profit. The dining room, where politicians and staff could eat during the day, was always overflowing with visitors. Two months after Black Tuesday—when the stock market crashed in 1929, plunging the country into the Great Depression—the board of the United Methodist Building was planning a costly expansion, adding apartments that could hold an additional three dozen tenants.[16]

But the country's economic doldrums—and a rising backlash against the Eighteenth Amendment—soon cast a shadow over the Methodist Church's glorious experiment. Rents were down across Washington by 1930, and it was a struggle to keep the building even half full.[17] Meanwhile, other Protestants began to criticize the denomination. In an editorial published in early 1931, the editors of *The Christian Century*, the flagship mainline Protestant magazine, shook their fingers at the Methodists' unilateral incursion into political affairs, which they saw as undermining a broad Protestant voice. "Does the Methodist Church, as such, desire to bring direct denominational pressure to bear upon the national government?" they wrote. "Any such concentration of ecclesiastical officialism at the nation's capital goes against the instinct of American Protestantism. . . . In the interest of our common Protestantism, we believe that the wedge which Methodism has unwittingly started to drive into American democracy should be withdrawn by the removal of [its] headquarters . . . from the capital city."[18] By the close of 1933, the harshest blow had been struck: the states ratified the Twenty-first Amendment, ending Prohibition.

The passage of the Twenty-first Amendment was an undisputable confirmation of Protestant leaders' loss of political power, and the United Methodist Building never achieved the status of its founders' dreams. Instead of building insider clout for Methodist leaders, the building slowly morphed into first an ecumenical, then an interfaith, gathering place. The fight for temperance persisted well into the 1950s, with Methodist leaders continuing to enthusiastically lobby Congress for restrictions on alcohol and tobacco, but even that emphasis began to fade. Increasingly, the inhabitants of the building championed a broader set of peace and equality issues. In the 1960s, the United Methodist Building was a gathering place for groups and agencies demonstrating for civil rights and protesting the Vietnam War; a decade later, supporters of the Equal Rights Amendment used the building as a center for their activities.

Today, as they approach the building's hundredth anniversary, the stewards of the United Methodist Building say their charge has expanded. Rather than sticking to the original mission—to be a "Protestant presence" on Capitol Hill—they have rented office space to a wide array of faith-based organizations, including the Islamic Society of North America, Catholic Relief Services, and the General Conference of Seventh-Day Adventists. Susan Henry-Crowe, the general secretary of the United Methodist Church's Board of Church and Society, which runs the building, says that the task now is to be an inclusive religious voice for justice. "I think this building has the potential to help animate and articulate a voice for lots and lots of minorities, which is really important." Instead of representing vested and powerful faith traditions within white Protestant Christianity, Henry-Crowe wants the United

Methodist Church to leverage its infrastructure to augment the voices of religious communities who lack political or cultural clout.[19]

The Interchurch Center (New York City, 1960): White Mainline Protestant Ecumenism

PHOTOGRAPH BY DION SUJATMIKO. USED WITH PERMISSION.

The Interchurch Center (New York City, 1960),
with Riverside Church in background

On a Sunday afternoon in October 1958, thirty thousand people gathered in the shadow of a partially completed nineteen-story steel skeleton overlooking the Hudson River to watch President Dwight D. Eisenhower lay the cornerstone for the Interchurch Center in New York City's Morningside Heights neighborhood. Using a new silver trowel, Eisenhower mortared a marble stone from the agora in Corinth, Greece—where the New Testament records the Apostle Paul once preached—into a two-ton block of Alabama limestone. The cornerstone, he declared, symbolized "a prime support of our faith—the Truth that sets men free." [20]

Behind Eisenhower, on a blue-and-white-draped podium, sat a wide array of ceremonial speakers, including David Rockefeller, whose father, John D. Rockefeller, Jr., had provided the site for the center and given $2.65 million toward the $20 million building. In the audience before them, large colorful banners representing thirty-seven Protestant and Eastern Orthodox Christian denominations bobbed against the sky, among a throng of robed clergy and academics that the historian James F. Findlay, Jr., described as a "Who's Who of American Protestantism." Speaking just before the president took the podium, the Methodist pastor Ralph Sockman outlined the building's lofty mission. "The 2500 occupants of this building will not only at times worship together but they will work together for common objectives," he declared. "And it is by working together that we best develop 'the unity of the Spirit in the bond of peace.' We hold endless discussions of racial problems and church unity. It would be far better if we stopped talking so much about these problems and got together as races and churches to tackle together our common problems such as moral laxity, juvenile delinquency, and the dangers of war." [21] It was an extravagant celebration to inaugurate a building that its founders called "the nearest thing to a Protestant-Orthodox 'Vatican' that the modern world would ever see." [22]

While the United Methodist Building was an expression of a single Protestant denomination's influence and aspirations, by the 1950s it was clear that Protestant national influence could be maintained only by cooperative endeavors. The dedication of the Interchurch Center represented the apex of a new Protestant enthusiasm for ecumenical unity; while its animating core was clearly white Protestantism, it was notable that the ecumenical vision extended to include some Eastern Orthodox and even some historically African American denominations. The building was such an important symbol of this movement that it was included in an exhibit at the 1964 New York World's Fair, and more than ten thousand postcards featuring the building were sold in its opening year. The building was connected to another Rockefeller-funded religious institution, Riverside Church, by an underground pedestrian tunnel. Just a stone's throw away from Union Theological Seminary, mainline Protestantism's most prestigious school, and not far from the Episcopal Cathedral of St. John the Divine, it was intended to embody a bold experiment in Protestant Christian cooperation and scholarship.[23]

Through the middle of the twentieth century, the more liberal, predominantly northern, and wealthier Protestant denominations behind this ecumenical project developed into what came to be known as "mainline" Protestantism. These influential denominations became the public face of Protestant Christianity, most prominently through the National Council of Churches, which formed in 1950, and its predecessor organization, the Federal Council of Churches. The idea behind the new federation—which included thirty Protestant denominations—was that Christian work would be more effective if large numbers of churches could rally behind a single mission. In a memo urging John D. Rockefeller, Jr., to donate the plot of land that eventually became the Interchurch Center, National Council of Churches leaders wrote, "For over 30 years, Protestant leaders have voiced the hope that the major denominational organizations, as a tangible expression of their basic religious unity and common faith, might work together physically in close fellowship."[24] Housing all of these religious entities in a single structure would help create this physical sense of unity.

In 1948, before the National Council of Churches was formally established, the goal was to create what the original articles of incorporation described as a "Protestant Center." This goal was in keeping with the general sense among mainline Protestants that the chief threats facing their cause were secularism and Roman Catholicism. But as the early NCC tent broadened to include Eastern Orthodox Churches—who also had viewed Roman Catholicism as a competitor since the denominations broke apart nine hundred years earlier—Charles Raphael, a Greek Orthodox layman and lawyer, suggested that the name be changed to the "Interchurch Center."[25] The switch was officially made in 1956 ahead of the 1957 groundbreaking ceremonies. According to Francis Stuart Harmon, one of the center's chief promoters, it reflected a "top priority in ecumenical strategy" by officially including Eastern Orthodox churches under the banner of Christian unity. "The Easterners traced the origins of their historic churches back to the apostles and the missionary journeys of St. Paul," Harmon wrote. "Certainly any name chosen for our project should be acceptable to that community."[26] The Catholic Church—which of course also traces its origins back to the apostles—was notably absent; as the Interchurch Center's own historical account notes, it "was not even considered as a partner to ecumenical initiatives."[27]

At the Interchurch Center's official dedication ceremony, visitors were invited to wander through a corridor lined with documents related to American religious freedom. After gazing at a display dedicated to "the basic theme that it is faith in God and understanding of his laws which provide sanction for human freedom," exhibit goers would walk past panels showing early American documents that guaranteed religious liberty, ending with a display case showing the evolution of "In God We Trust" on American money.[28] The point was clear: America was a pluralistic but fundamentally religious country, and the Protestant-led ecumenical movement—with its powerful symbolic incarnation in the Interchurch Center—was positioning itself to be the official voice of American religiosity.

But the vision of the Interchurch Center was almost immediately outstripped by reality. Already, in its first decade, the building proved difficult to fill with tenants. In 1960, part of the center was taken up by one of NASA's computer operations; neighboring Columbia University also rented office space. Efforts to engage the local community met with limited success: the center hosted a series of meetings and symposia, operated its own choir, and held daily church services, which were discontinued in 1970, due to sparse attendance. The building burst into the news again in 1969 because of the actions of one of its tenants. James Forman, a black militant activist, made headlines when he interrupted a formal Sunday morning service at Riverside Church to read aloud his "Black Manifesto," which demanded $500 million in reparation payments from the NCC and affiliates for black economic development.[29] The New York Supreme Court eventually barred Forman from the building, but not before half of the two thousand employees who worked in the Interchurch Center stayed home from work for a day in solidarity with his demands.[30]

By the 1980s, when the thirty-year leases signed in 1959 began to come up for renewal, the center was losing some of its most important tenants. In 1983, after the northern and southern branches of the Presbyterian Church decided to merge into one entity, the northern arm announced that it would move its headquarters out of the Interchurch Center, where it had occupied 163,000 square feet of office space.[31] The departure left the center with one third of its rentable space untenanted, a dramatic financial blow. But filling the empty offices wasn't the only problem: the building's ratio of secular to church-related agencies had never exceeded 25 percent. If religious tenants couldn't be found to replace the Presbyterian Church, the center's status as a hub of faithful activity could be severely curtailed.

The truth was that the longed-for spirit of ecumenical activity had never fully materialized, even when the building was new. For example, the NCC's administration failed even in their attempts to convince the tenants to create a building-wide phone system. Over time, the desire for denominational self-sufficiency—and the growing sense that New York City was the home of an elite East Coast liberal establishment that had little to do with ordinary Americans—overpowered the ecumenical dream. Christian unity was ultimately overshadowed by more basic concerns about keeping churchgoers in their pews.

In 2013, the National Council of Churches—the organization that had first pushed for the creation of an ecumenical Christian center— announced that it was moving out of the Interchurch Center as part of a larger effort to consolidate operations. The reasoning was, in part, financial: the move was accompanied by staff downsizing, and leaving the Interchurch Center would save the organization nearly half a million dollars a year. But the departure was also symbolic. In a statement announcing the closure, NCC president Kathryn Lohre admitted, "This consolidation will free us from the infrastructure of a bygone era, enabling us to witness more boldly to our visible unity in Christ, and work for justice and peace in today's rapidly changing ecclesial, ecumenical and inter-religious world."[32]

Today, the building's tenants are a hodgepodge of Protestant and ecumenical organizations, interfaith groups, and secular nonprofits—including a bicycling advocacy group, nonreligious educational organizations, and several Alcoholics Anonymous affiliates. Only about one third have missions related to the Protestant or ecumenical movement, another third could be characterized as either Jewish or interfaith organizations, and the final third of the building's tenants have missions unrelated to religion.[33] Its advocates' lofty vision of a center for Christian collaboration and growth, birthed at the height of Protestantism's cultural and political power, never materialized. Like the United Methodist Building, its current executive director, Paula Mayo, notes that although its name has not changed, the Interchurch Center has expanded its mission to include organizations working on "community development, educational initiatives and inter-cultural and religious exchange."[34]

The Crystal Cathedral (Garden Grove, California, 1980): White Evangelical Protestant Resurgence

On May 17, 1980, *The New York Times* published a glowing account of the consecration of the Crystal Cathedral, a spectacular new evangelical church in Orange County, California. "Beverly Sills sang, Frank Sinatra sent his congratulations, and church public relations agents declared that some people were already calling it 'the most important religious structure to be built since the Cathedral de Notre Dame de Paris,'" the reporter gushed.[35] The vast and glittering structure, sheathed in more than ten thousand panes of glass, seated nearly three thousand people. The cathedral was home to Dr. Robert Schuller, one of the nation's first television evangelists, whose *Hour of Power* service was broadcast on TV and radio stations across the country.

The Crystal Cathedral was one of the first megachurches to emerge

The Crystal Cathedral (Garden Grove, California, 1980)

from the revival of charismatic white evangelical Protestantism in the late 1970s, when white evangelical Protestants helped to sweep Ronald Reagan into office, demanding a return to traditional American and explicitly Christian values. To many—including the mainstream media and even mainline Protestant leaders themselves—the evangelical expression of White Christian America seemed to burst suddenly onto the scene. But while mainline Protestants were pursuing their ecumenical project, evangelicals were establishing rival institutions to compete for control of White Christian America. Instead of emphasizing ecumenical and even interreligious coordination, social justice, and international cooperation, they emphasized conservative doctrinal orthodoxy, personal salvation, and a call for the United States to become an explicitly Christian nation with a divinely favored mission in the world.[36] And as mainline Protestants began to lose their power, the evangelical wing of

White Christian America was poised to fill the vacuum, not only with growing churches but with a sophisticated communications network that brought their vision of Protestantism into American living rooms. The Crystal Cathedral was an early expression of this evangelical resurgence.

For all of its pomp and pizzazz, the Crystal Cathedral's origins were humble. In 1955, Schuller opened the Garden Grove Community Church, where—clad in a suit and tie—he would deliver sermons from the roof of a drive-in snack bar while his wife played the organ. "Churchgoers" parked in cars below would listen through the drive-in speakers and honk their horns instead of saying "amen." [37]

In the early years of his ministry, Schuller evangelized in the community around him by knocking on thousands of doors. A savvy marketer, Schuller asked his early parishioners to drive in separate cars, so the lot would look fuller. [38] After just two years, Sunday morning services were packed. In 1957, when Schuller invited Dr. Norman Vincent Peale, a popular proponent of Christian "positive thinking," to speak at Garden Grove, the masses of people who flocked to the service caused a traffic jam on Interstate 5. [39] Schuller's devotion to Peale's style of ministry—which emphasized making people feel good about themselves rather than "teaching" or "converting" them—proved to be a wild success. "I decided to adopt the spirit, style, strategy and substance of a 'therapist' in the pulpit," he remembered later. [40] It was the foundation for the "theology of self-esteem" that transformed Schuller into one of the most influential Christian pastors of the late twentieth century.

Schuller was one of the pioneers of a new conservative Christian trend that explicitly tied Christian worship to consumer culture. Calling his church a "shopping center for God," he marketed his vision to the prosperous, suburban white Christians who were thronging to southern

California.[41] In the early 1960s, he hired the famed architect Richard Neutra to build his first Garden Grove church. This gleaming, modernist predecessor to the Crystal Cathedral gave congregants a choice: they could sit inside the long, low, flat-roofed church, or they could park their cars outside and listen to the sermon on the radio. The church was designed with huge, movable glass walls so that Schuller could press a button in the pulpit and step out onto a balcony to address the parking lot directly, full of the cars that Schuller affectionately called "the pews from Detroit."[42] In 1967, with his congregation approaching five thousand, Schuller expanded again, building a thirteen-story "Tower of Hope" topped with a ninety-foot neon cross. The building was, in the words of architectural historian Thomas Hines, "more prominent than anything on the Orange County landscape except the nearby 'Matterhorn' at Disneyland."[43]

Around the time the Tower of Hope was built, Schuller began to tap into the promise of media evangelism. Inspired by Billy Graham's visit to Los Angeles in 1969, when the famed evangelist held a ten-day "crusade" in the Anaheim Stadium with nearly 400,000 attendees, Schuller launched the *Hour of Power* in February 1970, a taped version of his service that was first broadcast on a local TV station. The show—which quickly catapulted him into the national spotlight—featured interviews with celebrities like Mickey Rooney, Charlton Heston, and Ray Kroc, the founder of McDonald's. In all of his "episodes," Schuller presented a sunny, celebrity-infused theology in which accepting Christ was the first step toward personal self-fulfillment. He was the precursor of today's "prosperity gospel" ministers, men like Houston's Joel Osteen, who preach that God favors the faithful with material wealth and success. It was a message that Christians were ready to hear: By 1976, Schuller had eight thousand members in his Garden Grove congregation, and his shows had a weekly viewership of three million. By 1978, he was ranked as one of the twenty most influential religious figures in the nation.[44]

Riding this wave of popularity, Schuller turned his attention to an even more ambitious project: the Crystal Cathedral. With the help of professional fundraisers and a million-dollar gift from two wealthy congregants, he approved the $19.5 million design by postmodernist architect Philip Johnson for a soaring structure shaped like a four-pointed Bethlehem star. Like his Garden Grove church, the Crystal Cathedral featured two ninety-foot doors that would open during services to include the people sitting outside in their cars. Inside was one of the world's largest organs, with more than sixteen thousand pipes. A reflecting pool ran the length of the main aisles, decorated on either side with ferns and potted plants. Instead of pews, worshippers would sit in folding, padded theater seats. At its opening, *Newsweek* dubbed the Crystal Cathedral "one of the most spectacular religious edifices in the world."[45]

Schuller took this visually stunning space and used it to stage extravagant religious spectacles. The annual "Glory of Easter" and "Glory of Christmas" pageants featured professional casts of actors, a full orchestra, Hollywood-grade costumes, and live animals like peacocks, donkeys, and camels. Angels would fly high above the audience's heads and descend at speeds of more than twenty miles per hour. The performances would even include special effects like thunder, lightning, and earthquakes.[46]

Schuller's success was made possible by the booming suburbanization of Orange County, which began in the 1950s and grew through the 1980s. After Walt Disney opened his first theme park, Disneyland, just five miles from Garden Grove in 1955, the area began to transform from a sleepy backwater to one of California's most desirable destinations. The residents who flocked to live in the region's newly built subdivisions were nearly uniformly wealthy, white, Protestant, and politically conservative. Orange County was ripe for a white Christian conservative awakening.[47]

When he opened the Crystal Cathedral in 1980, Schuller was one of a handful of high-profile conservative Christian preachers who were transforming the face of American evangelicalism. Some of Schuller's peers were overtly political, casting their lot with the Republican Party and mobilizing their followers against issues like gay rights, women's rights, and abortion. But Schuller's message was a subtler conservatism, a pro-family ethos that revolved around an axis of personal success, echoing broader Republican economic messages about the evils of dependency and government handouts without specifically endorsing policies or candidates. Failure, he told his congregation, was a matter of personal choice. This was a message that appealed to the white, upwardly mobile, suburban Christians who gathered on Sundays in his sparkling cathedral, or tuned in to watch the *Hour of Power*. The appeal of megachurches like Schuller's was simple—they validated and encouraged a powerful trifecta of material success, personal growth and fulfillment, and political conservatism. Schuller's theology was contained in his Possibility Thinker's Creed: "When faced with a mountain I will not quit. I will keep on striving until I climb over, find a pass through, tunnel underneath, or simply stay and turn the mountain into a gold mine! With God's help!"[48]

Schuller's ministry was in the vanguard of the megachurch movement, a powerful new force in White Christian America's life. In 1970, there were only ten of these religious hubs—each with at least two thousand members—in the United States. By 1990, there were five hundred, and by 2005, there were fifteen hundred. By 2011 the rate of growth had slowed, but the number of megachurches continued to increase to more than sixteen hundred. While only about 10 percent of Americans attend megachurches, they continue to be a robust expression of evangelical Christianity in the country, particularly in their local communities.[49] The parishioners who fill the padded seats in the average megachurches are 82 percent white and overwhelmingly evangelical in their theological orientation. Today, these churches are religious goliaths, with an average annual budget of nearly $6 million. Estimates show that 85 percent are located in the suburbs outside major cities. Many feature satellite campuses, where services from the main church are streamed through huge television screens, creating competition for small, rural churches. Like Schuller, who was one of the architects of church-as-entertainment, most megachurch services incorporate drums, rock music, and high-tech visual displays to draw in their congregants. They also emphasize self-help and optimism in the face of struggle as central features of Christian life. The title of one of Schuller's books, *Turning Hurts into Halos*, could be a mantra for the entire movement.[50]

But if demographics had set Schuller on a swift path to success, the shifting regional profile of Orange County set the stage for his downfall. Beginning in the 1970s and 1980s, immigrants from Central America and South Asia began to move into the region, creating a demand for Catholic parishes, Buddhist temples, and Islamic mosques. Today, Orange County is home to the country's third-largest concentration of Asian Americans, thanks to a growth rate of 41 percent between 2000 and 2009. During that same period, whites lost their majority status in the county, their percentage declining by 9 points in less than a decade.[51]

By the time Robert Schuller stepped down as lead pastor of the Crystal Cathedral in 2006, the church was already beginning to lose membership. But under the leadership of Schuller's son, Robert Jr., the evangelical empire began to unravel swiftly. The church was deeply in debt, thanks to the building of the $40 million International Center for Possibility Thinking in the early 2000s, a 58,000-square-foot "welcome center" for visitors to the Garden Grove campus. A bitter family feud among Schuller's children forced Robert Jr. out within two years, leaving Schuller's daughters and their husbands to try to come up with solutions to the church's increasingly dire financial difficulties. By the time Sheila Schuller Coleman took over in 2010, the Crystal Cathedral's mortgage was $21 million and the church had a budget shortfall of $55 million. Meanwhile, the congregation was hemorrhaging members, raising questions about how the Schullers could continue to maintain such a lavish and expensive campus. Volunteers—instead of paid gardeners—tended the Crystal Cathedral's forty lush green acres, and the yearly window washings of the church's ten thousand glass panels were canceled.[52] But even these cutbacks couldn't heal the Schullers' financial wounds, and by the end of 2010, the Crystal Cathedral had filed for Chapter 11 bankruptcy.[53] In 2012, the Roman Catholic Diocese of Orange County bought the Crystal Cathedral for $57.5 million.[54]

As the Diocese of Orange County began to embark on renovations of the space—soon to be home to the area's 1.3 million Catholics—it renamed the building Christ Cathedral, officially marking the end of one of the most prominent expressions of white evangelical Protestant vitality.[55] The demographic differences between the two congregations couldn't have been starker. Schuller's church—with ten thousand members at its peak—had been predominantly white, while Christ Cathedral would draw from a Catholic population so large and ethnically diverse that Christ Cathedral held multiple daily masses in English, Spanish, and Vietnamese.[56]

In October 2014, six months before Robert Schuller's death, nuns in white habits and priests in long purple robes led the first Catholic mass in the church next door to the cathedral.[57] Inside the cathedral, Schuller's sanctuary was being torn apart and rebuilt, his pulpit replaced with an altar and a bishop's seat. Instead of light pouring onto congregants, the renovation plans included tall walls that would direct churchgoers' attention toward the priest and the central altar. "What we have to do is transform a space that was designed for the liturgy of the word in a TV studio environment," the diocese's liturgical consultant explained in a promotional video.[58] At an early mass held at the new campus, one Catholic parishioner told the *Los Angeles Times*, "We don't like to leave the old place, but look at this new place! And look at all the people together, for the same reason. *Es un milagro* [It is a miracle]."[59] Schuller's evangelical Protestant vision, dependent on the demographic strength of White Christian America, had been decisively eclipsed by the twenty-first century's wave of multiethnic Catholicism.

From Monuments to Memorials

Great buildings are symbolic expressions of power, capturing within their structures the aspirations and concerns of their builders in a particular historical moment. Each of these three historic buildings tells an important part of the story of White Christian America's rise and decline. Over the last half century, the United Methodist Church and even the National Council of Churches have been culturally disarmed, and Schuller's ministry has been completely bankrupted. Built as monuments to Protestant power, they ultimately became memorials to a White Christian America that never realized its aspirations.

But each in different ways has also become a harbinger of the new religious America and the place of white Protestants within it. The Methodist Board of Church and Society has altered its original mission and is using its considerable remaining assets to give a home and a voice to groups that just a generation ago would have been seen as fringe groups or even threats to white Protestant power: Muslims, Catholics, Seventh-Day Adventists, and others. The Interchurch Center, with the loss of its flagship tenants, has followed suit, expanding its scope well beyond its name to include Jewish groups, a Catholic magazine, interfaith groups, and community development and educational organizations. The building's transformation is mirrored in one of its largest new tenants, Auburn Seminary. Founded more than 150 years ago as a Presbyterian seminary, Auburn has transformed itself into a broad interfaith institution working across religious lines on a range of social justice issues. Finally, the white evangelical Protestant Crystal Cathedral has been rechristened as a multicultural Catholic parish. Each of these transformations marks a phase in the demise of White Christian America and highlights the realities of the new religious landscape. While the descendants of White Christian America still wield considerable financial assets and cultural influence, their future import will depend less on imposing presences than on strategic partnerships and alliances.

Understanding White Christian America

A Primer

What is "White Christian America"? It's related to the term "WASP" (White Anglo-Saxon Protestant), which is often used to describe the country's traditional cultural and religious core. Like WASP, White Christian America traces its roots to northern Europe, and its religious character is historically Protestant. But it is broader than "WASP." First, it goes beyond northern mainline Protestantism to include southern evangelical Protestantism. Second, White Christian America is a more inclusive and neutral term than WASP, describing the view as it appears from within.

Throughout the book, I use the term White Christian America to describe the domain of white *Protestants* in America. In the twentieth century, White Christian America developed along two main branches: a more liberal mainline Protestant America headquartered in New England and the upper Midwest/Great Lakes region and a more conservative evangelical Protestant America anchored in the South and lower Midwest/Ozark Mountains region. Geography is the most visible but also the most superficial division between the two groups. Historically, they were also marked by differences in social class and by their perspectives on race relations in the wake of the Civil War and Reconstruction. Their differences are rooted in disagreements over fundamental tenets of theology, approaches to diversity, and accommodations to the modern world and science.

In the early 1920s, a Protestant denominational controversy burst onto the national stage with such drama that a writer for the *New York Evening Post* declared that it was "getting to be more interesting to go to church than to stay at home and read newspapers."[60] The three major Protestant denominations—Baptists, Methodists, and Presbyterians— had already suffered schisms along North-South lines before the Civil War. Now two factions, known as Fundamentalists and Modernists, were furiously debating the extent to which Christianity could be compatible with the past century of scientific innovation.

Many Protestants had already begun, by the mid-nineteenth century, to adjust their faith to greet the modern world. The emerging genre of biblical criticism—which treated the Bible not as divine revelation but as a historical document created by people in a particular moment—grew in prominence alongside new scientific theories like evolution. These Modernists welcomed the new scholarship, even when it challenged traditional conceptions of their faith. They adapted their notion of the creation of the world to incorporate Darwinism, a model that was called "theistic evolution." They pushed to include evolution in the science curricula of the country's newly forming public school system, arguing that children should be armed with all available scientific knowledge.

Protestant Fundamentalists were horrified by these concessions. Responding to biblical criticism and the theory of evolution, Fundamentalists emphasized the Bible's truth and authority, prophesying a literal second coming where Jesus would descend physically from heaven.[61] They argued that allowing evolution to be taught in schools would lead to a denial of Christian doctrine, destroying America's moral and spiritual core. Curtis Lee Laws, the editor of a widely distributed Baptist periodical and the person credited with coining the term "Fundamentalist" in 1920, defined their response as "a protest against that rationalistic interpretation of Christianity which seeks to discredit supernaturalism."[62] By the end of the 1920s, twenty-three states had debated some kind of measure to restrict or outlaw evolution in the schools, although only three states—Tennessee, Mississippi, and Arkansas—ultimately voted to make the teaching of evolution a crime.

The 1925 Scopes "Monkey Trial" was the high-water mark of this debate. John Scopes, a Tennessee schoolteacher, had broken state law by teaching evolution. Clarence Darrow, a humanist and member of the American Civil Liberties Union, defended Scopes, while William Jennings Bryan, a Presbyterian former presidential candidate and one of the most famous orators of his day, stepped in to prosecute the young educator. Over nine hot days in Dayton, Tennessee, Darrow and Bryan sparred over the inerrancy of the Bible and parents' rights to dictate what their children would be taught in the public schools. Bryan, who had made his name by defending the Populist wing of the Democratic Party at the turn of the twentieth century, characterized the Modernists as a cabal of intellectual elitists who were trying to tear religion out of the hands of the people.

Scopes lost—a surprise to no one—but the massive press corps that had sent two million words of copy about the trial back to their home newspapers and magazines excoriated Bryan, who made an infamous attempt to scientifically defend the literal account of creation in the Book of Genesis as part of the trial. "Darrow has lost this case," wrote the journalist H. L. Mencken, who was the first to refer to the unfolding events in Dayton as the "monkey trial." "But it seems to me that he has nevertheless performed a great public service by fighting it to a finish and in a perfectly serious way. . . . It serves notice on the country that Neanderthal man is organizing in these forlorn backwaters of the land, led by a fanatic, rid of sense and devoid of conscience."[63] Bryan, victorious yet defeated, died in Dayton within a week of the trial's close.

The gaping wound between Modernists and Fundamentalists proved impossible to heal. While fights over theological doctrine and church authority had been a familiar part of white Protestant life throughout its nearly four-hundred-year history, the Modernist/Fundamentalist controversy exposed deep epistemological fault lines, with those who came to be known as mainline Protestants embracing modernism and evangelical Protestants championing the fundamentalist outlook. Historian David A. Hollinger called this struggle the "Protestant dialectic, within which the two great rivals for control of the symbolic capital of Christianity defined themselves in terms of each other."[64] Historian Martin

Marty, in his three-volume history of American religion, also noted the significance of this rift, tracing the beginning of White Christian America's downfall to the 1920s. "Whoever asked the question, 'Will America remain Protestant and Anglo-Saxon?' now had to ask, 'Which *kind* of Protestant?'" he wrote. This divide left what remained of the Protestant establishment "ever less prepared to hold its place of dominance in American culture in the decades to come."[65]

Until its high-water mark in the mid-1960s, around the time New York's Interchurch Center was built, the wealthier and more socially influential mainline Protestant branch of White Christian America was its most visible manifestation at the national level. At the beginning of the twentieth century, white mainline Protestants believed that they were on the verge of "The Christian Century." In the last hundred years of the millennium, they predicted, Christian principles would finally begin to shape national policy and world events. Heady with confidence, they emblazoned the name on the masthead of a magazine launched just before 1900. *The Christian Century* grew to become mainline Protestantism's flagship magazine, a force not only among white mainline Protestants but also in elite political and business circles. In 1908, thirty-two denominations joined together to form the Federal Council of Churches (FCC), which grew into the National Council of Churches in 1950.

Council leaders racked up impressive accomplishments and accolades. They played an important role in the formation of the United Nations, including adding the historic amendment that called for an international declaration of human rights. Presidents Harry S. Truman and Dwight D. Eisenhower were especially attentive to their work—one of their own, John Foster Dulles, chaired the U.N. committee of the FCC and later was appointed secretary of state by Eisenhower. *Time* magazine—headed by Henry R. Luce, son of Presbyterian missionaries to China—frequently featured the FCC's leaders in its pages and on its cover. And prominent members received international recognition for their work in building its impressive institutions; Methodist lay leader John R. Mott, for example, received the Nobel Peace Prize in 1946 for his leadership of the YMCA and foreign missions work.[66]

During the decades in the middle of the twentieth century, mainline Protestants wielded influence not only through these official bodies but also via individual members who carried their values and their agenda into the halls of power. Hollinger summarized the cultural dominance of white mainline Protestants this way:

> Persons at least nominally affiliated with these denominations controlled all branches of the federal government and most of the business world, as well as the nation's chief cultural and educational institutions, and countless state and local institutions. If you were in charge of something big before 1960, chances are you grew up in a white Protestant milieu.[67]

By the last few decades of the twentieth century, however, after the best efforts of a well-funded ecumenical movement failed to unite the mainline Protestant denominations, the northern arm of White Christian America began to lose both its influence and its membership.

Overshadowed on the national stage up through the 1960s, and without the wealth and social connections of their mainline cousins, white evangelical Protestants nonetheless built a formidable set of institutions. And as the mainline Protestant world weakened—in part because of evangelical challenges to it—evangelical Protestants were well positioned to promote an alternative Protestant Christian worldview, becoming the new face of White Christian America.

White evangelical leaders founded the National Association of Evangelicals (NAE) in 1942 as a direct challenge to the Federal Council of Churches. In 1947, to compete with the mainline Protestant's flagship Union Theological Seminary, evangelicals founded Fuller Theological Seminary in Pasadena, California, as a cross-denominational training ground for evangelical ministers. In 1956, to counter the influence of *The Christian Century*, L. Nelson Bell, known as an aggressive fundamentalist and segregationist, founded *Christianity Today*. To do so, he leveraged the reputation of his famous son-in-law Reverend Billy Graham and the wealth of Sun Oil magnate J. Howard Pew—a disgruntled conservative Presbyterian who later became a key Barry Goldwater supporter and co-founded the Pew Charitable Trusts.

The two Protestant branches' opposing worldviews can be seen with striking clarity in just a few of their midcentury activities. While the FCC and NCC were working to establish the U.N. and international standards for human rights, the NAE launched serious campaigns in both 1947 and 1954 to insert a reference to "Jesus of Nazareth" into the Constitution of the United States. When the National Council of Churches convened 237 clergy to address foreign policy and international relations issues in 1959, *Christianity Today*'s founding editor, Carl F. H. Henry, charged that 105 of them had "Communist affiliations."[68] Henry also regularly featured articles by J. Edgar Hoover in the pages of the magazine with titles suggesting the importance of a stalwart Christianity for resisting the dangers of communist influence: "Soviet Rule or Christian Renewal?" and "Communist Propaganda and the Christian Pulpit."[69] And importantly, without the easy access mainline Protestants enjoyed to mainstream media, white evangelical Protestants built an impressive array of radio stations, publishing houses, and television networks to widely promote their vision of White Christian America.

As white mainline influence faded and white evangelicals began to be the dominant cultural voice in the late 1970s, their claim to represent an unrealized "Moral Majority" had enough credibility to be plausible. But it also betrayed a defensive undertone. Instead of confidently ushering in "the Christian Century" with a vision of international cooperation with all people of good will, their goal was to restore and protect a distinctly Protestant Christian America, which would then allow the United States to fulfill its divine mandate in the world. The white Christian conservative movement dominated the American political and cultural consciousness in the 1980s, 1990s, and even into the mid-2000s. But in the last decade, even this second wave of Protestant energy has begun to wane.

As powerful as White Christian America was throughout the twentieth century, it is important to offer a few notes on its boundaries. Together, white mainline and evangelical Protestants were the beneficiaries of White Christian America, an inheritance they each simultaneously contested and strongly guarded. WCA certainly marshaled other Christian groups in the service of particular causes, as when the mainline Protestant churches included Eastern Orthodox and even some historically black denominations—but not Catholics—as part of the ecumenical umbrella organization that built the Interchurch Center. In the 1990s and 2000s, despite some internal trepidation, evangelical Protestants also expanded their political coalitions to include conservative white Catholics and Mormons. But these tent-broadening efforts were largely politically expedient concessions. They were not intended to weaken white Protestant dominance over the American religious and cultural landscape. On the contrary, these tactics were designed to shore up the two branches' competing claims to White Christian America's mantle in the face of both internal competition and outside challenges like secularism and religious disaffiliation.

Even when outsider groups gained a seat at the mostly Protestant table, they were indelibly marked by their historical experience of being outside the mainstream. White Protestants claimed an identity that was integral to the national narrative from its beginning. That is why—although I may occasionally cite the more expansive term "white Christians" in the following chapters—I use the term "White Christian America" to refer to the cultural domain populated exclusively by white mainline and evangelical Protestants.

The Social World of White Christian America

For most of the twentieth century, in White Christian America the terms "Christian" and "Protestant" were virtually synonymous. Questions like "And where do you go to church?" felt appropriate in casual social interactions or even business exchanges. White Christian America was a place where few gave a second thought to saying "Merry Christmas!" to strangers on the street. It was a world of shared rhythms that punctuated the week: Wednesday spaghetti suppers and prayer meetings, invocations from local pastors under the Friday night lights at high school football games, and Sunday blue laws that shuttered Main Street for the Sabbath.

In its heyday, a set of linked institutions reinforced White Christian America's worldview across generations: the Young Men's Christian Association (YMCA), the Boy Scouts, the Masonic Lodge, and the local country club with limits or even outright bans on membership for Catholics, Jews, and ethnic minorities. White Christian America had its golden age in the 1950s, after the hardships and victories of World War II and before the cultural upheavals of the 1960s. June Cleaver was its mother, Andy Griffith was its sheriff, Norman Rockwell was its artist, and Billy Graham and Norman Vincent Peale were its ministers.

To be sure, this seemingly seamless world was never as all encompassing as it pretended. It always operated parallel to the rich religious and cultural domain of African American Protestants. It tacitly acknowledged the notion of the "triple melting pot" offered by sociologist Will Herberg in his 1955 landmark analysis of the American religious tapestry, *Protestant, Catholic, Jew*, but it never saw these as more than theoretical concessions.[70] For most of the nation's life, White Christian America was big enough, cohesive enough, and influential enough to pull off the illusion that it was the cultural pivot around which the country turned—at least for those living safely within its expansive confines. But this artifice weakened as White Christian America shrank in size and the power of its institutions dwindled.

The remains of White Christian America can still be seen in the town squares of county seats in the South and Midwest. They are also visible in our oldest cities, where Protestant churches with tall steeples were erected centuries ago to keep a watchful eye over the centers of civic and business power. Today, many of these churches still preserve their core functions: conducting weekly worship services, leading Sunday Schools for children, and organizing charitable work for those in need. But even though the physical structures cast shadows as long as they did in the past, their cultural reach has shortened significantly. There are, to be sure, pockets of the country where the spirit of White Christian America still seems alive and well—like midwestern and southern exurbs, where lively megachurches have followed the outmigration of whites from cities, and rural communities, where churches and pastors continue to have vital social roles. But even within these reassuringly insular settings, it's no longer possible to believe that White Christian America sets the tone for the country's culture as a whole. And that realization—both for those inside and outside WCA's domain—marks something genuinely new in American life.

Why White Christian America Matters Now

Today, many white Christian Americans feel profoundly anxious. As is common among extended families, WCA's two primary branches, white mainline and white evangelical Protestants, have competing narratives about WCA's decline. White mainline Protestants blame evangelical Protestants for turning off the younger generation with their antigay rhetoric and tendency to conflate Christianity with conservative, nationalistic politics. White evangelical Protestants, on the other hand, blame mainline Protestants for undermining Christianity because of their willingness to sell out traditional beliefs to accommodate contemporary culture.

This book aims to tell a story that rises above intra-family feuding, examining White Christian America as a single dynasty. The key question here is not why one white Protestant subgroup is faring worse than another, but why white Protestantism as a whole—arguably the most powerful cultural force in the history of our country—has faded. This is a story of theology and culture, but it is also a story of powerful demographic changes.

These changes are both visceral and symbolic, affecting everyday religious communities as well as lofty American ideals. The transformations of the iconic religious buildings discussed above are emblematic of broad shifts within the religious world. But there are also striking symbols of change in our national government. There is, for example, no underestimating the impact of our first African American president taking up residence in the White House. The intensely negative reactions to his presidency among some whites—in particular, a series of challenges to the authenticity of his citizenship and his faith—were certainly fueled by the fact that he does not come from the world of White Christian America. In the judicial branch of the federal government, it is also notable that as of 2010—with the retirement of John Paul Stevens, a Protestant, and the 2010 confirmation of Elena Kagan, a Jew—for the first time in its history, the U.S. Supreme Court has no Protestant justices.[71] The current U.S. Supreme Court is comprised of six Catholics and three Jews. To put that into perspective, there have only been twelve Catholics in the 225-year history of the Court, half of whom occupy seats on the bench today. Similarly, only eight Jews have ever served on the Court, three of whom are sitting justices today.[72]

There have also been dramatic shifts on the ground. In 2004, the same year that Americans reelected George W. Bush as president, the U.S. Census Bureau made waves by predicting that by 2050 the United States would no longer be a majority-white nation.[73] Four years later, when Americans elected Barack Obama as their first African American head of state, the Census Bureau lowered that threshold year to 2042.[74] When Obama was reelected in 2012, population experts forecasted that by 2060 whites will see their numbers *decline* for the first time in American history, while the number of people who identify as multiracial will nearly triple and the number of Hispanics and Asians will more than double.[75] Mark Mather, a demographer with the Population Reference Bureau, summed up the magnitude of these shifts for *The New York Times*: "No other country has experienced such rapid racial and ethnic change."[76]

These racial and ethnic changes are dramatic, but they only partially account for the sense of dislocation many whites feel. In order to understand the magnitude of the shift, we have to also assess White Christian

America's waning cultural influence. Although the declining proportion of WCA members can be explained in part by immigration patterns and lower birth rates among white Americans, the other critical factor in declining influence is religious, most notably religious disaffiliation among younger white Americans.[77] It's impossible to grasp the depth of many white Americans' anxieties and fears—or comprehend recent phenomena like the rise of the Tea Party in American politics, the zealous tone of the final battles over gay rights, or the racial tensions that have spiked over the last few years—without understanding that, along with its population, America's religious and cultural landscape is being fundamentally altered.

One reason why the discussions of demographic change have been less focused on religion is that the U.S. Census Bureau has not asked about religious affiliation since 1946; in fact, current law forbids the Census from asking about Americans' religious beliefs.[78] Fortunately, during the last four decades—the period of the most intense transition—the social sciences began to more systematically measure religious affiliation and change. This analysis draws on two of the largest collections of social scientific survey data in existence: the long-running General Social Survey, conducted between 1972 and 2014 by the National Opinion Research Center at the University of Chicago, and the trove of more than 150,000 telephone interviews conducted by Public Religion Research Institute (PRRI) between 2013 and 2015 among random samples of the U.S. adult population. In examining the transitional moment in which we live, this book will draw on this data and other sources to document the demise of White Christian America.

Some recent events demonstrate the importance of coming to terms with the passing of White Christian America. In 2014 and 2015, the cities of Ferguson, New York, and Baltimore became hotbeds of protests after white police officers killed unarmed black men. These events have again brought issues of race to the forefront of American consciousness. Nonwhite Americans largely responded to these events with outrage and saw them as obvious examples of racially driven patterns of violence and discrimination against minorities. Many whites, by contrast, regarded the police killings of unarmed black men as isolated incidents. The national turmoil spurred by these events signal the need for white Protestants to deal with the legacies of slavery and segregation and to engage with the country outside the shrinking confines of White Christian America.

In June 2015, the U.S. Supreme Court announced its decision to legalize same-sex marriage nationwide. For the conservative evangelical descendants of White Christian America, this was another isolating moment. While most white mainline Protestants supported the court ruling, as did majorities of Catholics and Jews, white evangelical Protestants remain strongly opposed. Virtually all of the major white evangelical organizations—from the National Association of Evangelicals to the Southern Baptist Convention—doubled down on their opposition to gay marriage ahead of the ruling and reiterated their "no compromise" position afterward. As one the few major religious groups who remain strongly opposed to same-sex marriage, white evangelicals—especially if they continue to battle fiercely in the courts despite having lost the war—will set the tone for their future relationships with their own younger members and the broader society, not to mention the millions of gay and lesbian Americans.

As sympathetic or unsympathetic as one may be to white Christians' plight at this critical juncture in American history, one simple fact remains: White Christian America will be survived by significant numbers of its descendants. There is much at stake for the country in whether these survivors retreat into disengaged enclaves, band together to launch repeated rounds of what the sociologist Nathan Glazer has called "defensive offensives"[79]—in which a formerly powerful majority recasts itself as a beleaguered minority in an attempt to preserve its particular social values—or find a way to integrate into the new American cultural landscape.

2

Vital Signs: A Divided and Dying White Christian America

America the Diverse

WTF? @CocaCola has America the Beautiful being sung in different languages in a #SuperBowl commercial? We speak ENGLISH here, IDIOTS.

—@iResistAll

#Characters in these Cola commercials, from Mexicans to Indians, learn to #SpeakAmerican already! Or better don't be in em.

—@RealTrueCon

If you're complaining about the biracial Cheerios couple & the multilingual Coke commercial, you can buy a one-way ticket back to the 60's.

—@fleaskeys[1]

It's hard to imagine a more quintessentially American cocktail than the Super Bowl, Coca-Cola, and "America the Beautiful." But in 2014,

---

when Coca-Cola set aside its well-known polar bear mascot and instead debuted "It's Beautiful," a one-minute ode to American pluralism, the company stepped into dangerous territory. In the Super Bowl ad, the camera panned over Americans clad in everything from cowboy hats to yarmulkes to hijabs—including an interracial gay couple at a roller rink with their daughter—over a soundtrack of "America the Beautiful" sung in seven different languages.[2]

This particular blend of American symbols proved to be a volatile one. The ad spot immediately eclipsed the game, where the Seattle Seahawks were steamrolling the Denver Broncos.[3] Viewers whipped out their smartphones and computers and began to do battle online. By the fourth quarter, Twitter had lit up with trending hashtags defining the virtual opposing teams: #speakAmerican vs. #AmericaIsBeautiful. The skirmish was not confined to the Internet's trolls. Even former Republican congressman Allen West took the time to weigh in, writing on his blog:

> I am quite sure there may be some who appreciated the commercial, but Coca Cola missed the mark in my opinion. If we cannot be proud enough as a country to sing "American [sic] the Beautiful" in English in a commercial during the Super Bowl, by a company as American as they come—doggone we are on the road to perdition. This was a truly disturbing commercial for me, what say you?[4]

For its part, Coca-Cola released a press statement before the game that straightforwardly described the ad as one that "features real people enjoying each other and a Coke."[5] Perhaps anticipating some pushback, the company also included a quote from Katie Bayne, a Coca-Cola executive: "With 'It's Beautiful,' we are simply showing that America is beautiful, and Coke is for everyone."[6]

But the visceral responses to the ad indicate that for many Americans, "simply showing" their country's diversity and pronouncing it "beautiful" was a provocative act.

Why should a seemingly feel-good commercial spark such profound anger and bitter disappointment? A look at the changing racial and religious face of America provides some clues. Figure 2.1 illustrates the current diversity of the American religious landscape. Two features immediately jump out. First, the proportion of white Christians in the country, while still comprising the largest single wedge in the pie chart, has slipped below a majority to 47 percent. Moreover, if that measure is restricted to include only the descendants of White Christian America—white mainline Protestants and white evangelical Protestants—the number decreases to only about one third (32 percent) of Americans.* Second, religiously unaffiliated Americans—a group that is growing rapidly—comprise more than one in five Americans (22 percent) today.[7]

FIGURE 2.1 The American Religious Landscape

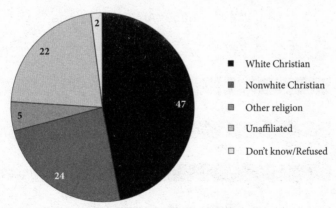

- White Christian
- Nonwhite Christian
- Other religion
- Unaffiliated
- Don't know/Refused

Source: PRRI, American Values Atlas, 2014.

*Aside from white Protestants, the larger white Christian group includes white non-Hispanic Americans who identify as Catholic, Orthodox, or other non-Protestant traditions.

Figure 2.2 digs deeper into these numbers and provides some insight into what the future may hold. Like an archaeological excavation, the chart sorts Americans by religious affiliation and race, stratified by age—demonstrating at a glance the decline of white Christians among each successive generation. This generational snapshot uncovers a striking finding: today, young adults (ages 18–29) are less than half as likely to be white Christians as seniors (age 65 and older). Nearly seven in ten (67 percent) American seniors are white Christians, compared to fewer than three in ten (29 percent) young adults. Although the declining proportion of white Christians is due in part to large-scale demographic shifts—including immigration patterns and differential birth rates—this chart also highlights the other major force of change in the religious landscape: young adults' rejection of organized religion. Young adults are three times as likely as seniors to claim no religious affiliation (34 percent versus 11 percent).[8]

FIGURE 2.2 Religious Affiliation by Age

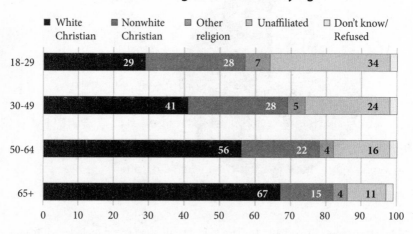

Source: PRRI, American Values Atlas, 2014.

These charts capture the story of a changing country—a tale that goes deeper than shifting demographics or the decline of particular religious denominations. The American religious landscape is being remade, most notably by the decline of the white Protestant majority and the rise of the religiously unaffiliated. These religious transformations have been swift and dramatic, occurring largely within the last four decades. Many white Americans have sensed these changes taking place all around them, and there has been some media coverage of the demographic piece of the puzzle. But while the country's shifting racial dynamics alone are certainly a source of apprehension for many white Americans, it is the disappearance of White Christian America that is driving their strong, sometimes apocalyptic reactions. Falling numbers and the marginalization of a once dominant racial and religious identity—one that has been central not just to white Christians themselves but to the national mythos—threatens white Christians' understanding of America itself.

The Declining Numbers of
White Christians in America

The previous two charts tell us where the country is and hint at where it's heading, but they don't explain how we got here. To understand just how fundamentally the American religious landscape is being altered, we need to look back to the 1970s, when—despite the growing acceptance of Catholics and Jews into the mainstream—Protestantism was still pervasive enough to be thought of as America's default faith.

As Figure 2.3 shows, nearly two thirds (63 percent) of Americans identified as Protestants in 1974, while approximately one quarter (26 percent) identified as Catholic. Only a sliver of the population claimed no religious affiliation (7 percent).[9]

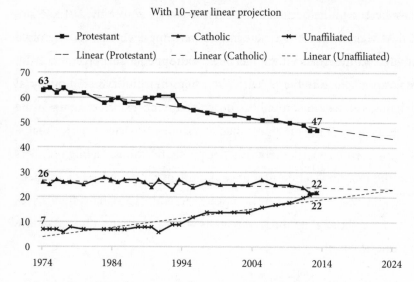

FIGURE 2.3 Religious Change in the U.S. (1974–2014)

With 10–year linear projection

Source: General Social Survey, 1974–2012; PRRI, American Values Atlas, 2013–2014.

These numbers remained mostly steady until the 1990s, when something unusual happened: the numbers of Americans who identified as Protestant began to slip. At the same time, more and more Americans were reporting to pollsters that they had no particular religious affiliation. Two thousand eight was the last year on record in which Protestants as a whole—not just white Protestants—represented a majority of the country.[10] By 2014, the religiously unaffiliated rivaled Catholics' share of the religious marketplace, with each group making up 22 percent of the American population.[11] Looking ahead, there's no sign that this pattern will fade anytime soon. By 2051, if current trends continue, religiously unaffiliated Americans could comprise as large a percentage of the population as Protestants—a thought that would have been unimaginable just a few decades ago.

Moreover, the past quarter century's religious revolution is almost entirely due to the decline of *white* Protestants, as we can see in Figure 2.4. As recently as 1993, a majority (51 percent) of Americans identified as white Protestants, but that percentage dropped to 32 percent by 2014. Meanwhile, the number of black Protestants remained steady at around one in ten Americans, while Hispanic Protestants gained strength, making up 4 percent of Americans by 2014.[12]

FIGURE 2.4 Protestants as Percent of Population by Race (1974–2014)

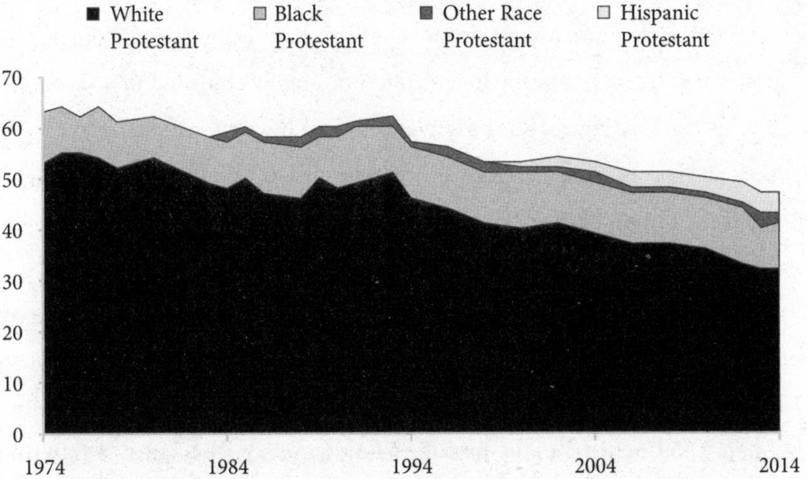

Source: General Social Survey, 1974–2012; PRRI, American Values Atlas, 2013–2014.

Looking still closer, it is clear that the downward trajectory of white Protestants has been due to declines among both mainline and evangelical Protestants. In the late 1980s, the two main branches of the White Christian America family tree were relatively equal in size: white mainline Protestants comprised 24 percent of the population, while white evangelical Protestants accounted for 22 percent of the population. But beginning in the 1990s and continuing into the early 2000s, leaders of the evangelical sector of White Christian America made much hay of what they called "mainline decline." Dr. Albert Mohler, president of the Southern Baptist Convention's flagship Southern Seminary, was a prominent voice in the chorus of evangelical critics who took the flagging mainline numbers to be a vindication of the evangelical project. Mohler's 2005 essay "When Will They Ever Learn? Mainline Decline in Perspective," was typical of these critiques:

> The mainline denominations have been losing members by the thousands for decades. Many of these churches have become so theologically inclusive, politically liberal, and doctrinally confused that there is no compelling reason for anyone to join anyway. . . . Sadly, they reject the one way out of their crisis—a return to biblical authority, Gospel preaching, and theological orthodoxy.[13]

As Figure 2.5 shows, it's true that mainline numbers dropped earlier and more sharply—from 24 percent of the population in 1988 to 14 percent in 2012, at which time their numbers stabilized. But beginning in 2008, white evangelical Protestant numbers began to falter as well. White evangelical Protestants comprised 22 percent of the population in 1988 and still commanded 21 percent of the population in 2008, but their share of the religious market has now slipped to 18 percent.[14]

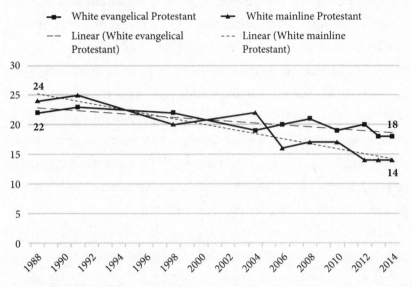

FIGURE 2.5 White Evangelical Protestants vs.
White Mainline Protestants (1988–2014)

Percent of population

Source: General Social Survey, 1988–2012; PRRI, American Values Atlas, 2013–2014.

Robert Putnam and David Campbell, in their important book *American Grace*, found corroborating evidence of decreases in both the mainline and evangelical branches of the white Protestant population, mirroring the patterns above—earlier and steeper declines among white mainline Protestants, followed by later significant declines among white evangelical Protestants. Using the General Social Survey to measure retention rates for each group, Putnam and Campbell found that mainline Protestant retention rates began to fall among people who came of age between 1920 and 1960, stabilizing at about 60–65 percent. In other words, as they put it, "for the last half century roughly one-third of the people raised in one of the mainline Protestant denominations has left the faith, mostly to become evangelical or none."[15] White evangelical Protestants, by contrast, retained approximately three quarters of their children for most of the twentieth century. However, among those who came of age in the 2000s, the retention rate plunged to 62 percent, a number comparable to that of their mainline cousins.[16]

A comparison of the current affiliation patterns of the oldest and youngest Americans, for example, reveals that white evangelicals have actually lost more ground than white mainline Protestants across current generations (Figure 2.6). White evangelical Protestants constitute 27 percent of seniors (age 65 and older), but only 10 percent of Americans under 30 years of age—a loss of nearly two thirds from the oldest to the youngest generation of adults. By contrast, white mainline Protestants—who saw a reduction in their numbers two decades before evangelical numbers began to dip—account for fewer (20 percent) seniors but 10 percent of

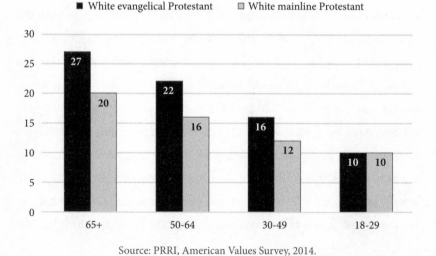

FIGURE 2.6 White Evangelical Protestants vs. White Mainline Protestants

Percent of population by age

■ White evangelical Protestant   ▢ White mainline Protestant

Source: PRRI, American Values Survey, 2014.

younger Americans. This still represents a 50 percent decline in market share across generations, but it is less steep than the evangelical decline.[17]

As a result of both lower birth rates among whites and the loss of younger members to disaffiliation, the median age among white Protestants overall has risen by seven years since 1972. In 1972, white Protestants' median age was 46 years old, only slightly higher than the median age for the American population (44 years old).[18] Today, white Protestants' median age is 53, while Americans as a whole have a median age of 46.[19] Notably, by 2014, there was no difference between the median ages of white evangelical and mainline Protestants; white evangelical Protestants' median age was 53, compared to white mainline Protestants' median age of 52.[20]

These indications of white evangelical decline at the national level are corroborated by internal membership reports during the same period from the Southern Baptist Convention (SBC), the largest evangelical Protestant denomination in the country. The 2015 report showed that SBC membership fell for the eighth year in a row.[21] The denomination's official *Baptist Press* reported that the 200,000-member plunge in 2014 represented the largest single drop in membership since 1881.[22] Writing on the faculty blog of Southeastern Baptist Theological Seminary, Ed Stetzer, the denomination's chief statistician, summed up the findings this way:

> From 1950 till 2007 [the SBC] showed growth—impressive growth—while other denominations were declining. . . . In 2008 there was a flurry of articles and debates about these numbers. National leaders spoke of this as a blip. It wasn't then—I think everyone now agrees—and it isn't now. The Southern Baptist Convention is declining and, if the trend continues, the decline will accelerate.[23]

Stetzer drove the long-term trends home in what he called "the chart of concern" (Figure 2.7), which traces the year-to-year growth percentage between 1950 and the present. This chart shows clearly that the recent dip in membership is not an anomaly—it's the result of a much longer trend of declining growth rates, which finally fell into negative territory in 2007.

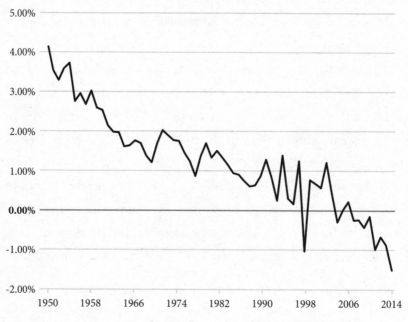

FIGURE 2.7 Declining Growth Rate Among Southern Baptists (1950–2014)

Source: SBC Annual Church Profile, 1950–2014, provided by Lifeway Research.

These numbers point to one undeniable conclusion: white Protestant Christians—both mainline and evangelical—are aging and quickly losing ground as a proportion of the population.

White Christian America's Homeland

A quick look at a map of the United States' religious population shows that, despite the massive shifts in religious affiliation over the past few decades, the historical homeland of White Christian America remains recognizable. Despite their diminishing numbers, the descendants of White Christian America retain a dominant presence in a significant number of states (Figure 2.8).

FIGURE 2.8 States Where White Protestants Remain Dominant

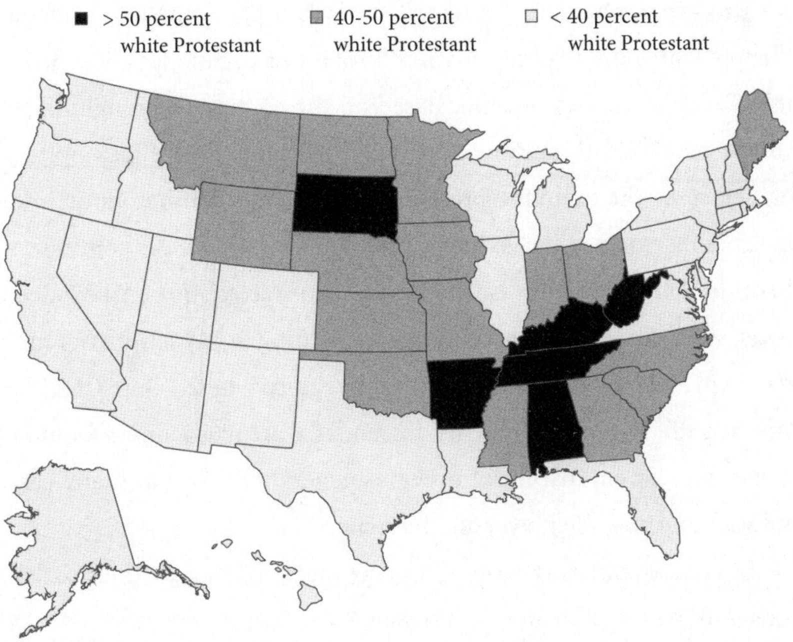

Source: PRRI, American Values Atlas, 2014.

There are six core states in which white Protestants have held on to a majority of the population. With the exception of South Dakota—which earns this status because of its very small racial minority population—these states are anchored in the Deep South (Alabama, Arkansas, and Tennessee) and Appalachia (Kentucky and West Virginia). There are sixteen additional states in which white Protestants comprise between 40 and 50 percent of the population. With one exception, these peripheral states wrap the core states in a contiguous blanket that covers much of the remainder of the South and the Midwest, extending as far west as Montana and Wyoming. Maine sits as a lone outpost of White Christian America in New England, largely due to its lack of racial and ethnic minorities; it is, at 95 percent white, the most racially homogeneous state in the country.[24]

This geographic segregation, particularly in the South and Midwest, often obscures the realities of white Protestant decline for those living in WCA's historical homeland. Based on the continued strength of the white evangelical Protestant population in states like Mississippi and Tennessee or the mainline presence in states like Minnesota or Iowa, one might imagine that White Christian America could continue to thrive indefinitely within isolated pockets of the country. And indeed, many white Americans are temporarily holding at bay a full awareness of the encroaching diversity. Within the regions where White Christian America still reigns supreme, its descendants are maintaining a kind of vitality that is reminiscent of previous generations, and in many cases still wield formidable power and influence.

But this vitality is shadowed by a cognitive dissonance their parents and grandparents did not experience. Even in the staunchest strongholds of White Christian America, the incursion of the Internet and national cable news has made it impossible for WCA's contemporary descendants to assume that their own beliefs are universal. Today, daily doses of devotionals on radio and TV, lessons in church services, the political fight to homeschool children, the growth of private Christian academies, and the themes of Christian radio are as much inoculations against outside contagions as tools for internal spiritual formation.

Over the coming years, regardless of their defense strategies, the slow tectonics of demographic and religious change will finally reach these communities. The meeting place of the Hindu Temple Society in Brandon, Mississippi, is one compelling example. Mississippi is among the most heavily white Protestant states in the country, with nearly half the state identifying as either white evangelical (37 percent) or white mainline (9 percent) Protestant. Brandon, a town of some twenty thousand people, is the county seat of Rankin, just one county over from the state capital of Jackson. The Hindu diaspora into Mississippi took root in the late 1960s when basic scientists began moving into the state in order to teach at various universities. A wave of Indian physicians moved into Mississippi starting early in the 1970s, followed by businessmen in the mid- to late 1980s.

The first Hindu Temple, built in 1986, was modest in structure. As more resources became available, this structure was converted into a community hall, and a larger temple, built according to Hindu architectural standards, was planned. The new temple was consecrated in 2010. Its striking white facade, topped by a tall, intricately carved pyramid-shaped tower, provides a sharp visual reminder of the growing diversity of America's religious population and the decline of white Christian cultural dominance, even in the heart of the Deep South.[25]

Struggles for Admission to
White Christian America

Within the domain of White Christian America, white Protestants have been locked in an internal dispute over who will carry on the family name. As the twentieth century progressed, the mainline and evangelical factions each declared themselves to be WCA's true descendants and set up competing theologies, cultures, and institutions to secure this position. Each, in different ways, policed the boundaries of the white Protestant realm and sought to limit who could lay claim to the coveted twin adjectives of "white" and "Christian." But this intra-family strife ultimately weakened white Protestantism, and as their members declined in both proportion of the population size and power, white Protestants were increasingly compelled to form new alliances.

Over the course of less than a century, white mainline Protestants have moved from assertions of denominational power in the 1920s, to the midcentury ecumenical efforts that included outreach to Eastern Orthodox Christians and African American Protestants, and finally, in more recent times, to new interfaith partnerships. On the other hand, the major expressions of white evangelical Protestantism have moved from the first formal efforts at white evangelical cooperation in the 1940s, to the conservative Christian political movements in the 1980s and 1990s, and more recently to ad hoc alliances with white Catholics and some Greek Orthodox leaders around specific issues such as opposition to same-sex marriage and abortion.

These developments demonstrate that necessity is the mother of collaboration. At key historical moments, the need to resist and outflank competing forces—Catholicism, secularism, and often each other—drove white Protestants to form expedient alliances, highlighting common interests while conveniently overlooking differences. These alliances, they hoped, would allow them to claim the WCA birthright, which conferred on its holder the ability to speak for the moral center of the country.

Catholics and White Christian America

While white evangelicals and mainline Protestants scuffled for control of White Christian America, Catholics were still struggling to be accepted into the American mainstream. Many Catholics who would be called "white" today, even those of northern European descent such as Irish immigrants, found the entry door to White Christian America doubly barred: they were often considered neither white nor authentically Christian. In his book *Whiteness of a Different Color: European Immigrants and the Alchemy of Race*, Matthew Frye Jacobson documents how Irish immigrants were frequently categorized as "Celts" in nineteenth- and early-twentieth-century immigration policy and court rulings, although their classification often depended on region and the proximity of other immigrant groups that were deemed further from a northern European racial ideal. For example, Jacobson notes that "an Irish immigrant in 1877 could be despised as a Celt in Boston—a threat to the republic—and yet a solid member of The Order of Caucasians for the Extermination of the Chinaman in San Francisco, gallantly defending U.S. shores from an invasion of 'Mongolians.'"[26]

The religious conflicts between Protestants and Catholics, always tinged with race, were fierce. As late as the early twentieth century, white Protestant attempts to keep Catholics outside the boundaries of Christianity could still spark outright violence. On the evening of August 11, 1921, a Catholic priest named Father James Coyle was reading on the porch of his rectory in Birmingham, Alabama, when Edwin Stephenson, a Methodist minister, approached him. Earlier that day, Father Coyle had performed the marriage ceremony for Stephenson's daughter, Ruth, to a Catholic man of Puerto Rican descent. Furious, Stephenson pulled out his pistol and shot Coyle three times, killing him. Stephenson was a member of the Ku Klux Klan, which was making a violent revival in the South. So was Hugo Black, his defense attorney (although Black rose three decades later to serve as one of the most liberal justices on the United States Supreme Court).[27] Stephenson was acquitted for Coyle's murder in the midst of one of the most virulently anti-Catholic periods in U.S. history.

In 1928, Al Smith emerged as an embodiment of Protestant fears about Catholic power. Smith, who had served four terms as governor of New York, was running as the Democratic candidate against a Quaker, Herbert Hoover. During Smith's brief campaign, from September to November 1928, the country was engulfed in a tempest of suspicion and fear. Photos of the newly completed Holland Tunnel were distributed nationwide with a warning that Smith intended to extend the tunnel underneath the Atlantic Ocean so that he could take secret orders from the pope.[28] The Ku Klux Klan entered the fray, with one leader mailing thousands of postcards that read, "We now face the darkest hour in American history. In a convention ruled by political Romanism, anti-Christ has won." With messages like these, the KKK placed Catholicism firmly outside the domain of White Christian America, painting the Catholic Church—and its adherents—as un-Christian and thus un-American.

The KKK fed a persistent strain of anti-Catholicism throughout the early twentieth century, but concerns about the proliferation of Catholic parochial schools—and resentment over requests for public tax dollars to support them—echoed widely within the mainline Protestant community, which was pushing for universal public education for children. During the oral arguments in a 1947 Supreme Court case that dealt with whether a New Jersey township could reimburse parents of Catholic schoolchildren for busing expenses, Justice William O. Douglas passed a jocular note to Hugo Black—now, more than two decades after the shooting of Father Coyle, an associate justice on the high court—warning, "If the Catholics get public money to finance their religious schools, we better insist on getting some good prayers in public schools or we Protestants are out of business." [29]

These anti-Catholic views within the Protestant establishment persisted through the middle of the twentieth century. At the end of his four-decade career as owner and editor of *The Christian Century*, Charles Clayton Morrison presided over a series of editorials addressing America's religious future: an eight-part series by field editor Harold Fey in 1944–1945 titled "Can Catholicism Win America?" and a sixteen-part series he penned himself in 1946, "Can Protestantism Win America?" The articles formed what was essentially a single long-running argument that Catholicism threatened not only Protestantism, but also democratic governance. Morrison argued essentially that Roman Catholicism—far from being a legitimate Christian religion that should be a partner in ecumenical cooperation—was essentially a hostile power to be contained. For him Catholicism was "a self-enclosed system of power resting on the broad base of the submission of its people, whose submission it is able to exploit for the gaining of yet more power in the political and cultural life of the secular community." [30] As historian Elesha Coffman summed it up in *The Christian Century and the Rise of the Protestant Mainline*, "To Morrison, as to many Protestants at the end of [World War II], Roman Catholicism threatened the entire American project." [31]

In 1959, John F. Kennedy announced his intention to run for president, reopening the question—closed since Al Smith's defeat three decades earlier—of whether Americans were ready for a Catholic president. After Kennedy defeated Hubert Humphrey to secure the Democratic nomination, many influential Protestant leaders returned to the anti-Catholic rhetoric that had doomed Smith, arguing that Kennedy's Catholic faith would trump his allegiance to the Constitution. Speaking for a coalition of 150 Protestant clergy, Norman Vincent Peale warned, "It is inconceivable that a Roman Catholic president would not be under extreme pressure by the hierarchy of his church to accede to its policies with respect to foreign interests."[32]

But the national milieu had changed substantially since the 1920s. An interfaith coalition of religious leaders headed by Reinhold Niebuhr, a prominent mainline Protestant theologian, wrote a rejoinder to Peale, condemning his letter for "opening the floodgates of bigotry."[33] Kennedy himself offered a nimble and sure-footed response to the fears about his Catholic loyalties. Speaking before an assembly of Protestant ministers in Houston in September 1960, he delivered a now famous speech on the separation of church and state. He chastised the ministers as un-American for disqualifying him as a candidate for president because of his faith, saying:

I believe in an America where the separation of church and state is absolute, where no Catholic prelate would tell the president (should he be Catholic) how to act, and no Protestant minister would tell his parishioners for whom to vote; where no church or church school is granted any public funds or political preference; and where no man is denied public office merely because his religion differs from the president who might appoint him or the people who might elect him.[34]

Not everyone was convinced. "No matter what Kennedy might say, he cannot separate himself from the Church if he is a true Catholic," said Ramsey Pollard, president of the Southern Baptist Convention. "All we ask is that Roman Catholicism lift its bloody hand from the throats of those who want to worship in the church of their choice."[35] But Kennedy's victory over Richard Nixon in one of the closest presidential elections in American history decisively quashed the notion that America could not abide a Catholic president.

The next three decades saw occasional collaboration between the mainline Protestant guardians of White Christian America and Catholics. For example, white mainline Protestants marched beside Catholics in the civil rights movement, while white evangelical Protestants stayed largely on the sidelines. But in 1994 an alliance formed on the other side of WCA's family tree. As Bill Clinton's 1992 election was causing Republican political operatives to rethink their strategies, a group of white evangelical Protestant leaders decided that it might be time to reconsider their historic reluctance to join forces with Catholics. Meanwhile, white conservative Catholics—finding themselves in a politically divided and ethnically transforming church—also saw an opportunity to increase their influence. In short, after more than a century of uneasy and sometimes downright hostile relations, conservative white Protestants and Catholics realized in the 1990s that they needed each other.

In May 1994, more than three dozen Roman Catholic and evangelical Christian scholars and leaders from the conservative end of the political spectrum publicly endorsed a statement declaring their commitment to a shared "Christian mission in the third millennium." The document, titled "Evangelicals and Catholics Together," pledged to reduce conflicts between the denominations and work together on issues where they found common cause. The impetus for the groundbreaking statement came from Charles Colson—a former Nixon aide who went to jail after the Watergate scandal, converted to Christianity, and founded the influential evangelical prison ministry program Prison Fellowship— and Father Richard John Neuhaus, a theologian who helped publish the conservative-leaning Catholic magazine *First Things*. No ecclesiastical bodies or denominations approved the statement, but according to Neuhaus, Vatican officials had given the document their blessing.[36]

The evangelical-Catholic rapprochement was an unparalleled display of ecumenism between two groups that had historically been at odds. Declaring a shared commitment to the Christian faith was itself a radical act. Since the Protestant Reformation in the sixteenth century, Protestants and Catholics had disputed who deserved the label of "Christian." So why, at the end of the twentieth century, were Catholics and evangelicals officially declaring a truce? In the wake of the 1970s, they had found common cause in three emerging culture war issues: abortion, gay rights, and religion in public schools.

The potential for this alliance was not immediately obvious. After the Supreme Court ruled against school prayer in 1962, some evangelical Christians cheered the victory as a necessary check against Catholics' persistent demands for public funding for parochial schools.[37] Meanwhile, throughout the 1960s and into the early 1970s, abortion remained almost exclusively a Catholic issue. While Catholics watched in panic, eighteen states liberalized their antiabortion statutes between 1967 and 1973.[38] Then in 1973, the Supreme Court legalized the procedure nationwide. In this same period, the Southern Baptist Convention adopted a 1971 resolution calling for legal abortion in a broad range of circumstances that included not just rape and incest, but "damage to the emotional, mental, and physical health of the mother."[39]

But by the end of the 1970s, it was clear to conservative Catholic and evangelical leaders that a partnership might be necessary to stem what they saw as the rising tides of secularism and liberalism. Part of their calculation was political: Catholics had been loyal Democratic voters since the days of the New Deal, but Republican strategists speculated that they could peel these voters away from the Democrats by emphasizing issues like abortion. The Democratic Party's refusal to endorse an antiabortion amendment in 1976 was, for many Catholic leaders, a slap in the face. "The platform makes it official," Rev. Edward O'Connell, a Catholic leader, wrote at the conclusion of the 1976 Democratic National Convention. "The Democratic Party doesn't want Catholics."[40] White evangelical leaders had, by the late 1970s, repudiated their cautious acceptance of abortion. In 1979, the Southern Baptist Convention reversed its earlier conditional support for abortion, throwing its institutional weight behind a proposed constitutional prohibition on abortion.

As the conservative evangelical political movement ascended in the 1980s, evangelical leaders like Moral Majority founder Jerry Falwell reached out to Catholic voters, urging a kind of ecumenical conservative religious coalition. These overtures were not immediately successful, in part because other evangelicals attacked Falwell for his willingness to work with Catholics. In 1980, Bob Jones, Jr., an ultraconservative evangelical leader, censured Falwell's alliance with the Catholic antifeminist activist Phyllis Schlafly, declaring that Falwell could not be considered a biblical fundamentalist because of his work with Schlafly and other Catholics.[41] But by the mid-1990s, denunciations like Jones's had all but disappeared, as it became evident that white evangelical Protestants alone were insufficiently powerful to sway elections and set policy agendas at the national level.

In 2014, during the second term of President Obama's presidency,

Catholic and evangelical leaders celebrated the twentieth anniversary of their alliance. They were working more closely together than ever before in a campaign to allow religiously affiliated companies—both for-profit and nonprofit—to opt out of a provision in the Affordable Care Act (aka Obamacare) that required employers to provide no-cost birth control coverage to their employees. "We recognize we have common cause with Catholic University of America and other Catholic institutions in defending religious liberty," said Philip Ryken, the president of the flagship evangelical institution, Wheaton College, as he announced a joint lawsuit against the Obama administration. "We're, in effect, co-belligerents in this fight against government action." [42]

In 2015, ahead of the widely anticipated U.S. Supreme Court ruling on the constitutionality of state same-sex marriage bans, the Evangelicals and Catholics Together coalition issued "The Two Shall Become One Flesh: Reclaiming Marriage," a sweeping manifesto against gay marriage. In the document, they declared that same-sex marriage was a "graver threat" to America than divorce or cohabitation. "A faithful Christian witness," they wrote, "cannot accommodate itself to same-sex marriage." The message was clear: those who applauded gay marriage's recent gains could not consider themselves truly Christian. [43]

The Evangelicals and Catholics Together movement over the last twenty years provided the theological justification for a project that political and religious leaders saw as increasingly necessary, not only for conservative Americans' political success but for the continued national deployment of white Christian clout. As the political gap widened between white mainline and evangelical Protestants, it helped give evangelicals an advantage in their contest to be the face of White Christian America. And as the overall numbers of white Protestant Christians began to slip in the late 1990s, expanding the tent to include white

Catholics helped perpetuate the illusion that White Christian America was still the country's dominant religious culture.

But even this radical move is unlikely to succeed. Compounding the losses among the evangelical descendants of White Christian America, today the number of white Catholics is also diminishing. In 1990, white Catholics comprised a solid 22 percent of the American population; by 2014, that number had fallen by nearly half, to 13 percent of Americans.[44] Today, *former* Catholics—most of them white and relatively young—make up 15 percent of the total adult population.[45] The only reason that the Catholic population overall has maintained its stable one quarter of the population is that Hispanic Catholics—who now comprise 8 percent of the population—are replacing disaffiliating and dying white Catholics.

The Mormon Moment

In the struggle to move from the margins of American religious life, Mormons had to travel a longer road than Catholics. In the majority opinion for the 1878 Supreme Court case *Reynolds v. United States*, Chief Justice Morrison Waite underscored one of the fundamental challenges of American jurisprudence: "The word 'religion,'" he wrote, "is not defined in the Constitution." Waite was tasked, in the *Reynolds* case, with determining whether the country's federal antibigamy statute violated the religious freedom of Mormons who believed in plural marriage. He concluded that while the Constitution protected freedom of religious *belief*, the same privilege did not necessarily extend to freedom of religious *action*. Polygamy was a fundamental social taboo, comparable to human sacrifice—one that the United States was not obligated to protect.[46]

The *Reynolds* case was one of the flash points in a century-long national debate about whether Mormonism—founded in upstate New York in 1830 by the twenty-four-year-old farmer Joseph Smith—could be considered a religion. In the years after *Reynolds*, this controversy shifted in key to whether Mormons, with their serious theological differences with traditional Protestant Christianity, could be accepted within the White Christian American fold. Even today, substantial numbers of evangelical Protestants do not consider Mormonism to be a Christian faith. However, the tone of these accusations has shifted markedly over the past fifteen years, as Mormons became increasingly accepted members of the white Christian conservative political coalition. This status was cemented in 2012, when Mitt Romney, a Mormon, ran as the Republican presidential candidate and carried 79 percent of the white evangelical vote.[47]

In the mid-nineteenth century, Joseph Smith was routinely denounced as a charlatan and a fraud. During the early years of their history, Mormons were the frequent targets of violence. A large group of Mormons settled in Missouri in the 1830s after Smith declared that his followers would inherit the land for their "City of Zion." After a series of clashes with local militias, the Missouri governor, Lilburn Boggs, issued a military order declaring that Mormons "must be treated as enemies, and must be exterminated or driven from the state, if necessary, for the public good." After relocating to neighboring Illinois, Smith petitioned the government for a measure of home rule, including the right to establish his own municipal militia. He was killed in 1844 by a mob in the town of Carthage.[48]

Fleeing the perpetual threat of bloodshed, Smith's successor, Brigham Young, led the midwestern Mormon community into the relative safety of the unsettled West, where they began to openly practice plural marriage. The Mormons' efforts to establish their own government were widely regarded as dangerous signs of a budding theocracy. In a floor speech to the House of Representatives in 1854, Caleb Lyon of New York launched into an invective against Mormon settlers in the West, constructing an unmistakable opposition between Mormonism and Christian America. "Let us, as Christians, follow and legislate in the doctrines of Christ, not of Joe Smith; let us take the holy Gospel, not the Book of Mormon. . . . Point me to a nation where polygamy is practiced, and I will point you to heathens and barbarians," he said. "It seriously [affects] the prosperity of States, it retards civilization, it uproots Christianity. . . . Let us nip this evil in the bud, for the sake of morality, religion, and Christianity." [49]

Mormonism's critics frequently resorted to racial slurs to characterize the "barbarism" that Mormonism represented. Like Catholics, Mormons were not initially considered to be "white." Instead, Mormonism was compared to Islam and Mormons to African, Asian, and other "uncivilized" peoples that also embraced polygamy. Mormons were seen as their own distinct "race," prone to the sexual vices of these "barbaric" foreigners. [50]

In 1887, Congress voted to dis-incorporate the Church of Jesus Christ of Latter-day Saints and seize its property, a law that was upheld by the Supreme Court in 1890. [51] That year, faced with institutional annihilation, Mormon church president Wilford Woodruff issued a "Manifesto" abandoning plural marriage, a decision that has been contested by renegade Mormon sects ever since. This repudiation of polygamy pacified the federal government, which allowed Utah to become a state in 1896. It also paved the way for the "Americanization" of Mormonism, which slowly unfolded over the course of the twentieth century. [52]

The second half of the twentieth century was a watershed period for American Mormons, as they became increasingly integrated into the fabric of American life. In 1968, Mitt Romney's father, George Romney—a successful Mormon businessman, the former governor of Michigan—was a contender for the Republican presidential nomination, which eventually went to Richard Nixon. His candidacy would have been unthinkable at the turn of the twentieth century, when Mormons were, according to Martin Marty, "safely describable as the most despised large group" in America.[53]

Romney's political ascendancy signaled that Mormons were entering the mainstream. Mormons were an increasingly sizable proportion of the American religious population—church membership in the two decades after World War II more than doubled, bringing their numbers to two million by 1963—and the church was expanding quickly outside its once insular home in Utah.[54] In 1965, the Mormon Tabernacle Choir sang at Lyndon B. Johnson's inauguration, and sports stars like Gene Fullmer, a boxing champion, talked openly to the media about their commitment to their Mormon faith.[55]

In the 1970s, Mormon evangelism was expanding internationally, to great success. In 1984, the sociologist Rodney Stark predicted that the world's nearly six million Mormons could multiply to 260 million by the year 2080, if their growth rate held steady. Mormonism, according to him, was about to become "the first major faith to appear on earth since the prophet Muhammad rode out of the desert."[56]

But although Mormons were becoming increasingly numerous and visible in the public eye, prominent Protestant leaders continued to question their religious credentials. Anti-Mormon suspicion had an unexpected revival with the rise of the Christian Right, as preachers like Jerry Falwell began to decry Mormonism as a "wolf-in-sheep's-clothing" religion.[57] They also feared Mormons' proselytizing zeal as a threat to their own church memberships. In the early 1990s, the Southern Baptist Convention's Sunday School Board created an instructional kit called "The Christian Confronting the Cults" that covered five religious groups: the Mormon Church, Jehovah's Witnesses, the Worldwide Church of God, the Unification Church (the "Moonies"), and Christian Scientists. An article titled "Bizarre Theology Does Not Prevent Mormonism's Growth" ran in a 1997 issue of *SBC Life*, the Southern Baptist Convention's official magazine. It instructed readers to "pray for friends and family members who are ensnared by the attractive nature of Mormonism but are unaware of its unbiblical doctrines."[58]

White evangelicals in general—and Southern Baptists in particular—also saw the growth of the Mormon Church as a barrier to their larger goal of returning America to its traditional Protestant roots. In 1998, the Southern Baptist Convention decided to take the challenge to the Mormon Church's doorstep. They held their annual convention in Salt Lake City, where they kicked off a massive evangelism campaign. To accompany a blitz of proselytizing throughout the state of Utah, the Southern Baptists produced a video titled *The Mormon Puzzle* and a book called *Mormonism Unmasked*, which promised to "lift the veil from one of the greatest deceptions in the history of religion."[59]

These theological attacks on Mormonism were largely limited to an evangelical subculture. *The Christian Century*, consistent with its general orientation toward respecting diversity, began to accept Mormonism's self-understanding as a branch of Christianity in the 1970s. But the charges that Mormonism was a cult did strike a chord among the population as a whole, a belief that was likely amplified by a series of scandals related to renegade polygamous Mormon sects in the 1990s and early 2000s. In 2007, a Gallup poll showed that more Americans had an unfavorable view of Mormonism (46 percent) than a favorable view (42 percent). When asked their first association with the "Mormon Church," associations were negative by a nearly two-to-one margin. Eighteen percent of Americans said "polygamy," and an additional 20 percent cited negative associations such as "cult," "secretive," or "false beliefs." By contrast, just 7 percent responded with some variation on "good people/caring/kind/strong morals," along with an additional 15 percent who offered descriptions such as "devout," "Christian," or "clean/healthy lifestyles."[60] But Mitt Romney's campaign for president in 2012 would have a significant impact on these negative judgments—especially among white evangelical Protestants.

In December 2007, Mitt Romney rose to address the assembled crowd at the George H. W. Bush Presidential Library in College Station, Texas. Romney, the son of the 1968 presidential candidate George Romney and a former governor of Massachusetts, had announced his candidacy for the Republican nomination for presidency earlier that year, but nine months later he was still struggling to gain traction among the GOP's conservative Christian base—thanks, in part, to his Mormon faith. One of his rivals, the evangelical Mike Huckabee—who as an ordained Baptist minister was the clearest representative of traditional White Christian America—played the "bizarre theology" card in a *New York Times Magazine* interview by insinuating that Mormons believed that Jesus and the devil were brothers.[61]

Drawing an explicit parallel between his political career and that of John F. Kennedy, Romney reassured his audience that his presidency would not be tainted by influence from the Mormon Church. "Let me assure you that no authorities of my church, or of any other church for that matter, will ever exert influence on presidential decisions," he said. "I will put no doctrine of any church above the plain duties of the office and the sovereign authority of the law."[62] Romney's attempt to quell fears about his religion wasn't convincing enough for Republicans in the 2008 Iowa caucus, where he lost badly to Huckabee. But four years later, Romney returned as the Republican front-runner and forced Christian conservatives to confront the very real possibility of a Mormon president.

In June 2011, *Newsweek* magazine ran a cover story speculating about whether the country was in the midst of a "Mormon Moment." In addition to Romney, Jon Huntsman, another Mormon, was running in the Republican presidential primary. Mormon characters formed the backbone of popular television shows like *Big Love* and *Sister Wives*, which focused on the daily realities of plural marriage. The satirical musical *The Book of Mormon* had just won nine Tony Awards and set Broadway records for ticket sales. While this media exposure did not produce positive publicity for the Mormon Church, it did generate unprecedented national focus on their faith. Sensing the opportunity, the Mormon Church decided to launch a public relations campaign called "I'm a Mormon," featuring the personal stories of Mormons who defied commonplace stereotypes. They produced a sophisticated website (http://www.mormon.org/people) where users could enter their gender, age, and ethnicity, and the website would display profiles of Mormons who shared their demographic characteristics. Meanwhile, Mormon "distinctiveness," *Newsweek*'s Walter Kirn argued, was becoming a part of American popular culture:

> David Neeleman, the Mormon founder and former CEO of JetBlue Airways, brought lessons from his church to his company, donating most of his salary to a fund for needy employees and regularly shedding his suit and tie for a flight attendant's uniform. Management guru Stephen Covey has sold millions of books translating core elements

of the upstanding, upwardly striving Mormon outlook into a method for becoming a "highly effective" person. Stephenie Meyer's extraordinarily popular *Twilight* novels and films give vampires a Mormon makeover, with a lead character, Edward Cullen, serving as a sexy model of moral purity and chastity. And the list goes on.[63]

Romney lost the 2012 election, and Mormonism has faded from center stage. In retrospect, it seems fair to ask whether there really was a "Mormon moment" at all, at least if that meant full acceptance of the Mormon candidate's religion. Although Romney was the subject of about twice as much religion-related media as Obama,[64] less than half (45 percent) of Americans overall could correctly identify Romney's religion as Mormon, even after he had secured the GOP nomination and the campaign was in full swing in May 2012.[65] After the election, the vast majority of U.S. adults said that they learned either "not very much" (32 percent) or "nothing at all" (50 percent) about the Mormon religion during the presidential race. Less than one third of American adults (29 percent) were able to give the right answer for two basic, factual questions about the history and sacred texts of the Mormon Church, the same percentage that answered both of those questions correctly in 2010.[66]

Still, Romney's candidacy had moved Americans toward broader cultural acceptance. Public attitudes toward Mormons softened during and after the 2012 election, especially among evangelical Christians. Among white evangelical Protestants, Romney's favorability as a candidate rose from 39 percent in the fall of 2011[67] to 67 percent by May 2012,[68] and white evangelical Protestant voters supported him at the polls roughly as strongly as they had supported George W. Bush. When asked in December 2012 for one-word impressions of the Mormon religion, more Americans mentioned positive terms such as "good," "dedicated," and "honest" (24 percent) than prior to the election in 2011 (18 percent).[69]

Nearly one hundred years ago, white Protestant Christianity fractured over debates about evolution and the inerrancy of the Bible. Nonetheless, white Protestants maintained indisputable dominance over American cultural and political life. For the first two thirds of the twentieth century, white mainline Protestants were the most visible face of White Christian America at the national level. But beginning in the 1970s—due to the twin forces of demographic change and religious disaffiliation—white mainline Protestants began to rapidly decline in both power and numbers. In this vacuum, white evangelical Protestants began to assert themselves as the face of White Christian America, only to find their own numbers dropping by the first decade of the twenty-first century.

As white mainline Protestants passed from the national political scene, Republican Party operatives and conservative white Protestant and Catholic leaders began to weave together an increasingly capacious alliance. This broader alliance, they hoped, would sustain White Christian America. But as we will see in the next chapter, even the groups gathered under this broadened tent no longer have the numbers or the cultural authority to dominate American public life.

3

Politics: The End of the White Christian Strategy

Barack Obama and the Twilight of White Christian America

In 1960, John F. Kennedy had the distinction of being the first commander in chief to break White Christian America's succession of presidents stretching back more than two centuries to the founding of the Republic.[1] While Kennedy's battles with anti-Catholic sentiment were significant, religious discrimination has never found American soil fully nourishing. If WCA could not embrace him as a fellow Protestant, they could at least claim him as white.

But race-based slavery was firmly anchored within the colonies for more than 150 years before the country's founding, and it flourished within the United States for nearly another century. Even after the Civil War, legal racial discrimination hung on in many forms for another hundred years, and the Civil Rights Act of 1964 is only two to three generations behind us. As a result, Protestant-Catholic disputes have been more easily eradicated, while racial prejudice has the stubborn resilience of a weed that breaks off at the ground level, leaving the taproot intact.

The crossing of the color line at Barack Obama's inauguration in January 2009 presented the most visible symbolic challenge to White Christian America's hold on the country. Despite bitterly cold weather in Washington, attendance at the inauguration was the highest in decades, perhaps in history. Prominent African American leaders, both Democrat and Republican, commemorated the occasion. Some Americans even extolled this moment as the beginning of a "post-racial" nation. But the end of the white Christian monopoly did not come without loud protests. Obama was the object of multiple attempts—using race, religion, and even his citizenship status—to mark him as unfit to hold the office of the presidency, before he had even taken up residency in the White House.

On the religion front, Obama was accused simultaneously of being associated with the controversial leader of a liberal Christian church and of being a Muslim. During the 2008 presidential campaign, Obama was criticized for his relationship with his longtime Chicago pastor, Rev. Jeremiah Wright, whom Obama had called his "spiritual mentor."[2] Reporters uncovered sermons in which Wright harshly criticized the U.S. government—using the inflammatory phrase "God damn America"— and issued stinging critiques of white racism. Obama eventually distanced himself from Wright and resigned his membership in Wright's church, saying that the pastor's "rants" were "appalling."[3]

The episode highlighted both Obama's race and his affiliation with the United Church of Christ, one of the oldest mainline Protestant denominations in the country. But even well into his presidency, long after the Wright controversy was over, Obama continued to struggle with widespread perceptions that he was not a Christian. In 2012, just before he was reelected, a Public Religion Research Institute (PRRI) survey found that nearly four in ten (39 percent) voters did not know the president's religious affiliation, and approximately one in six (16 percent) reported that they thought Obama was a Muslim. Among white evangelical Protestant voters, the number saying Obama was a Muslim rose to nearly one in four (24 percent)—almost as many as those who could correctly identify his religion as Protestant (28 percent).[4]

This confusion about Obama's religious beliefs was due neither to his inability to articulate his faith nor his unwillingness to do so.[5] As a candidate in 2008, Obama offered a theologically sophisticated account of how his faith connected with his life and work as an elected official.[6] A few years later, in 2011, Obama gave an unusually personal speech about his faith at the National Prayer Breakfast. In the speech, he explained, "It is the biblical injunction to serve the least of these that keeps me going and that keeps me from being overwhelmed."[7] Despite Obama's consistent testimony to his Christian faith, many white Christians were either unable or unwilling to see him as an embodiment of their own religion. Obama's problem of being perceived by many white Christians as a religious other were compounded by his race and his Kenyan ancestry on his father's side.

Some of Obama's critics even questioned his American citizenship. Strangely enough, this conspiracy theory, which came to be known as "birtherism," had its roots in emails from Hillary Clinton supporters, sent as her campaign was faltering in the spring of 2008.[8] The notion that Obama was not actually an American citizen fit hand in glove with the idea that he was not Christian. These assertions were picked up and promoted widely by conservative commentators and media outlets during the general election and well into his first term as president. In 2010, a CNN poll found that more than one quarter (27 percent) of the country harbored some doubts about the legitimacy of Obama's citizenship.[9]

Based on analysis of online comments on the subject in *The New*

York Times and *The Wall Street Journal*, Matthew Hughey, a sociologist at Mississippi State University, argued that these rumors were fueled by the fact that Obama's election had challenged many whites' central cultural assumption—that the White Anglo-Saxon Protestant (WASP) was the only authentic model of citizenship.[10] In an April 2011 editorial following the release of Obama's long-form birth certificate, which mostly quelled these rumors, *The New York Times* editorial board concluded, "It is inconceivable that this campaign to portray Mr. Obama as the insidious 'other' would have been conducted against a white president."[11]

Despite the messy aftermath, Obama's inauguration was indisputably the end of the white Christian presidency. It was not, however, the end of the white Christian political strategy. That would come four years later.

The Politics of Nostalgia

Two weeks after Barack Obama's reelection in November 2012, an alarmist email went out from the Christian Coalition of America, the organization founded in 1989 by Pat Robertson that became the backbone of the Christian Right in the 1990s. The centerpiece of the message was an image of a white family bowing their heads to say grace before a Thanksgiving meal (Figure 3.1). The photo's caption read: "Saying grace before carving a turkey at Thanksgiving dinner, Pennsylvania, U.S., 1942." Below, the email's text reminded readers that "the United States of America is the only nation where Thanksgiving has its roots in a Judeo-Christian tradition." Even today, it went on, "most Americans . . . see this holiday as an expression of their faith."

But the kicker was a lament that revealed the Christian Coalition's despairing view of what the election meant for the country's direction:

We will soon be celebrating the 400th anniversary of the first Thanksgiving and God has still not withheld his blessings upon this nation, although we now richly deserve such condemnation. We have a lot to give thanks for, but we also need to pray to our Heavenly Father and ask Him to protect us from those enemies, outside and within, who want to see America destroyed.

With only an image and a few hundred words, the email conjures up an idyllic memory of White Christian America. The choice of a

FIGURE 3.1 Email from Christian Coalition of America, November 21, 2012

From: Christian Coalition of America <newsletters@cc.org>
Date: Wednesday, November 21, 2012 9:52:55 PM
Subject: Christian Coalition of America Wishes You and Your Family a Happy Thanksgiving

Christian Coalition of America
...defending America's Godly heritage

Thanksgiving Day

Saying grace before carving a turkey at Thanksgiving dinner, Pennsylvania, U.S., 1942 black-and-white photograph transports the mind back to a "simpler" time. The picture's composition closely resembles Norman Rockwell's iconic depiction of an American Thanksgiving in "Freedom from Want," also painted in November 1942 and published in *The Saturday Evening Post* on March 6, 1943.[12] Thanksgiving 1942 came less than a year after the attack on Pearl Harbor drew the United States into World War II. Patriotic sentiment and a sense of shared national purpose were high, and for most white Americans the racial tensions of the 1960s were not yet on the horizon. The photo's setting in Pennsylvania evokes heartland America.[13]

The family in the photo is plainly Caucasian, and the practice of praying before the meal denotes them as Christian. The email text leads with a quote from the King James version of the Bible, securing their Protestant affiliation. Moreover, the characteristics of the table and the room—with some signs of affluence but no servants—mark it as middle-class, and the position of the father figure at the head of the table depicts traditional gender norms. The multiple layers of meaning in this single image make it a nearly perfect exhibit of the lost utopian world of White Christian America.

But the newly reelected president embodied a very different story. President Obama's second inaugural address, with its forward-thinking narrative of moral progress, presented a striking contrast to the nostalgic lament of the Christian Coalition email. Obama framed the speech with an opening reference to the Declaration of Independence, then painted a portrait of struggle and progress in living up to the Constitutional principle of equality. He described the present moment as the continuation of "a never-ending journey to bridge the meaning of those words with the realities of our time." The crescendo of his address echoed Martin Luther King, Jr.'s "I Have a Dream" speech, but expanded its reach in significant ways:

We, the people, declare today that the most evident of truths—that all of us are created equal—is the star that guides us still; just as it guided our forebears through Seneca Falls, and Selma, and Stonewall. . . .

It is now our generation's task to carry on what those pioneers began. For our journey is not complete until our wives, our mothers and daughters can earn a living equal to their efforts. (Applause.) Our journey is not complete until our gay brothers and sisters are treated like anyone else under the law—(applause)—for if we are truly created equal, then surely the love we commit to one another must be equal as well. (Applause.) Our journey is not complete until no citizen is forced to wait for hours to exercise the right to vote. (Applause.) Our journey is not complete until we find a better way to welcome the striving, hopeful immigrants who still see America as a land of opportunity—(applause). . . .

That is our generation's task—to make these words, these rights, these values of life and liberty and the pursuit of happiness real for every American.[14]

If most readers of the Christian Coalition email found comfort in its black-and-white depiction of a bygone era, they were almost certainly dismayed by President Obama's speech. Among the Christian Coalition's audience, Obama's speech was not a harbinger of progress but a disturbing celebration of moral disarray. The two divergent and competing narratives—one looking wistfully back to midcentury heartland America and one looking hopefully forward to a multicultural America—cut to the heart of the massive cultural divide facing the country today.

A PRRI survey question captured the breadth and depth of this cultural gulf: "Since the 1950s, do you think American culture and way of

FIGURE 3.2 Opinions About Changes in American Culture Since 1950s

Since the 1950s, do you think American culture and way of life has mostly changed for the better, or has it mostly changed for the worse?

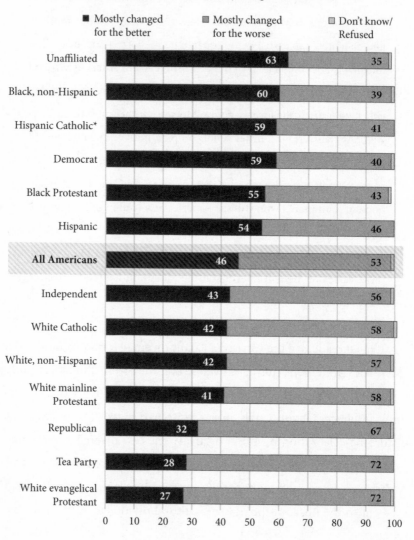

■ Mostly changed   ■ Mostly changed   ☐ Don't know/
for the better   for the worse   Refused

*Sample size is less than 100 (N=98). Results should be interpreted with caution.
Source: PRRI 2015 American Values Survey.

life has mostly changed for the better, or has it mostly changed for the worse?" (Figure 3.2).[15]

The question of whether American culture has gone downhill since the 1950s divides Americans overall, with a majority (53 percent) saying it has changed mostly for the worse, compared to 46 percent who say it has changed mostly for the better. But we can see stark cleavages by race and religion. More than seven in ten (72 percent) white evangelical Protestants and nearly six in ten (58 percent) white mainline Protestants say American culture and way of life has changed for the worse since the 1950s. Roughly six in ten white Catholics (58 percent) agree with their fellow white Christians that American culture has changed for the worse since the 1950s.

Meanwhile, approximately six in ten Hispanic Catholics (59 percent) say the opposite—that American culture has changed for the better. Approximately six in ten (63 percent) religiously unaffiliated Americans also say American culture and way of life has changed for the better since the mid-twentieth century, as do majorities of African American Protestants (55 percent). Overall, the pattern is unambiguous: most white Christians—along with groups in which they constitute a majority, like the Tea Party—believe that America is on a downhill slide, while strong majorities of most other groups in the country say things are improving.

The End of the White Christian Strategy

This cultural divide illustrates the far-reaching political and cultural consequences of White Christian America's demise. We are witnessing the end of the era. For the first time in more than five decades, an appeal to a sentimental vision of midcentury heartland America is not a winning political strategy. To understand the post-Obama milieu, it is necessary to understand the "White Christian Strategy," a political tactic employed primarily by the Republican Party beginning with the campaigns of Barry Goldwater and Richard Nixon in the mid-1960s and ending with Mitt Romney's failed presidential run in 2012.

From the Southern Strategy to the White Christian Strategy

What I am calling the White Christian Strategy is an outgrowth of the Southern Strategy, a tactic developed by political conservatives and the Republican Party in the mid-1960s to appeal to white southern voters who were angry with the Democratic Party for its support of civil rights. The Southern Strategy picked up momentum through two critical transition moments, one in the 1960s and one in the 1980s, which political scientists Merle and Earl Black identified as the two iterations of the "Great White Switch."[16]

Prior to the civil rights movement, most white Southerners were loyal members of the Democratic Party. But with the passage of landmark civil rights legislation like the Civil Rights Act of 1964 and the Voting Rights Act of 1965, Republican Party strategists saw an opportunity to coax disgruntled white southern voters into their camp.[17] The first Great White Switch began in the 1964 presidential race, when Barry Goldwater ran an explicitly anti–civil rights campaign under the Republican banner. Goldwater lost, but his run loosened the historic ties between the Democrats and the South. In that year, for the first time since the Civil War, more southern whites voted for the Republican candidate than for the Democrat, setting a precedent that has held true for every subsequent presidential election.[18] In 1968, Richard Nixon struck a deal with South Carolina Senator Strom Thurmond—promising to oppose court-ordered busing to integrate schools, name a southerner to the Supreme Court, and pick someone acceptable to the South for his running mate—which secured Southern support for his campaign.[19] Following Nixon's success, Republican Party strategists continued to hone these racial wedge tactics in the South, giving them a prominent place in the GOP's national political playbook.[20]

A confluence of three events kept the Southern Strategy from fully taking hold in the mid-1970s. The Watergate scandal and Nixon's subsequent resignation in 1974—coupled with national weariness over the war in Vietnam—tarnished the GOP's image, making Republican candidates an unappealing electoral prospect.[21] Then in 1976, the Democrats nominated Jimmy Carter, a Southern Baptist, Sunday-school-teaching Georgia governor who seemed the ideal antidote to southern discontent. Many Goldwater white Southerners had high hopes for Carter, the first born-again Christian to occupy the White House. But he quickly proved indifferent to their agenda.[22] He refused to roll back civil rights protections and supported controversial women's rights legislation like the Equal Rights Amendment.[23] To the consternation of those who opposed Supreme Court decisions that outlawed school prayer in the early 1960s,[24] Carter's fealty to separation of church and state openly challenged the growing evangelical Protestant movement that sought to reverse these dramatic social changes.[25] Carter's election in 1976 was only a temporary stay in what would ultimately be a decisive judgment against the Democratic Party by white, mostly Christian voters in the South. In an ironic twist, it was disappointment with Carter's moderate politics that transposed the Southern Strategy into an overtly religious key.[26]

By the time Carter took office, evangelicals were just beginning to emerge into the national spotlight as a powerful interest group.[27] The Reverend Jerry Falwell, an independent Baptist pastor in Virginia, was one of the major architects of this transformation.[28] Setting out to capitalize on the growing discontent among conservative white Christians, in 1976 he launched a nationwide series of "I Love America" rallies that explicitly linked his faith to a political agenda: opposition to feminism, homosexuality, and pornography. The crowds that thronged to his rallies were tangible evidence that Falwell had struck a nerve.[29] Over the next few years, he became an increasingly vocal critic of the Carter administration. By 1979, he had officially founded the Moral Majority, a political organization that threw its weight behind a Republican rising star: Ronald Reagan.[30]

Reagan was the spark that Falwell needed to turn the White Christian Strategy into a true political force. The California governor's ability to connect with white conservative Christians was unparalleled—he understood their potential as an electoral engine and spoke eloquently about their concerns. At the 1980 Religious Roundtable's National Affairs Briefing, Reagan was introduced as "God's man." Turning to the roomful of prominent white Christian leaders, he said: "I know you can't endorse me, but I want you to know that I endorse you."[31]

Just as Reagan helped carry Falwell's message onto the national stage, Falwell played a critical role in propelling Reagan into the White House. In 1980, the Moral Majority ran more than $10 million in ads supporting Reagan.[32] Although in that election cycle many southern white voters were still registered as Democrats and voted for state-level Democratic candidates, they crossed party lines to vote for Reagan at the top of the ticket.[33] Over the next eight years, Reagan presided over the second Great White Switch, the decade of transition when many southern whites shed their long-standing affiliation with the Democrats and began to not only vote for Republican presidential candidates but to identify as Republicans.[34]

The alliance between the Republican Party and the emerging Christian Right, helmed by Falwell, proved to be an unstoppable political union. The Reagan presidency gave white Christian conservatives the attention of a sitting president and bolstered their fundraising capabilities. Flush with cash, groups like the Moral Majority began to build an impressive political machine.[35] The Christian Right's religious rhetoric and extensive organizing at the local level, in turn, gave the GOP a new tool for driving a wedge between the Democrats and white southern voters. Leaders like Falwell brought a new, moral language to these old political maneuvers, allowing the goals of the Southern Strategy—the acquisition of white Christian voters in the South—to be pursued under more respectable auspices.[36] As a result, the White Christian Strategy that arose from this partnership became an integral part of the Republican Party's strategic playbook.

When the Moral Majority officially disbanded in 1989, declaring its mission accomplished, other leaders and organizations moved to consolidate its gains and propel the White Christian Strategy forward into the 1990s.[37] Pat Robertson and Ralph Reed of the Christian Coalition of America, James Dobson of Focus on the Family, and Gary Bauer and Tony Perkins of the Family Research Council spoke for White Christian America through a proliferation of statewide and local chapters of their organizations. These conservative titans continued to rally their followers by leveraging white Christians' discomfort with the country's growing secularism and pluralism, and calling for a return to what they portrayed as America's Protestant Christian roots. By the end of the decade, these groups had become a staple of Republican politics virtually everywhere, although their presence was strongest in the South and Midwest.[38]

The leaders of the Christian conservative movement won support by extolling the virtues of an orderly bygone era, where white Protestant Christian beliefs and institutions were unquestionably dominant and there were clearly defined roles for whites and nonwhites, men and women. For these groups, the allure of the black-and-white image of a family Thanksgiving meal lay in this utopian vision of "true" America.

George W. Bush's election in 2000 showed that the White Christian Strategy was still viable. According to political scientist John Green, one of the most astute observers of conservative Christian political activism, the Christian Right played a key role in the Republican primaries by boosting Bush's campaign over his rival John McCain, who had publicly called leaders of the Christian Right "agents of intolerance."[39] In the general election in November 2000, Green reported that 80 percent of the Christian Right's voting bloc supported George W. Bush.[40] These voters also certainly played a role in securing Bush's razor-thin electoral victory over Al Gore in key battleground states.

If the Moral Majority reigned over the 1980s and the Christian Coalition dominated the 1990s, the 2000s were the decade of James Dobson's Focus on the Family. Dobson, an evangelical Christian psychologist and author with a flair for both self-promotion and institution building, had been a prominent Christian Right figure in the 1990s, but with Bush's election he began to use his media empire as a tool for political activism.[41] By the time of Bush's reelection campaign in 2004, Dobson's broadcasting juggernaut consisted of daily radio addresses with a bigger audience than NPR and ten monthly magazines with a subscriber base of 2.3 million. The sprawling Focus on the Family campus in Colorado Springs processed so much mail that it qualified for its own zip code.[42]

Dobson was one of the engineers of the 2004 "Values Voters" campaign, which buoyed Bush's re-election and the passage of more than a dozen state-level bans on same-sex marriage. After the 2004 election, Christian conservative leaders like Dobson, Perkins, and Ralph Reed (now at the Faith and Freedom Coalition after a stint as a Republican operative) flaunted poll numbers showing that conservative Christians—who had turned out in record numbers, urged on by the gay marriage bans—were the key to Bush's success.[43] While the causal claims are debatable, there is no doubt that white evangelical Protestants turned out in high numbers and that nearly eight in ten (79 percent) pulled the lever for Bush.[44]

But by the end of Bush's second term, the resurgence of White Christian America's evangelical wing began to lose steam. The year 2007 brought with it a succession of symbolic events. Most prominently, Rev. Jerry Falwell, founder of the Moral Majority, died on May 15. Just a few months later on September 5, Rev. D. James Kennedy—the Florida megachurch pastor and founding board member of the Moral Majority whom *Rolling Stone* magazine called "the most influential evangelical you've never heard of"—died as well. Between 2007 and 2008 alone, Focus on the Family laid off nearly 250 workers, approximately one fifth of its workforce.[45] By 2011, it was operating with half the staff it had employed in 2002.[46]

The National Association of Evangelicals, the organization founded as a conservative counterweight to the National Council of Churches, spent 2007 plagued by public scandal and infighting. The NAE entered the year functioning with an interim head after NAE president Ted Haggard resigned in November 2006 following revelations that he had been having sexual liaisons with a male prostitute.[47]

Perhaps most tellingly, 2007 was the year that it became clear that the Christian Right had lost its ability to influence the nominating process for Republican Party presidential candidates.[48] The Council for National Policy, a small, secretive but powerful group that includes a who's who of Christian Right leaders, emerged from its 2007 meeting at a Florida resort without coming to consensus on a GOP horse to back in the 2008 election, despite the presence of Mike Huckabee, who—as an ordained Southern Baptist minister—was one of their own.[49] They remained divided throughout the Republican primaries, from which John McCain emerged triumphant. Again in 2012, over 150 conservative Christian leaders attended a private meeting at a Texas ranch looking for an alternative to Romney, at least in part because of their reticence about his Mormon faith. Despite voting overwhelmingly to back Catholic candidate Rick Santorum, they were unable to halt Romney's march to the nomination.[50]

But the White Christian Strategy had not quite run its course. The GOP continued to rely on this strategy in national elections, and with the election of Barack Obama, white Christian conservatives rallied in a new and unexpected way.

The Rise of the Tea Party

On a rainy day in April 2009, less than three months into Barack Obama's presidency, protesters swarmed the park across from the White House. Some wore tea bags affixed to their glasses or umbrellas, while others preferred a projectile approach, tossing boxes of tea bags over the fence and onto the White House lawn.[51]

It was Tax Day, and the group of demonstrators on Pennsylvania Avenue was just one of the hundreds of groups across the country who had gathered to demonstrate against government overspending—specifically, the Obama administration's $787 billion stimulus package. The protests had taken inspiration from an unlikely source. In February 2009, from the floor of the Chicago Board of Trade, CNBC commentator Rick Santelli launched into a rant about President Obama's housing bailout plan, which was designed to help some homeowners refinance high interest mortgages to avoid foreclosure. Santelli's monologue culminated in a cry for a second "Tea Party," in the spirit of the 1773 protest against British import taxes.[52] On Tax Day, protesters across the country waved placards with messages like "Abolish the I.R.S.," "Less Government More Free Enterprise," "We Miss Reagan," and "Honk if You Are Upset About Your Tax Dollars Being Spent on Illegal Aliens."[53]

The demonstrations were the first stirring of a nationwide movement that came simply to be called the Tea Party, and the protesters weren't just angry about the stimulus plan. By the fall of 2009, Tea Party groups had coalesced in opposition to President Obama's health care reform law, which organizers decried as a dangerous form of government overreach.[54] They turned the first part of their title into an acronym—"Taxed Enough Already"—and with help from Fox News, which gave the movement round-the-clock coverage, the Tea Party soon became a regular feature of the media landscape.[55] In January 2010, Republican Scott Brown won a special election to fill the late Ted Kennedy's Massachusetts Senate seat, a surprising upset that fueled the Tea Party's momentum.[56] Polls around the 2010 midterm elections showed that about one in ten Americans considered themselves a part of the Tea Party movement.[57]

The handful of national Tea Party organizations that sprang up in 2009 and 2010, such as FreedomWorks and the Tea Party Express, officially branded theirs as a libertarian movement—opposed to government overspending in general and to Obama's health care reform law in particular.[58] On the ground, however, the Tea Party conveyed other undercurrents of distress. Signs and T-shirts at Tea Party marches featured images of President Obama as an African witch doctor, a mugger holding Uncle Sam from behind in a chokehold, or with the disfigured smile of Batman's Joker.[59] Rand Paul, a Kentucky ophthalmologist and the son of the perennial libertarian presidential candidate Ron Paul, muddied his victory in the 2010 Republican Senate primary with a controversy over his inability to say whether he would have voted for the 1964 Civil Rights Act.[60] These overtones, along with the fact that Tea Party members were overwhelmingly white, fueled accusations that their virulent reaction against the federal government was actually a symptom of their discomfort with the nation's first black president.[61]

But most of the early coverage of the Tea Party missed something vitally important: its connection to the Christian Right. Just before the November 2010 elections, PRRI, in partnership with The Brookings Institution, released one of the first surveys to map the demographics of the Tea Party.[62] Some of its findings were foreseeable—compared to the general population, Tea Party supporters were likelier to be white and supportive of small government—but others upset the conventional wisdom about the budding movement. Despite the official assertions that the Tea Party represented a new libertarian surge, nearly half (47 percent) of Tea Party supporters reported that they also considered themselves a part of the Religious Right or Christian conservative movement. Moreover, they were mostly social conservatives, with views on issues like abortion and same-sex marriage that would have dismayed libertarian purists. Nearly two thirds (63 percent) of Tea Party members said abortion should be illegal, and only 18 percent favored allowing gay and lesbian couples to marry. This new research showed definitively that the Tea Party, far from representing a new strain of libertarian populism, was in fact another revival of White Christian America.

A subsequent PRRI survey, conducted in 2013, brought the link between the Tea Party and the Christian Right into even sharper focus.[63] Contrary to Tea Party leaders' claims to libertarianism, the survey showed that the two segments of the American population operated in almost completely separate spheres. More than six in ten (61 percent) libertarians reported that they did not consider themselves part of the Tea Party movement, while only approximately one quarter (26 percent) of Tea Party members said they identified as libertarians. Twice as many Tea Partiers (52 percent) said they were part of the Religious Right or Christian conservative movement.

The Tea Party is animated by a narrative of cultural loss that allows it to function as a continuation of the White Christian Strategy. The Obama presidency provided a unique focal point for many white Christian voters, who already felt as if familiar cultural touchstones were disappearing at every turn. Shifting social norms, declining religious affiliation, changing demographics, and a struggling economy—all were embodied in one powerful symbol: a black man in the White House.

The appeal of a return to an idealized past can be seen across a number of attitudinal measures. Like white evangelical Protestants, large numbers (70 percent) of Tea Party members agree that American culture and way of life has changed for the worse since the 1950s.[64] A remarkable three quarters (73 percent) of Tea Party members agree with the statement, "Today discrimination against whites has become as big a problem as discrimination against blacks and other minorities," compared to just 45 percent of Americans overall.[65] More than half (55 percent) of Tea Partiers agree that the United States *today* is a Christian nation—compared to only 39 percent of Americans as a whole.[66]

Overall, the Tea Party movement is best understood as a socially conservative movement with deep roots in White Christian America; as it gained momentum, the Tea Party became the natural receptacle of many Christian Right concerns. Its national leaders have been only minimally successful at maintaining a thin libertarian veneer over what is at its heart a socially conservative movement. The Tea Party continues to log some victories in local races, and in midterm and primary elections with lower turnout. It was not, however, a major factor in the 2012 presidential election. Milt Romney's defeat in 2012 showed that despite its appearance of vitality, the Tea Party is better understood as a late-stage expression of a White Christian America that is passing from the scene.

The Romney Campaign and the White Christian Strategy

Early in the evening on November 6, 2012, the atmosphere at the Mitt Romney Victory Party at the Boston Convention and Exhibition Center was electric with anticipation. Fox News's coverage of the incoming returns from the 2012 presidential election resounded from TV monitors. The crowd cheered and waved miniature American flags as Republican strongholds like West Virginia and Indiana rolled in for Romney.[67]

Upstairs at the Westin Waterfront Boston Hotel, the candidate and his family watched the same coverage. Romney had written a 1,118-word victory address earlier in the day—but no concession speech, he said. "I feel like we put it all on the field. We left nothing in the locker room. We fought to the very end, and I think that's why we'll be successful," he told reporters aboard his plane as they flew from his last campaign stop in Pittsburgh to Boston for the election night festivities. An eight-minute fireworks display over the Boston Harbor was planned to celebrate his win.[68]

Romney and his advisors were confident, going into election day, that they would win. The public polls showed a close race, but the Romney campaign insisted that Obama couldn't match the record-breaking levels of support from ethnic minorities that had propelled him to the White House in 2008.[69] They preferred instead to rely on their own "unskewed" polls that assumed a whiter, older, and more conservative electorate—more like the people who turned out in 2010, the year of the Tea Party surge. Romney and his team were relying on their white Christian base to carry the day, optimistic that the composition of the 2008 electorate was an anomaly.

Then New Hampshire and Pennsylvania, two sought-after swing states, went for Obama. They were quickly followed by Michigan, Minnesota, and Wisconsin—all states with large populations of white working-class voters, whose discontent with the president was supposed to ensure Romney's victory. The documentary *Mitt*, a behind-the-scenes account of Romney's quest for the presidency, shows the faltering mood as the evening wore on. Just before the networks called Ohio—the pivotal swing state—for Obama, one of Romney's sons turned to his father. "I just can't believe you're going to lose," he said. "I just don't believe it's possible."

Even after Fox News declared Obama the winner, Republican strategist Karl Rove appeared live, arguing that his own polling numbers showed that Romney could still take Ohio. His unwillingness to concede the race prompted Fox News host Megyn Kelly to ask incredulously, "Is this just the math that you do as a Republican to make yourself feel better or is it real?" When Rove continued to insist that Romney still had a chance, Kelly laughed and wrapped the segment abruptly, saying, "That's awkward."[70]

The Romney campaign's incredulity was justifiable. They had hit or exceeded most of their electoral targets. Romney tirelessly pursued political independents, who GOP strategists believed would lead them to the White House. Obama had won independent voters by 8 percentage points in 2008, but Romney won them by 5 percentage points nationally—and by 10 points in Ohio.[71] He also won the senior vote by 12 points, up from McCain's 8-point margin.

Most significantly, Romney increased his margins among white voters overall, taking McCain's 12-point margin to an impressive 20 points. White Christian voters, too, fell solidly in the Romney camp. Romney maintained McCain's 11-point advantage over Obama (55 percent vs. 44 percent) among white mainline Protestants and performed well among white Catholic voters, increasing McCain's 5-point margin over Obama to 19 points (59 percent vs. 40 percent). Among white evangelical Protestants, a group that refused to fall behind Romney until the end of the primaries, Romney performed better than McCain and as well as George W. Bush, winning a remarkable 79 percent of their votes.[72]

From the Republican perspective, there were no obvious failures. White turnout did dip slightly compared to previous election cycles, but a greater proportion of white voters who showed up at the polls cast their ballot for Romney than for the Republican candidate in past years.[73] Advantages the Obama campaign might have retained among lower- and middle-income whites also evaporated.[74]

So how could Romney have lost? As analysts began to tally the numbers from the 2012 election, the answer quickly became apparent. The traditional Republican coalition—heavily dependent on white Christians—simply no longer added up to a majority. Black voter turnout jumped between 2008 and 2012, making 2012 the first presidential election in which black turnout exceeded white turnout.[75] Although turnout among Hispanic voters actually dropped compared to 2008, more

Hispanic voters cast ballots thanks to rapid population growth in the intervening four years. The Census Bureau revealed that the number of Hispanic Americans who voted for president increased by about 1.5 million from 2008 to 2012, to a record 11.2 million. (Notably, the number of Hispanic Americans who *didn't* vote increased even more.)[76] And Obama increased his vote share among Hispanic voters from 67 percent in 2008 to 71 percent in 2012. In post-election analysis, the Associated Press concluded that if the composition of the electorate in 2012 had looked the way it did in 2004, Romney would have narrowly defeated Obama.[77]

It was clear that the Romney campaign had doomed itself from the start by using an outdated playbook. The Romney campaign—with its largely successful execution of a campaign that ended in defeat—marks a milestone: the end of the White Christian Strategy for presidential elections.

The 2013 GOP Autopsy Report

In the midst of the handwriting over the lost election, with an eye toward the changing electorate, Republican operatives set out to give the party's strategy a much needed makeover. In December 2012, Republican National Committee chairman Reince Priebus named a task force to provide a thorough analysis of the party's failings and chart a way forward. "The Republicans need a new business model, and a new product for the new century," a GOP pollster told *The Washington Post*. "It's not just a problem of one candidate or one campaign."[78]

The GOP's "autopsy report," as it came to be known, was released in March 2013 with much fanfare.[79] The ninety-seven-page document promised "an honest review of the 2012 election cycle and a path forward for the Republican Party to ensure success in winning more elections."[80] Republicans would not be able to win a presidential election, the report explained, without rebranding their conservatism to appeal to women, ethnic minorities, and young people, who saw the party as narrow-minded and out-of-touch. Focus groups revealed that many Americans dismissed the GOP as a collection of "stuffy old men."[81]

In the report, the task force offered a slate of ambitious policy prescriptions. Noting that the party relied overwhelmingly on white voters, they declared that it was time to start doing serious outreach to the growing Hispanic population. The report recommended that the GOP "elevate Hispanic leaders within the party infrastructure," reach out more aggressively to Hispanic faith communities, and commit more resources to voter registration and mobilization among ethnic minorities.[82] But the Republican Party's hard-line stance on immigration policy—including Romney's controversial suggestion that politicians should make it impossible for illegal immigrants to find work, forcing them to "self-deport" to their home countries—had not positioned the party well for this kind of outreach. Just months after the GOP autopsy report was released, a PRRI survey of the American Hispanic community found that in an open-ended question about perceptions of the Republican Party, just one in ten (11 percent) Hispanics offered a positive comment. A similarly small number (12 percent) said they thought the GOP cared about people like them.[83]

To address the equally glaring issue of the youth vote—Romney won voters older than 30 by 1.8 million votes but lost voters younger than 30 by five million votes—the report proposed a change in tone. Antigay rhetoric in particular, they suggested, was alienating Millennials, who saw same-sex marriage as the civil rights issue of their day. The report stopped short of endorsing gay marriage, but made it plain that Republican politicians lambasted gay rights at their peril.

When it came to the GOP's core constituency—conservative white Americans—the report was more oblique. It did not, for example, mention the Tea Party. The authors recommended that the party "increase its base" by eschewing conventions and caucuses—which require a small, active core of supporters and tend to dampen turnout—in favor of primaries, which would "invite" more voters into the party.[84] They also suggested that the party halve the number of debates and shorten the primary season in an effort to lessen the exposure more mainstream candidates might have to Tea Party challengers from the right.

At the time of its release, the report was lauded for its honesty by commentators on both the left and the right. *New York Times* columnist Thomas B. Edsall praised the authors for their "remarkably hard-headed diagnosis" of the party's "internal discord and vulnerability."[85] At *The Washington Post*, the conservative analyst Jennifer Rubin wrote, "the report is controversial and bold, not the usual political pabulum designed to avoid ruffling feathers. . . . The RNC is taking a risk here, one that is badly needed."[86]

But Tea Party leaders lashed out against the recommendations, saying they represented the opinions of the Republican elite, rather than the grassroots groups that were crucial to the party's electoral success. Some criticized the proposed reforms to the primary season, saying that they unfairly limited the influence of Tea Party candidates, and especially their ability to push mainstream Republicans to the right during the early stages of campaigns.[87]

Others condemned the report's accommodating language on social issues such as gay marriage and immigration. "Here is a rule of politics which just does not change, ever: When Republicans distinguish themselves from Democrats, they almost always win, and when they don't, they almost always lose," Brent Bozell, chairman of the Tea Party group

For America, told *The Hill*.[88] Rush Limbaugh also blasted the report, saying the authors were "totally bamboozled."[89] The solution, in his eyes, was for the party to become more conservative, not less.

For all its bold policy directives, the RNC's autopsy report had little effect on the immediate actions of the Republican majority in the House of Representatives. Held hostage by a united Tea Party minority, the House repeatedly rejected the Senate's bipartisan efforts to pass an immigration reform bill. But one year after the release of the report, the mood at GOP headquarters was surprisingly sunny. In March 2014, RNC chairman Priebus told reporters at a press breakfast that the Democrats were facing a "tsunami-type election" in the upcoming November midterms, predicting that the GOP would take the Senate and even pick up some congressional seats.[90]

On the same day, the Democratic National Committee issued a report mocking the Republicans' "rebrand" failure.[91] The GOP, the Democrats contended, had only pretended to make changes. Its policies still catered to a narrow base of white conservatives while alienating minorities, women, and young voters.

It turned out that both parties were correct. GOP candidates generally ignored the RNC task force's recommendations—and not just on immigration reform. But when the 2014 midterms came, the party triumphed, winning nearly every contested race in the country, scooping up more governors' mansions, and taking decisive control of Congress.[92]

The GOP's success wasn't due to a change in strategy. In fact, Republican candidates deliberately returned to the tactics that lost Romney the White House in 2012. This was a calculation tailored for the composition of the midterm electorate. As the voter pool shrinks in midterm elections it skews more heavily toward older white voters—voters who also tend to be conservative Christians. The turnout rate for the 2014 midterms was shockingly low; at only 36 percent of eligible voters, it was the lowest in seventy-two years.[93] In fact, going back to 1900, the only two other national elections with similarly paltry turnout occurred just ahead of the Great Depression and in the midst of World War II. Because so many voters stayed home in 2014, white Christians exerted a disproportionate influence over the election's outcome.

The Shrinking White Christian Voter Pool

But the empirical trends indicate that these are short-term gains, and the delays in acting on the GOP task force's recommendations may prove costly for 2016 and other future presidential campaigns. As Figure 3.3 illustrates, the stair-step downward trajectory of white Christian presence in the electorate over the last three decades is stunningly clear. In 1992, when Bill Clinton was elected to his first term as president, nearly three quarters (73 percent) of the electorate was white and Christian. By 2012, white Christians' influence had declined precipitously, comprising only 57 percent of the electorate. A linear forecast line based on these trends demonstrates that the White Christian Strategy will yield diminishing returns in each successive national election cycle. White Christians will likely make up 55 percent of voters in 2016 and drop to 52 percent of voters by the following presidential campaign in 2020. If current trends hold steady, 2024 will be a watershed year—the first American election in which white Christians do not constitute a majority of voters.

The chart demonstrates that every midterm election, the GOP essentially gets to rewind the clock. Low turnout among young and minority voters allows the GOP to carry over whatever advantage they had

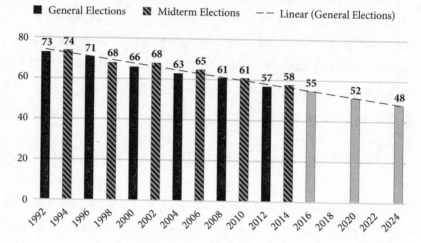

**FIGURE 3.3 White Christians as a Proportion
of the Electorate (1992–2014)**

With 10–year linear projection

■ General Elections   ◪ Midterm Elections   – – Linear (General Elections)

Source: National Exit Polls, 1992–2014.

in the last presidential election among white Christian voters into the following midterm election. But even this "midterm time warp" GOP advantage is fading over time. Newt Gingrich's 1994 revolution relied on an electorate that was 74 percent white and Christian. The more recent Tea Party wave of 2010 banked on an electorate in which 61 percent of voters were white and Christian. And the 2014 Republican gains leveraged an electorate that was only 58 percent white and Christian.

For GOP leaders, the reliably Republican midterm constituency may seem like a bonus—a chance for the party to make up ground and reinforce their connection with their base. But in other important ways, it's a distraction that undermines the GOP's long-term goal of creating a more diverse electoral coalition. In this light, it's easy to see why the Republicans refused to pass immigration reform or loosen their rhetoric on gay rights with a year to go before the midterms.

These actions could have created havoc among their most reliable supporters, thus threatening their chances of retaking the Senate. But it's clear that these appeals to white Christians, while helpful in some short-term fights, sealed the fate of the Romney campaign in 2012 and will likely set the GOP back when it turns to the task of reclaiming the White House in 2016.

Together, Figures 3.4 and 3.5 demonstrate the shortsightedness of the GOP's continued reliance on the White Christian Strategy in this climate. As data from the National Exit Polls demonstrate (Figure 3.4), in 1992 the voting coalitions of both George H. W. Bush and Bill Clinton were mostly white and Christian (86 percent and 60 percent respectively). This spread remained steady through both Clinton elections in the 1990s, but the religious composition of partisan voting coalitions subsequently began to drift apart in the 2000s. Even as the proportion of white Christian voters in the electorate dropped from 73 percent in 1992

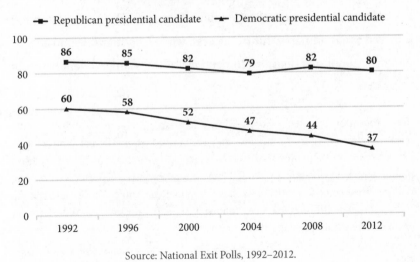

FIGURE 3.4 Reliance on White Christian Votes by Party (1992–2012)

Source: National Exit Polls, 1992–2012.

to 57 percent in 2012 (Figure 3.3), Republican Party candidates including Romney have continued to rely on voting coalitions in which approximately eight out of every ten supporters are white and Christian.
Democratic candidates, by contrast, have more closely followed the
changing demographics in the country. Whereas Bill Clinton's winning
coalition in 1992 was 60 percent white Christian, Obama's winning coalition in 2012 was only 37 percent white Christian. The result is that the
white Christian strategy has left Republicans dependent on a steadily
shrinking slice of the electorate.

Figure 3.5* uses 2012 post-election data from PRRI to further illus-
trate the challenges for the GOP. Even a quick glance at this chart reveals
the disadvantage Romney and future Republican presidential candidates face: the racial and religious composition of Romney's political
coalition mirrored the country's oldest voters, while Obama's coalition
looked like Millennials.

For Republicans, this chart should be alarming. Nearly eight in ten
(79 percent) of Romney's coalition were white Christian voters, and approximately half of those were white evangelical Protestants. This group
has been an important anchor for Republican politics in the past, but it
is flawed as a roadmap to future success: white Christians overall constitute only about one quarter (26 percent) of the youngest generation of

*The proportion of voters who are white Christians in Figure 3.5 differs slightly
from numbers in Figure 3.4 because they are derived from different samples. Figure 3.4 relies on the national exit polls, which survey actual voters as they leave
polling places on election day, while Figure 3.5 relies on self-reported vote among
self-identified voters on PRRI's post-election American Values Survey, a telephone
survey conducted in the first week following the 2012 election. All differences in
estimates are within the margin of error.

FIGURE 3.5 The Obama and Romney Coalitions

Among 2012 voters by religious affiliation and age

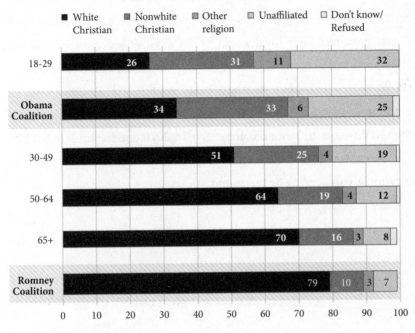

■ White   ■ Nonwhite   ▨ Other   ▨ Unaffiliated   ▢ Don't know/
   Christian   Christian   religion   Refused

	White Christian	Nonwhite Christian	Other religion	Unaffiliated	Don't know/Refused
18-29	26	31	11		32
Obama Coalition	34	33	6		25
30-49	51	25	4		19
50-64	64	19	4		12
65+	70	16	3		8
Romney Coalition	79	10	3		7

Source: PRRI, Post-election American Values Survey, November 2012.

voters, and white evangelical Protestants comprise (only 12 percent of this youngest voting cohort).

Democrats may depend heavily on religiously unaffiliated voters, but they have also rounded out their coalition with percentages of other subgroups that mirror the demographics of younger Americans. The bloc of religiously unaffiliated voters is expanding quickly, comprising one quarter of Obama's voting coalition and about one third (32 percent) of young voters under the age of 30. Perhaps most notably, Obama's reliance on white Christian voters was less than half of Romney's.

•   •   •

Although the Romney campaign missed it, the math here is simple. In 2016 and beyond, the shrinking white Christian voter pool will probably continue to support Republican candidates as much as they have in the past, but their loyalty will help the GOP less and less. By the 2024 presidential election, even if the GOP nominee could secure every single white Christian vote, these votes would land 3 points short of a national majority. The data point to one unavoidable conclusion: if the GOP wishes to remain competitive in 2016 and beyond, the White Christian Strategy, one of the most dependable tactics in the Republican playbook, will need to be put to rest.

4

Family: Gay Marriage and White Christian America

"Same Love" at the Grammys

When we say music has the power to bring people together at the Grammys, we mean it. . . . This song is a love song not just for some of us but for all of us. And tonight we celebrate the commitment to love by some very beautiful couples . . . with an uplifting song that says whatever God you believe in, we come from the same one. Strip away the fear, underneath it's all the same love.

—Queen Latifah, introducing Macklemore and
Lewis at the 56th Grammy Awards

At the 56th Grammy Awards on January 26, 2014, the rapper Macklemore appeared before a soaring but spare backdrop, decorated with illuminated outlines of doors and windows that evoked the pointed arches and swooping vaults of Gothic church architecture. As Macklemore, Ryan Lewis, and the singer Mary Lambert launched into "Same Love," a nominee for Song of the Year, electric white lines glimmered into place to form the outlines of stained glass windows. The lyrics of the first verse contained a sharp indictment of many religious groups responses to same-sex relationships.

America the brave still fears what we don't know
And "God loves all his children" is somehow forgotten
But we paraphrase a book written thirty-five-hundred years ago.

As the performance continued, lights rose on a swaying multicultural chorus dressed in the satiny black robes and white stoles of a gospel choir accompanied by a full band. Warming to the performance, Macklemore finished the second verse about marriage equality—declaring "Damn right I support it." As he pointed his finger to the sky, a surge of applause washed over the room.

At the top of the stage, Grammy Award winner Queen Latifah strode through a pair of tall double doors while thirty-three diverse couples—straight and gay, multiracial and interracial—filed into the theater's aisles and faced each other. Queen Latifah, who had earlier registered with the state of California as a wedding officiant, asked the couples to exchange rings. As she pronounced them legally married, the white outlines in the backdrop burst into a rainbow of colors, gleaming like the windows of a cathedral. Madonna walked onstage in an all-white pantsuit and cowboy hat and began to sing a ballad version of her 1986 hit "Open Your Heart to Me." The camera panned to close-ups of the newlywed couples crying, hugging, and singing along, while the crowd jumped to their feet in a standing ovation.

The performance ended on an emotional high note with a musical call and response. The choir sang the opening words of Corinthians 13:4–8, a scripture commonly read at Christian weddings, while

Madonna and Lambert echoed their own line, "I'm not crying on Sundays."

Love is patient

Love is kind

Love is patient

Love is kind

(I'm not crying on Sundays)

Love is patient

(I'm not crying on Sundays)

Love is kind

(I'm not crying on Sundays)

The song's lyrics came out of the performers' deeply personal, negative experiences with religion. Macklemore wrote the main lyrics after experiencing the negative attitudes toward his gay uncles from both churches and the hip-hop scene. Lambert's echo line, "I'm not crying on Sundays," flowed from her experience as a lesbian Christian attending Mars Hill Church in Seattle, a prominent evangelical megachurch, where she regularly heard sermons and teachings that being sexually active with someone of the same gender, no matter what the context, was a sin. In an interview with the *Seattle Post-Intelligencer*, Lambert recalled that she would "come home from services and cry, ashamed and apologizing to God for being who she was."[1]

The performance wasn't just remarkable because of the musicians' support for the legalization of same-sex marriage. It was also a direct challenge to religious opposition to gay rights, mounted in front of 28.5 million American viewers on a Sunday night. The song was not so much an antireligion invective as it was an indictment of religion using its own principles and symbols. It took particular aim at the socially conservative branches of evangelical Protestant Christianity. The first verse argues that Christians who oppose gay rights are missing the forest for the trees by zeroing in on specific verses written in ancient cultural contexts while missing the vital message that "God loves all his children." The second verse goes even further, proclaiming that the sermons and liturgies of those who "preach hate" cannot be holy or anointed, because they contradict the basic spirit of the gospel. But the song ends on a different note, a kind of invitation, by repeating a biblical text and a reference to the pain that many gay Christians have experienced in church literally in the same breath.

Notably, the performance was not broadcast on MTV or VH-1, where a younger audience would safely embrace it. Instead, it played in living rooms across the country on CBS, during prime time. Its appearance on CBS was significant because for years the network had trailed the other major broadcasters in featuring pro-gay advertisements or even gay characters in their programming. In 2004, CBS refused to run an ad sponsored by the United Church of Christ, a mainline Protestant denomination, promoting the inclusion of gay and lesbian people in churches.[2] In the ad, two bouncers standing outside a church refused to admit a gay male couple. It ended with the words: "Jesus didn't turn people away; neither do we." Despite the fact that they had just featured a glut of campaign ads, CBS officials explained that they had rejected the spot because it ran afoul of the network's prohibition on "advocacy advertising." Six years later, in January 2010, CBS refused to air an ad for the gay dating site mancrunch.com, saying that it was "not within the Network's Broadcast Standards for Super Bowl Sunday."[3]

But CBS hit a turning point in July 2010, when the gay rights advocacy organization GLAAD gave the network a failing diversity grade for the second year running. At the end of the 2009–2010 TV season, GLAAD called out CBS for having no gay characters among its 132 series regulars—compared to eight gay characters at ABC, four at Fox, and three at NBC.[4] CBS entertainment president Nina Tassler responded by announcing that the network would be adding three gay characters to the next season. "We're disappointed in our track record so far. We're going to do it. We're not happy with ourselves," she said.[5] By the 2014–2015 season, CBS was still lagging behind the other major networks, but it had increased the number of gay regular series characters to six, or 3 percent of all its regular characters.[6]

Still, it's one thing to include gay characters in regular programming; it's quite another to feature a pro-gay rap song that openly criticizes Christian groups—*and* to host a large group wedding that includes same-sex couples—on prime-time television. The risky decision paid off commercially. The 56th Grammy Awards registered its second-highest viewer ratings in over twenty years—second only to the 2012 show, which aired one day after Whitney Houston's death.[7]

Rolling Stone declared: "Macklemore and Ryan Lewis turned their performance of pro-gay, pro-unity rap 'Same Love' into a piece of Grammy history tonight."[8] But it wasn't just a music industry milestone. This performance of "Same Love"—by Lambert and the duo who had just won four Grammys, including Best New Artist and Best Rap Album—on the country's most culturally cautious major broadcast network was a decisive sign that a tipping point had been reached.

Negative fallout from the 2014 Grammys was astonishingly muted. Bryan Fischer, the former spokesman for the American Family Association and a fervent opponent of gay rights, tweeted his objections ahead of the broadcast: "Heads up: Grammy telecast to feature sodomy-based wedding ceremonies." Fox News's Todd Starnes responded to the performance, tweeting, "I've never seen such a display of intolerance, bigotry and hatred. #Grammys #antichristian."[9] But these commentators had little company outside conservative Christian publications and social media circles. Two days after the show, Ed Stetzer, the head statistician for the Southern Baptist Convention, wrote a blog post at *Christianity Today*, "The Grammys, Grace, and the Gospel: 3 Things the Grammys Can Remind Christians." Stetzer acknowledged the show as another concrete reminder that conservative evangelical Christianity was losing the cultural center. "Views that were sidelined ten years ago (remember, Presidents Clinton and Obama were once opposed to gay marriage) are not just accepted, they are celebrated. . . . Times are a-changing."[10]

Opposition to Gay Rights and White Christian American Identity

During the rise of the Christian Right, evangelical leaders staked their communal identity on an unbridled opposition to gay rights—and at first they were strikingly successful. Opposition to gay rights was so widespread that the concept of nationwide "marriage equality" that became a reality in 2015 seemed a pipe dream to most activists and gay and lesbian Americans.

Faced with widespread intolerance and even violence, gay rights activists in the 1970s embarked on what seemed at the time like an ambitious crusade: passing laws banning discrimination on the basis of sexual orientation in employment and housing. It was a pressing concern, as discrimination against gays in the workforce was not only common in the private sector—it was the federal government's official policy. During the height of the Cold War, the government reacted to what historians have dubbed "the lavender scare."[11] In 1953, for example, President Dwight Eisenhower issued an executive order that prevented anyone who engaged in "sexual perversion" from holding a job in the federal government. Over the next two decades, FBI agents hunted down and fired thousands of gay and lesbian federal employees. Although other industries did not have similar blanket prohibitions, there was nothing to stop employers from summarily dismissing workers who were suspected of being gay, leaving many in perpetual fear of losing their jobs. By 1975, the push for workplace protections for gay and lesbian employees saw successes in revising federal government practices. Activists also began to make inroads into local ordinances by the late 1970s.[12] But these triumphs also catalyzed conservative Christian activists.

In January 1977, the Dade County Metro Commission in Miami, Florida, joined nearly thirty cities, including Los Angeles and New York, in banning employment and housing discrimination against gay and lesbian people. The decision caught the eye of Anita Bryant, a Christian gospel singer and former beauty queen living in Miami. Bryant, who was best known as the spokeswoman for Florida orange juice, became one of the key spokespeople for a movement to repeal the antidiscrimination ordinance, led by an efficient network of churches and Christian organizations.[13]

From the start, evangelicals' fears crystallized around the alleged threat posed by gay men. Arguing that gay men would molest children and try to "recruit" young boys to their "perverted, unnatural, and ungodly lifestyle," Bryant helped collect more than sixty thousand signatures—six times the number needed—to get a popular referendum against the ordinance on the ballot. She founded an organization called

Save Our Children and traveled throughout the South under its auspices, raising hundreds of thousands of dollars for advertising. Even before Miami's citizens were able to consider the referendum, Bryant had expanded her campaign to include local antidiscrimination laws in Minnesota and other states.[14] In 1977, when Miami voters approved the ballot initiative overturning the ordinance by a gaping two to one margin, Bryant declared the "normal majority" victorious. "With God's help, we will prevail in our fight to repeal similar laws throughout the nation which attempt to legitimize a lifestyle that is both dangerous and perverse," she announced.[15]

Bryant's coup in Miami made her into an evangelical icon. In 1978, a group of Southern Baptist pastors went so far as to campaign for her election as the first female vice president of the Southern Baptist Convention (although she lost). While Bryant's prominence in the Christian Right movement was cut short because of a divorce in 1980, her 1977 Miami victory was a defining moment for the nascent Christian Right.[16] Religious conservatives and Republican strategists were energized by her success. As the Christian conservative movement grew, it increasingly built its identity around the issue of gay rights, in part because leaders like Bryant were so popular. To many, her campaign against gay rights represented the first volley in a battle to roll back the secularizing effects of the 1960s Sexual Revolution and return the country to its Christian moral center.

A Republican state legislator from California named John Briggs, who also helped fight the Miami ordinance, returned home determined to bring similar changes to his state.[17] With the aid of Jerry Falwell and others, he introduced a broad ballot measure that would repeal the state's anti-discrimination law for gay teachers and give school districts explicit authority to fire teachers and other employees who were found to be either "engaging in" or "advocating, soliciting, imposing, encouraging, or promoting" sexual activity between "persons of the same sex."[18] Falwell organized California pastors in favor of Briggs's referendum, writing, "It is time that today's Christian generation stand up and speak out against the sin that is eating away at the very foundations of our nation."[19]

The Briggs campaign lost decisively at the ballot box, but its effects were far-reaching. As white evangelical leaders began to collaborate more closely with Republican politicians, opposition to gay rights became a fundamental element of their partnership. Throughout the 1980s and into the early 1990s, the struggle against any legal recognition of gay rights was central to the Christian Right's mission, and formed a cornerstone of white evangelicals' political character. The rise of AIDS made the gay community an even greater target for conservative activists, who decried the disease as God's judgment on homosexuals.[20] Republican senator Jesse Helms famously told *The New York Times* that federal funding for AIDS should be reduced because gay people contracted the illness through their "deliberate, disgusting, revolting conduct."[21] Helms' views weren't so far out of the mainstream; in 1992, a PSRA/*Times Mirror* poll found that 36 percent of Americans agreed that "AIDS might be God's punishment for immoral sexual behavior."[22]

Two major events in 1993 provided even more energy for the push against gay rights among Christian conservatives. In May, the Hawaii State Supreme Court ruled that denying marriage licenses to same-sex couples was a violation of the state constitution.[23] Then in July, President Bill Clinton instituted the "Don't Ask, Don't Tell" policy, a compromise that forbade military personnel from discriminating against or harassing closeted gay soldiers, while simultaneously excluding openly gay men and women from military service.[24] Republicans and Christian conservatives began organizing, and in 1996 Congress passed the federal Defense of Marriage Act, which defined marriage as the union of one man and one woman and allowed states to refuse to recognize same-sex marriages granted in other states; the law had bipartisan support in the House and the Senate, and President Clinton signed it.[25]

In 2001, now bolstered by the presence of a Republican in the White House, the Christian Right's antigay rhetoric hit a peak. Jerry Falwell, appearing on Pat Robertson's Christian Broadcasting Network television show two days after the September 11 attacks on the World Trade Center and the Pentagon, declared, "The pagans and the abortionists and the feminists and the gays and the lesbians who are actively trying to make that an alternative lifestyle, the ACLU, People for the American Way—all of them who have tried to secularize America, I point the finger in their face and say, 'You helped this happen.'" Robertson replied, "Well, I totally concur."[26]

The Dramatic Rise in Support for Same-Sex Marriage (2003–2015)

Courts and Legislatures: Changes in the Law

Because evangelical leaders made opposition to gay rights so central to their movement's identity, no issue captures White Christian America's loss of cultural power better than the rapid rise in public support for same-sex marriage. As recently as 2004, when the "values voters" campaign was instrumental in securing George W. Bush's reelection, opposition to abortion and same-sex marriage were still the two defining issues for the Christian Right. And as recently as the mid-2000s, evangelical leaders were still successfully utilizing opposition to gay marriage as a tool in the White Christian Strategy playbook. During the 2004 election, voters passed constitutional amendments against same-sex marriage in thirteen states.[27] At the end of 2004, there were sixteen states with constitutional bans on same-sex marriage,[28] and another twenty-nine states with statutory bans against same-sex marriage; gay couples could legally marry only in Massachusetts.[29]

Before the ink had fully dried on the draft of 2004 gay marriage bans, though, rapid fire actions in other states signaled that attitudes were beginning to shift. By 2006, the New Jersey legislature had passed a law allowing gay and lesbian couples to form civil unions,[30] and voters in Arizona rejected a constitutional ban on same-sex marriage, marking the first time a ballot measure to prohibit gay marriage had failed.[31] In 2007, New Hampshire followed New Jersey in legalizing civil unions.[32] The following year, Connecticut became the second state to legalize same-sex marriage.[33] In 2009, Vermont legalized same-sex marriage, as did Iowa, the first state outside New England to do so. Two thousand ten saw same-sex marriage become legal in New Hampshire and in the nation's capital, Washington, D.C. New York became the sixth and largest state to legalize same-sex marriage in 2011. And in 2012, President Obama became the first sitting president to voice approval for same-sex marriage.

But even as some lawmakers gradually began to push for gay marriage in their state legislatures, many continued to vigorously oppose it, creating a confusing and fraught political landscape. The tug-of-war between lawmakers, the public, and the courts over the issue of same-sex marriage was most visible in California. In 2007, the California legislature made same-sex marriage legal, but Republican governor Arnold Schwarzenegger vetoed the legislation.[34] The following year, the California Supreme Court ruled that gay and lesbian couples had a constitutional right to marry—but then voters overturned this ruling a few months later by narrowly passing Proposition 8, a constitutional amendment banning same-sex marriage.[35] In 2010, the Federal District Court in San Francisco found that Proposition 8 violated the U.S. Constitution, but marriages were not allowed to begin while the case was being appealed. Finally, in 2013, the U.S. Supreme Court ruled that Proposition 8's supporters lacked standing to defend the law and same-sex marriages resumed in California.

By early 2015—just twelve years after Massachusetts became the first state to allow gay and lesbian couples to marry legally—same-sex marriage was legal in thirty-seven states and the District of Columbia. Only thirteen state-level constitutional bans against same-sex marriage remained. On June 26, 2015, the U.S. Supreme Court issued its landmark ruling in *Obergefell v. Hodges*, declaring that all bans on same-sex marriage were unconstitutional. Justice Anthony Kennedy—a Reagan appointee who was the critical swing vote in the 5–4 decision, summarized the logic of the ruling this way in the majority opinion:

> Here the marriage laws enforced by the respondents are in essence unequal: same-sex couples are denied all the benefits afforded to opposite-sex couples and are barred from exercising a fundamental right. Especially against a long history of disapproval of their relationships, this denial to same-sex couples of the right to marry works a grave and continuing harm. The imposition of this disability on gays and lesbians serves to disrespect and subordinate them.[36]

The decision cleared the way for gay and lesbian couples to marry and to have their marriages recognized in all fifty states.

The Sea Change in Public Opinion

Compared to the fits and starts of the legal process, the increase in public support for gay rights in the twenty-first century has been remarkably steady. Figure 4.1 shows growing approval for same-sex marriage between 2003 and 2014, as measured by six leading national public opinion polls: PRRI, Pew Research, Gallup, CNN/ORC, ABC/*Washington Post*, and NBC/*Wall Street Journal*.

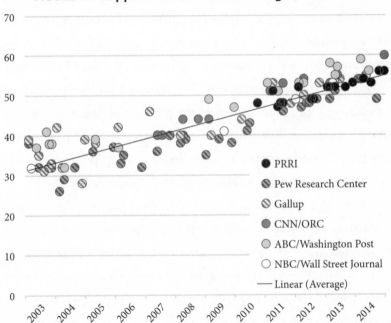

FIGURE 4.1 Support for Same-Sex Marriage (2003–2014)

- ● PRRI
- ◈ Pew Research Center
- ◍ Gallup
- ● CNN/ORC
- ○ ABC/Washington Post
- ○ NBC/Wall Street Journal
- — Linear (Average)

One of the earliest public opinion questions on the subject, included in the 1988 General Social Survey, found virtually no support for legalizing gay marriage. At the time, only about one in ten (11 percent) Americans supported allowing gay and lesbian couples to marry legally.

By the time Massachusetts became the first state to legalize same-sex marriage in 2003, support was still fairly low, with less than one third (32 percent) of Americans favoring same-sex marriage; nearly six in ten (59 percent) Americans were opposed to gay marriage, including 35 percent who were strongly opposed.[37] The next several years saw modest increases in support for gay marriage. By 2008, most surveys showed that approximately four in ten Americans favored allowing gay and lesbian people to marry legally, while a majority remained opposed.

Views shifted quickly during the following three years. By 2011, four different surveys, including one conducted by PRRI, recorded majority support for same-sex marriage for the first time.[38] By 2013, virtually every major national poll was reporting that more than half of Americans supported gay marriage. At the close of 2014, PRRI's American Values Atlas—based on interviews with over forty thousand Americans—showed that a solid majority (54 percent) of Americans favored allowing gay and lesbian couples to legally marry, while 38 percent were opposed.[39] This represents an astounding leap of 22 percentage points over the last decade and 43 percentage points since the late 1980s.

Although younger Americans, who support gay marriage in higher proportions than older Americans, are certainly driving these trends, support has been increasing proportionally across all generational groups. In fact, the generation gap in 2014 was comparable to the generation gap in 2003. In 2003, 45 percent of young adults (ages 18 to 29) favored allowing gay and lesbian people to marry, compared to 13 percent of seniors (age 65 and older), a 32-point generation gap. By 2014, support among the youngest American adults had increased to seven in ten (70 percent), but support had also risen to nearly four in ten (39 percent) among seniors—a 31-point generation gap. Put another way, support for same-sex marriage among the youngest and the oldest

Americans has increased by nearly equal amounts during the last decade: 25 percentage points among young Americans and 26 percentage points among seniors.[40]

Similarly, although conventional wisdom suggests that liberal strongholds in New England and on the West Coast are guiding these changes in opinion, support for same-sex marriage increased by more than 20 percentage points in every region of the country over the past decade. In 2003, support for same-sex marriage fell short of a majority in every region of the country. Between 2003 and 2014, support for allowing gay and lesbian couples to marry shifted from 42 percent to 64 percent in the Northeast, from 36 percent to 59 percent in the West, and

FIGURE 4.2 Allowing Gay and Lesbian Couples to Marry Legally

Percent who favor

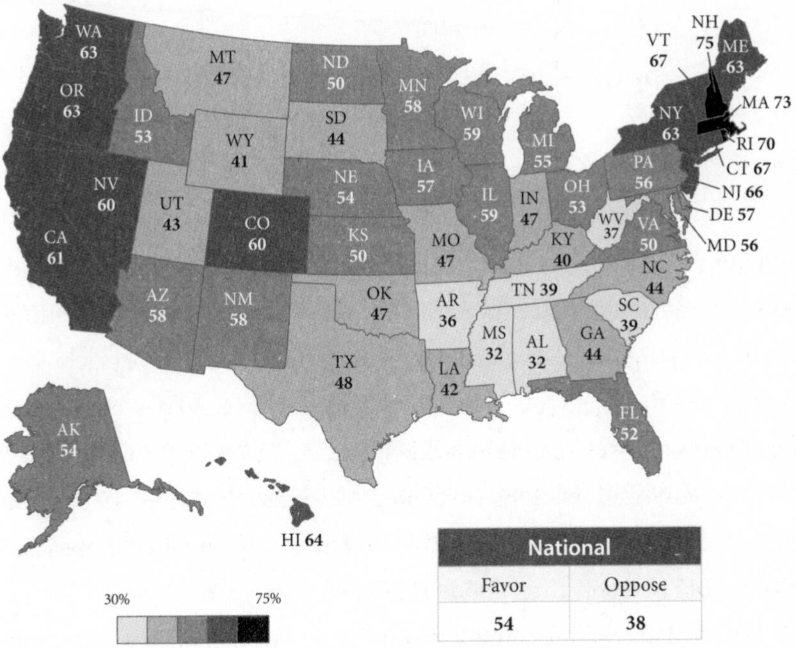

National	
Favor	Oppose
54	38

Source: PRRI, American Values Atlas, 2014.

from 33 percent to 54 percent in the Midwest. While the South remains the only region in which less than half support same-sex marriage (46 percent favor, 46 percent oppose), support has grown to match the opposition. At the end of 2014, the number of Southerners who favored same-sex marriage was 24 percentage points higher than it was in 2003 (22 percent).[41]

A look at a state map of support for same-sex marriage shows just how broad support had become by 2014 (Figure 4.2). In thirty-two states, at least half of residents favored same-sex marriage. Eleven states were roughly evenly divided. Most notably, there were only seven states—Kentucky, South Carolina, Tennessee, West Virginia, Arkansas, Alabama, and Mississippi—where majorities of residents opposed same-sex marriage.

Same-Sex Marriage and Religion

Support for Same-Sex Marriage Among Religious Groups

Religious affiliation has always influenced levels of support for same-sex marriage, although patterns within the religious landscape are shifting. Among all religiously affiliated Americans in 2003, when Massachusetts became the first state to legalize same-sex marriage, 28 percent favored legalizing same-sex marriage, while 63 percent were opposed. By 2014, support among all religiously affiliated Americans had risen 19 percentage points, and for the first time more religiously affiliated Americans favored (47 percent) than opposed (45 percent) gay marriage.[42]

By 2014, battle lines on the issue of same-sex marriage were no longer between religious and nonreligious Americans. Rather, debate was raging *among* religious groups—those who had shifted their positions to support same-sex marriage and those who were holding the conservative line. In 2003, nearly two thirds (65 percent) of religiously unaffiliated Americans favored same-sex marriage, but there were no other major religious groups in which a majority agreed. A decade ago, the most supportive religious groups were white mainline Protestants (36 percent support) and Catholics (35 percent support).[43] But by 2014, in addition to 77 percent of religiously unaffiliated Americans, majorities of Buddhists (84 percent), Jews (77 percent), white mainline Protestants (62 percent), white Catholics (61 percent), Hispanic Catholics (60 percent), Orthodox Christians (56 percent), and Hindus (55 percent) supported same-sex marriage.[44] American Muslims were roughly divided on the question, with a slim majority in opposition (43 percent in support and 51 percent opposed).*

On the other side, there were only four major religious groups in which solid majorities opposed same-sex marriage: white evangelical Protestants (66 percent), Mormons (68 percent), Hispanic Protestants (58 percent), and African American Protestants (54 percent). Of these, white evangelical Protestants and Mormons are the most prominent exceptions; they are the only religious groups in which fewer than three in ten support same-sex marriage (28 percent and 27 percent respectively).

This large spread in opinion among religious Americans—nearly 50 percentage points between white evangelical Protestants and Jews—has been compounded over the last decade by greater swings in opinion among some religious subgroups. While all religious groups saw double-digit shifts toward more support for same-sex marriage between

---

*Due to the relatively small sample size of Muslims, the eight percentage point difference here is not statistically significant.

2003 and 2014, the most conservative religious groups (particularly white evangelical Protestants) have been less influenced by these trends. For example, while white evangelical Protestant support for same-sex marriage grew to 16 percentage points between 2003 and 2014, support jumped 25 points among Catholics and 26 points among white mainline Protestants over the same period.

Outliers: White Evangelical Protestants and Mormons

As members of other religious groups—including the mainline Protestant branch of White Christian America—moved toward greater support for gay rights, the evangelical wing of White Christian America and Mormons have become increasingly isolated outliers in the religious landscape. In fact, identification as a white evangelical Protestant or Mormon remains one of the strongest single independent predictors of opposition to same-sex marriage. For example, the most prominent common characteristic of the seven states where majorities oppose same-sex marriage is the strong presence of those two groups. Figure 4.3 demonstrates just how strongly their presence affects a state's overall support for same-sex marriage. The chart sorts all fifty states by proportion of white evangelical Protestants and Mormons in the state's population, ranging from a low of 6 percent in New Jersey and New York to a high of 61 percent in Utah.

As Figure 4.3 demonstrates, there is a strong inverse relationship between the presence of white evangelical Protestants and Mormons and support for same-sex marriage within a state. In twenty-four states—including many in the West and Northeast—white evangelical Protestants and Mormons constitute less than one fifth of the population. In each of those states, there is majority support for same-sex marriage, ranging from 75 percent support in New Hampshire to 52 percent support in Florida. The remaining twenty-six states have higher percentages of white evangelical Protestants and Mormons—ranging from Texas at 20 percent to a high of 61 percent in Utah thanks to Mormons' outsized presence there. In twenty-one of these states, less than a majority of residents support same-sex marriage, with Mississippi and Alabama anchoring the bottom of the list at 32 percent each. The five states whose population is more than one-fifth white evangelical Protestant and Mormon *and* have a majority supporting same-sex marriage—Oregon, Nebraska, Ohio, Iowa, and Idaho—all share one attribute: they have comparable or greater numbers of religiously unaffiliated residents. These nonreligious Americans act as a counterweight to the states' white evangelical Protestants on the issue of gay marriage. For example, although 21 percent of Oregonians are white evangelical Protestants or Mormon, 63 percent of the state's residents support same-sex marriage. The explanation? Thirty-seven percent of Oregonians are religiously unaffiliated.

Although their numbers are falling, white evangelical Protestants continue to comprise 18 percent of the population nationwide and one quarter (25 percent) of Southerners. While their views are increasingly out of touch with mainstream opinion, their strong opposition to LGBT rights, combined with their geographic concentration, positions them to have a continued impact, at least for the near future, on these debates.

However, even among these outlier groups, generational differences make it clear that opposition to gay rights will ultimately lose its power as the culture war weapon of choice. Campaigns animated by antigay rhetoric are unlikely to appeal to younger religious Americans regardless of their religious affiliation. For example, 45 percent of young evangelicals (ages 18–29) and 43 percent of young Mormons favor same-sex

FIGURE 4.3 Presence of White Evangelical Protestants or Mormons vs. Support for Same-Sex Marriage

By state

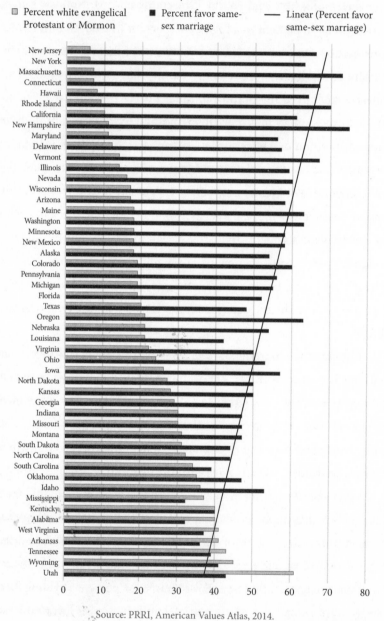

☐ Percent white evangelical Protestant or Mormon   ■ Percent favor same-sex marriage   —— Linear (Percent favor same-sex marriage)

Source: PRRI, American Values Atlas, 2014.

marriage, compared to only 19 percent of white evangelical seniors (age 65 and older) and 18 percent of Mormon seniors. Most notably, the data show that young Republicans have passed the tipping point; 53 percent of young Republicans now support same-sex marriage.

Moreover, unlike their elders, younger evangelicals are surrounded by friends who hold a range of views on LGBT rights. Approximately eight in ten (79 percent) white evangelical Protestant seniors (age 65 and older) say most of their friends oppose same-sex marriage. By contrast, among white evangelical Protestants under the age of 30, less than half (46 percent) say most of their friends are opposed. Nearly four in ten (37 percent) younger white evangelical Protestants say most of their friends support same-sex marriage, and 9 percent say their friends are evenly divided on the issue.[45]

The Impact of Church Opposition to Same-Sex Marriage on Young Americans

Although Americans who have disaffiliated from their childhood faith give a variety of reasons for leaving,[46] a number of studies have found that negative religious teachings about gay and lesbian people and relationships—that they are sinful, immoral, or perverse—are one of the significant factors driving younger Americans to abandon traditional religious institutions.[47]

In UnChristian: What a New Generation Really Thinks About Christianity, David Kinnaman, the president of the evangelical polling firm the Barna Group, analyzed the results of a 2006 survey among a random sample of 16- to 29-year-olds. The study found that the top three attributes young Americans associated with "present-day Christianity" were being antigay (91 percent), judgmental (87 percent), and hypocritical (85 percent). In fact, for members of this generation, who grew up with the conservative Christian political movements as Christianity's dominant expression, seven of the top ten attributes they used to describe contemporary Christianity were negative. Kinnaman's blunt conclusion was that "Christianity has an image problem" among American youth.[48]

Similarly, in their landmark 2010 study of the changing religious landscape, *American Grace*, sociologists Robert Putnam and David Campbell noted that younger Americans who reached adulthood after 1990 were marked by two prominent, interrelated traits: they were more liberal on gay rights and had lower rates of religious affiliation. They summed up the conflict this way:

> *This group of young people came of age when "religion" was identified publicly with the Religious Right, and exactly at the time when the leaders of that movement put homosexuality and gay marriage at the top of their agenda. And yet this is the very generation in which the new tolerance of homosexuality has grown most rapidly. In short, just as the younger cohort of Americans was zigging in one direction, many highly visible religious leaders zagged in the other.*[49]

Subsequent research from PRRI found that antigay teachings or stances by churches loom large among the specific reasons Millennials (ages 18–34) give for leaving the religion in which they were raised. Among Millennials who no longer identify with their childhood religion, nearly one third (31 percent) say that negative teachings about or treatment of gay and lesbian people were important factors in their disaffiliation from religion—roughly twice the rate (15 percent) of seniors (age 65 and older) who say the same.[50]

Moreover, more than seven in ten (72 percent) Millennials agree that religious groups are estranging young people by being too judgmental about gay and lesbian issues. Seniors are the only age group among whom less than a majority (44 percent) agree. The dilemma for many churches is this: they are anchored, both financially and in terms of lay support, by older Americans, who are less likely to perceive a problem that the overwhelming majority of younger Americans say is there.

Majorities of nearly every major religious group confirm the problem. Jewish Americans (79 percent), religiously unaffiliated Americans (74 percent), white mainline Protestants (61 percent), African American Protestants (58 percent), and Catholics (55 percent) all agree that negative, judgmental attitudes about LGBT people are creating barriers between churches and the younger generation. Indeed, the only major religious group to say that these judgments are *not* alienating young people are white evangelical Protestants (51 percent).[51]

The generational divides over LGBT rights are momentous for the evangelical branch of White Christian America and for conservative religious groups generally. What's at stake isn't just the outcome of political debates. Conservative religious groups' very future hinges on how willing they are to navigate from the margins toward the new mainstream. Because many conservative right-leaning religious leaders and organizations have self-consciously defined themselves through opposition to gay rights during the heyday of the Christian Right movement, they face thorny choices. To move away from strong opposition to same-sex marriage would spark a profound identity crisis and risk losing support from their current—albeit aging—support base. Refusing to reevaluate, on the other hand, may relegate conservative religious groups to cultural irrelevancy and continued decline, as more and more young people leave church behind.

The Road Ahead

In the wake of Americans' sea change in perspective on gay rights, the descendants of White Christian America are heading down one of three major paths. Most white mainline Protestants, along with a small but significant minority of white evangelical Protestants, have already joined most of the country on the road to acceptance. At the other end of the spectrum, a shrinking and graying sector of the white evangelical Protestant world is hunkering down under a "no compromise on marriage" banner, preparing to fight gay rights to the last man and the last dollar. A third group of leaders has conceded the loss of the war on gay marriage but is regrouping to fight a prolonged set of tactical battles around the concept of religious liberty.

Acceptance

Most members of the mainline Protestant branch of White Christian America have staked out a space among gay marriage supporters. The trend line of increasing support for same-sex marriage among white mainline Protestants has been even steeper than the general population's trajectory. By 2014, 62 percent of white mainline Protestants supported same-sex marriage, compared to 54 percent of Americans overall. By the time the U.S. Supreme Court legalized same-sex marriage in June 2015, nearly all of the major mainline Protestant denominations—including the Episcopal Church, the Evangelical Lutheran Church in America, the Presbyterian Church (USA), and the United Church of Christ— had officially sanctioned same-sex marriage.[52] The Disciples of Christ, although it has no official policy on same-sex marriage, supports the ordination of LGBT clergy and passed a 2013 resolution that affirmed "the faith, baptism and spiritual gifts of all Christians regardless of their sexual orientation or gender identity, and that neither are grounds for exclusion from fellowship or service within the church, but are a part of God's good creation."[53]

The notable exceptions among the major mainline Protestant denominations are the American Baptist Churches USA—the group of northern Baptists that parted ways with southern Baptists in the mid-1800s over slavery—and the United Methodist Church, each of which is officially opposed to same-sex marriage. However, the Methodists—the largest mainline denomination—have been engaged in a heated debate over this issue in recent years, complicated by their large international membership and the strong opposition of African Methodists in particular, who for example are projected to comprise approximately 30 percent of the delegates that the 2016 UMC General Conference, the body authorized to set policy and speak for the denomination.[54] Nevertheless, data from PRRI's 2014 American Values Atlas shows that at least in the American pews, the members of denominations have sided with their mainline kin on this issue. Among mainline Baptists, 53 percent favor same-sex marriage, while 39 percent are opposed; similarly, among Methodists, 51 percent favor same-sex marriage, while 40 percent are opposed.[55]

The prospects for acceptance of same-sex marriage within the evangelical world have historically been quite limited, to say the least. Given its role as a boundary-defining issue, moving away from the party line of staunch opposition has been a good way for an evangelical leader to lose his job. To give just one prominent example, Richard Cizik, the vice president of the National Association of Evangelicals (and a PRRI board member) was fired in 2009 after more than two decades of service for uttering even this qualified statement on air to NPR's Terry Gross: "I'm shifting, I have to admit. In other words, I would willingly say that I believe in civil unions. I don't officially support redefining marriage from its traditional definition, I don't think."[56] In announcing Cizik's resignation, NEA president Leith Anderson said that the remarks had caused members to lose trust in his leadership.

Although the evangelical branch of White Christian America's strong opposition to same-sex marriage is nearly unrivaled, it is not universal. Nearly three in ten (28 percent) white evangelical Protestants overall—and 43 percent of white evangelical young adults (ages 18–29)—favor same-sex marriage. And in recent years, several leaders have begun to break the taboo and articulate a serious theological case for supporting same-sex marriage. These leaders are addressing the significant minority who disagree with the prevailing evangelical position as well as the growing sector of evangelicals who are torn between their traditional theological beliefs and approaches to the Bible and increasing discomfort with the orthodox conclusions on this issue.

Following the legalization of same-sex marriage nationwide, a group of more than one hundred evangelical leaders signed an open letter celebrating the court's decision, with this core message:

> As Evangelical pastors and leaders, we believe that the gospel of Jesus Christ is a message of good news for all people. Following in the way of Jesus, we are compelled to be a voice for the voiceless and to fight for the dignity and equality of all people, regardless of their race, religion, ethnicity, sexuality, or gender identity. Today, the Supreme Court of the United States has ruled in favor of civil marriage equality for lesbian, gay, bisexual, transgender, and queer Americans. We join with millions of people around the country in celebration of this major step towards justice and equality for LGBTQ people in the United States.[57]

The document was endorsed by many prominent figures from the evangelical world: Richard Cizik, who had since founded the New Evangelical Partnership for The Common Good; David Gushee, a prominent Christian ethicist (and former PRRI board member) and author of *Changing Our Mind*, a rethinking of evangelical theological and moral assumptions about homosexuality;[58] Brian McClaren, a former pastor and leading Christian author; and Matthew Vines, an author and former pastor who caused a stir in 2012 when a video of a sermon in which he argued that the Bible does not address modern gay relationships, went viral.[59] Compared to other similar evangelical documents, which feature very few women, it is also notable that approximately one quarter of the endorsers were women.

Many of the evangelical endorsers of the open letter hail from the Baby Boomer or X Generations; they have taken stands for LGBT equality at great risk to their careers and reputations and have the battle scars to show for it. But perhaps the strongest sign that the ground is shifting even within white evangelical Protestant circles is that a number of older leaders who had long careers in the evangelical mainstream also signaled their change of heart. For example, Tony Campolo, an eighty-year-old popular speaker, author, and retired sociology professor at Eastern University, announced his support for same-sex marriage in early June 2015, and Jim Wallis of Sojourners announced his support in 2013. Campolo and Wallis are perceived to be within, but on the left edge of, the evangelical world, and therefore their support was not perhaps that surprising. But, notably, David Neff, the retired editor in chief of *Christianity Today*, who still writes a column for the flagship evangelical publication, also announced his support a few days after Campolo via a statement on his Facebook page. Neff wrote: "I think the ethically responsible thing for gay and lesbian Christians to do is to form lasting, covenanted partnerships. I also believe that the church should help them in those partnerships in the same way the church should fortify traditional marriages."[60]

Rather than leaving the fold, a critical mass of white evangelical leaders are laying the theological and cultural groundwork for a reassessment of what has been the untouchable third rail in white evangelical churches. This group remains a minority within the evangelical world, but it has established an important base for fellow evangelicals, both gay and straight, who do not want to choose between their faith and their support for LGBT equality.

Last Stands

> If there ever was a time when Christian people should fight for what they believe, this is it. Solidarity is critical. And yet, regrettably, some Christian leaders are saying that the battle has been lost, and that the family of the future will be increasingly compromised. Some have even told their constituencies to get used to same sex marriage. They are tragically wrong. . . . What would be the consequences of losing this cultural war? It would be a social and international disaster.
>
> —James Dobson, President, Focus on the Family (June 2011)

In June 2011, just after New York become the sixth and largest state to legalize same-sex marriage, James Dobson issued a lengthy call to action in Focus on the Family's newsletter.[61] The missive drew heavily from Dobson's 2004 book, *Marriage Under Fire: Why We Must Win This Battle* and from a 2009 manifesto, "The Manhattan Declaration: A Call of Christian Conscience."[62] The latter was signed by a coalition of more than 150 evangelical and Catholic leaders—including many of the architects of the Christian Right movement such as Gary Bauer, Charles Colson, and Dobson himself. It urged young Christians to hold the line on the issues that were the backbone of the expanded conservative White Christian America coalition: opposition to same-sex marriage and abortion.

With a sense of heightened urgency following the passage of the New York law, Dobson summarized the arguments of his book by mentioning nearly all of the elements of the Christian Right's standard case against gay marriage. He warned that the widespread legalization of same-sex marriage would lead to social anarchy where polygamy, marriage between cousins, and even marriage between "daddies and little girls" would follow in short order. Legal gay marriage would destroy the "traditional family" and harm children. Public schools would be forced to "endorse homosexuality in the curriculum," adoption guidelines would be dismantled, and churches "[would] be subjected to ever-increasing oppression and discrimination." The column ended with an apocalyptic crescendo—hinting that our current society may be so corrupt as to warrant a purging biblical flood—and described the dire consequences of inaction: "The culture war will be over, and the world will become 'as it was in the days of Noah' (Matthew 24:37, NIV). This is the climactic moment in the battle to preserve the family, and future generations hang in the balance."

In 2011, when public opinion polls first registered majority support for gay marriage Dobson's call for a last stand retained some plausibility. But it's difficult to see more recent efforts, launched well after the major battles have been lost, as anything other than last-ditch efforts in the face of certain defeat. Nonetheless, there is a significant contingent of the white evangelical old guard that is digging in and attempting to reinforce their position with conservative Catholic allies.

Take, for example, a 2015 statement by Evangelicals and Catholics Together, the influential coalition founded in 1994 to form common cause on conservative political issues, especially same-sex marriage. The document, titled "The Two Shall Become One Flesh: Reclaiming Marriage" and endorsed by many of the same leaders who backed the Manhattan Declaration, opens with a firm rejection of gay marriage: "There can be no compromise on marriage. We cannot allow our witness to be obscured by the confusions into which our culture and society have fallen."[63] In a key section called "A Parody of Marriage," the authors assert that same-sex marriage is more damaging to the institution of marriage than either divorce or cohabitation:

> An easy acceptance of divorce damages marriage; widespread cohabitation devalues marriage. But so-called same-sex marriage is a graver threat, because what is now given the name of marriage in law is a parody of marriage.

As the document continues, the authors argue that same-sex marriage threatens to unravel the fabric of the family—and even social reality itself.

> No one should doubt or deny what is at stake here. To sustain the fiction of same-sex marriage, the natural family must be deconstructed. . . . When society systematically denies the difference between male and female in law and custom, our fundamental dignity is diminished, the image of God within us is obscured, unreality becomes legally established, and those who refuse to conform are regarded as irrational bigots.

In case there was any remaining doubt about their position, the authors close by declaring, "faithful Christian witness cannot accommodate itself to same-sex marriage. It disregards the created order, threatens the common good, and distorts the Gospel."

The "Two Shall Become One Flesh" document calls conservative Christians to stay strong in their opposition to the sweeping, seemingly irreversible cultural changes around them. Yet rather than seriously analyzing these shifts, the authors set them aside as academic:

> *Within the span of a decade, same-sex marriage has not only been legally recognized, but its acceptance has been declared an index of one's status as a citizen committed to liberty and justice for all. How and why such a cultural and legal revolution has taken place so quickly is for historians and sociologists to explain.*[64]

There is evidence that these recent manifestos against same-sex marriage have found little support among the younger members of evangelical communities. When the authors of the 2009 "Manhattan Declaration" argued that younger evangelicals should take up the standard of the culture war and continue the fight against gay rights, Jonathan Merritt—son of a former Southern Baptist Convention president and a prominent voice in young evangelical circles—responded in his *Newsweek/Washington Post* column with the literary equivalent of a shrug. Merritt argued that these statements assert a false hierarchy of issues, with older generations contending that only a few "hot button" issues are worthy of attention. "Younger Christians believe that our sacred Scriptures compel us to offer a moral voice on a broad range of issues," Merritt wrote. "The Bible speaks often about life and sexuality, but it also speaks often on other issues, like poverty, equality, justice, peace, and care of creation."[65] Merritt pointed out that among the document's 140-plus signatories there were "no notable evangelicals under 40." In fact, the supporters of the 2015 Evangelicals and Catholics Together document were almost exclusively older white men. Rather than representing a plausible call to arms, these statements may be better understood, as journalist Dan Gilgoff wrote in *U.S. News & World Report*, as windows into "the fears of a graying generation of culture warriors."[66]

Conditional Surrender: The Christian Minority and the Religious Liberty Insurgency

Some younger leaders of White Christian America's evangelical wing are taking a more realistic measure of the prevailing cultural winds. Russel Moore, the head of the Southern Baptist Convention's Ethics and Religious Liberty Commission, was forty-one years old in 2013 when he took over the reins of the denomination's advocacy arm from Richard Land, then in his late sixties.

Some of Moore's rhetorical flourishes certainly echo the tone of the culture wars of the 1980s and 1990s. For example, he describes the goals of a personified Sexual Revolution this way: "The Sexual Revolution isn't content to move forward into bedrooms and dinner tables. The Sexual Revolution wants to silence dissent. The religious liberty concerns we are grappling with already will only accelerate."[67] In a 2014 blog post titled "Same-Sex Marriage and the Future," Moore called on his fellow conservative Christians to "thunder back with the old gospel that calls all of us to repentance and to cross-bearing."[68] Acknowledging the high levels of support for same-sex marriage among Millennials, Moore declared flatly, "If we have to choose between Jesus and Millennials, we choose Jesus."

But in this same article, and in a new book titled *Onward: Engaging the Culture Without Losing the Gospel*,[69] Moore also admonished some in White Christian America's old guard as false prophets who are using "talk radio sloganeering" to shore up their own status and line their pockets by telling conservative Christians what they want to hear. "This prophet implies that if we just sign checks to the right radio talk-show hosts, and have a good election cycle or two, we'll be right back where we were, back when carpets were shag and marriages were strong," he wrote. Moore contended that these voices—although they came from inside the Christian world—were also dangerous threats to traditional marriage, because they distorted reality and exploited a short-term financial opportunity with no real hope of winning the longer war. If Christians couldn't accurately read the signs of the times, in Moore's view, they would be ill prepared to face the future.

Rather than calling for a heroic last stand in the culture wars, Moore has urged the nation's largest Protestant denomination—and the cornerstone of White Christian America's evangelical wing—to stop pretending they are the moral majority and face cultural defeat. He described the urgency of the shift this way:

> Above all, we must prepare people for what the future holds, when Christian beliefs about marriage and sexuality aren't part of the cultural consensus but are seen to be strange and freakish and even subversive . . . for a world that views evangelical Protestants and traditional Roman Catholics and Orthodox Jews and others as bigots or freaks.

Moore's call is not for a total retreat from American culture. Rather, he has urged Christians to relinquish their status as defenders of a lost consensus and instead embrace their status as "strangers." Rather than seeking to change American minds on the larger issue of the moral acceptability of same-sex relationships, Moore argues that conservative

Christians should rally around a more limited movement to maintain their traditional view of marriage within their own communities.

Moore however doesn't call for evangelicals to fully disarm. He encourages his fellow evangelicals to defend their right to "religious liberty" in the public sphere. It's not completely clear, however, just how compatible these two strategic plans are. The degree to which each is emphasized and the nature of these religious liberty claims are both critical for understanding the future landscape.

The appeal to religious liberty is one that has long resounded in the American context—starting with the First Amendment to the Constitution. But its recent adoption by conservative white Christians reflects a departure from its traditional usage in church/state separation debates. Rather than being understood as a negative liberty protecting against interference with freedom of worship, white evangelical Protestant leaders have joined forces with conservative Catholic leaders to create a sweeping new expansion of religious liberty, one that is specifically designed for the aftermath of the lost war over same-sex marriage.

At its heart, the new doctrine of religious liberty asserts that individuals should be able to carry religious objections from their private life into their public roles as service providers, business owners, and even elected officials. Under this framework, small business owners who believe same-sex relationships are sinful on religious grounds would be legally allowed to refuse to sell products or offer services to gay and lesbian people. Such businesses might include bakeries and wedding photographers, as well as bed-and-breakfast establishments, pharmacists, even pediatricians treating children of same-sex couples. The "freedom" might even extend to individuals who find the general requirements of their jobs religiously objectionable, such as elected county clerks who issue marriage licenses, or front-line service providers such as doctors who do not want to provide services to gay or lesbian couples, or social workers who refuse to place foster kids with families headed by married same-sex partners.

Ross Douthat, a conservative Catholic who writes a regular column at *The New York Times*, penned one of the clearest and most concise rationales for this position, aptly titled "The Terms of Our Surrender." Douthat argued that these assorted calls for religious liberty exemptions around LGBT rights legislation are "a way for religious conservatives to negotiate surrender—to accept same-sex marriage's inevitability while carving out protections for dissent."[70] Seen in this light, the new religious liberty battles are best understood as a rearguard insurgency that is specifically designed to secure in isolated strongholds what White Christian America has lost on the field.

The Supreme Court's decision to legalize same-sex marriage nationwide was a nuclear event for the evangelical wing of White Christian America, which has for decades staked its identity on opposing this issue. While some of the old generals are embracing no-compromise positions, some evangelicals are advocating a change of heart. The shift they have suggested is essentially a defection, an attempt to rally with their mainline kin and their own younger cohort around acceptance of gay rights. But most of white evangelicals' energy and resources, at least for the short term, seem likely to be poured into the religious liberty battles being led by Russell Moore and the Southern Baptist Convention, in tandem with his conservative Catholic compatriots.

The days ahead will be defined by how each side—the cultural victors and the defeated from among the ranks of evangelical White Christian America—proceeds. Although Moore and others are calling for concessions from the winners, PRRI poll numbers from just before the

June 2015 Supreme Court ruling indicate that most Americans have little appetite for allowing individuals to discriminate because of personal religious beliefs. By nearly a two-to-one margin (60 percent vs. 34 percent), Americans oppose allowing a small business owner to refuse products or services to gay and lesbian people, even if doing so violates his or her religious beliefs.[71]

Given that concessions from the victors are not likely to be forthcoming, much will depend on how white evangelicals will navigate the inevitable tension—and perhaps, finally, the incompatibility—between Moore's call to embrace their cultural strangeness and accept a more modest political footprint, and his call to defend religious liberty, which could easily devolve into a desperate attempt to fight the lost war by other means.

5

Race: Desegregating White Christian America

Franklin Graham and #BlackLivesMatter

On August 9, 2014, a white Ferguson police officer named Darren Wilson shot and killed an unarmed black teenager, Michael Brown, sparking nationwide outcry.[1] The roiling protests in the majority-black St. Louis suburb—and the name "Ferguson" itself—became a powerful symbol of the country's troubled race relations, especially after a succession of additional high-profile cases where unarmed black men were killed by white police officers. Stories like Brown's filled the headlines throughout 2014 and 2015.

After the initial protests in Ferguson finally simmered down, chaos on the ground reignited on November 24, 2015, when a Missouri prosecutor announced that the grand jury had decided not to indict the white police officer who had shot Brown.[2] This decision was followed a week later by the news that a Staten Island grand jury also had decided not to indict the white police officer who strangled Eric Garner, an unarmed black man who was illegally selling cigarettes on the street.[3] A bystander's haunting cell phone video went viral, showing Garner rasping "I can't breathe!" while the officer refused to release his grip.

On Twitter, the conversation crystallized around a set of hashtags: #ICantBreathe (Garner's last words), #HandsUpDontShoot (a reference to the disputed claim that Brown had his hands up during at least part of the shooting), and #BlackLivesMatter, an umbrella hashtag that poignantly highlighted the conversation's stakes. Between the end of November and the first week of December 2014, these hashtags were trending globally. At the end of the year, Twitter produced an animated map showing the explosion of the hashtags across the world.[4]

Reactions to these events revealed a deep rift between white and black Americans generally, and white Christians and black Americans specifically. Not all white Americans were buying the narrative of racial injustice. On March 12, 2015, as protests in Ferguson passed the 200-day mark, two police officers were shot during a protest outside the Ferguson police station.[5] In response, the Reverend Franklin Graham, the son of the famed evangelist Billy Graham, fired off this missive to his 1.4 million Facebook fans:

> Listen up—Blacks, Whites, Latinos, and everybody else. Most police shootings can be avoided. It comes down to respect for authority and obedience. If a police officer tells you to stop, you stop. If a police officer tells you to put your hands in the air, you put your hands in the air. If a police officer tells you to lay down face first with your hands behind your back, you lay down face first with your hands behind your back. It's as simple as that. Even if you think the police officer is wrong—YOU OBEY.

Graham's post continued, admonishing President Obama to tell parents to "teach your children to respect and obey those in authority." More widespread respect for authority, he concluded, would have avoided "some of the unnecessary shootings we have seen recently."[6] Nearly 200,000 people "liked" the post on Facebook and it was shared more than 83,000 times.[7]

The younger Graham's remark was, for him, nothing special. Where his father, Billy Graham, remained cautious on the subject of race relations,[8] Franklin Graham has frequently courted controversy.[9] But this time, his post struck a nerve among the sizable number of white Americans who felt bewildered and resentful about the avalanche of news coverage highlighting the lethal use of force by white police officers on unarmed African Americans.

Graham's Facebook post prompted an angry open letter from a group of African American, Hispanic, and Asian American religious leaders, many of whom were fellow evangelicals:

> Frankly, Rev. Graham, your insistence that "Blacks, Whites, Latinos, and everybody else" "Listen up," was crude, insensitive, and paternalistic. . . . The fact that you identify a widely acknowledged social injustice as "simple" reveals your lack of empathy and understanding of the depth of sin that some in the body have suffered under the weight of our broken justice system. It also reveals a cavalier disregard for the enduring impacts and outcomes of the legal regimes that enslaved and oppressed people of color, made in the image of God—from Native American genocide and containment, to colonial and antebellum slavery, through Jim Crow and peonage, to our current system of mass incarceration and criminalization.[10]

This response was drafted by Dominique Gilliard, a young African American pastor at New Hope Covenant Church in Oakland, California, and a board member of the Christian Community Development Association, a Mississippi-based group that works to engage Christians in development work in poor communities. Four thousand five hundred endorsers joined the letter's thirty-one initial signers. When it was published in *Sojourner's* magazine, a left-leaning evangelical publication, it quickly became the most viewed page in the magazine's online history.[11]

On the heels of these clashes, the nation was rocked again on April 19, 2015, by the death of Freddie Gray, a young black man who died of severe spinal injuries while in the custody of the Baltimore police. Once again, there were protests—many violent—in the streets.

The Racial Perception Gap

To most African Americans, the protests of 2014 and 2015 were a long overdue indictment of the grim reality of racial injustice in the country. These recent events were seen against a historical backdrop of lynchings, all-white juries that refused to convict or even indict white perpetrators, and the disproportionate mass incarceration of black men.[12] *Time* magazine's stark May 11 cover captured their anger. Taken by an amateur photographer in Baltimore, the cover photo depicted an African American demonstrator fleeing a wall of police officers in riot gear. The text on the cover read, "America, 1968 2015. What Has Changed. What Hasn't."[13]

But many white Americans continued to be either baffled or frustrated by the coverage these cases were getting and began to openly resist the "Black Lives Matter" message. On Twitter, a competing #All-LivesMatter hashtag erupted. Prominent megachurch pastor Rick Warren launched an explicitly theological version of this reaction, with #AllLivesMatterToGod.[14] The clash even found expression at the local level. Two predominantly white Maryland churches that put up "Black Lives Matter" banners on their front lawns in solidarity with the movement found them vandalized—with the word "Black" spray painted over with an "X" on one banner and cut out of the other.[15] Even some white Democratic politicians used the retort, although not without consequences. For example, former Maryland governor and Democratic presidential candidate Martin O'Malley was forced to apologize for remarks he made at a liberal organizing conference. When activists demanded he address the issue of police brutality, shouting, "Black lives matter!," O'Malley responded by saying, "Black lives matter. White lives matter. All lives matter." The activists, who were predominantly black, responded by booing and shouting him down.[16]

While the legal terrain has certainly shifted since the 1960s, serious racial disparities remain in the criminal justice system. According to a *New York Times* investigation published in the wake of the Baltimore protests, both official and unofficial statistics show that African American civilians are far more likely to be killed by police than white people. In records where the race of the victim is identified, about three in ten victims are black—two and a half times their proportion of the population. The *Times* investigation also concluded that since the most reliable statistics don't indicate an uptick in these incidents in recent years, these disparities have been with us for some time.[17] Police violence has become more visible, however, thanks to bystanders who have captured racially charged encounters with cell phone videos. Widespread social media usage, too, has allowed protesters to amplify their concerns in ways that weren't possible even five years ago. In the wake of the Baltimore protests, President Obama emphasized that these clashes were part of an alarming pattern: "This has been a slow-rolling crisis. This has been going on for a long time. This is not new, and we shouldn't pretend that it's new."[18]

But for many white Americans, the stories of unfair treatment of blacks by police and the court system *did* feel new. And the fury with which African American protesters took to the streets after each death also challenged the cherished assumption that the country had moved beyond its racially troubled past into a "post-racial" era. African Americans have contended for decades—or even centuries—that the criminal justice system is stacked against them, but many white Americans continue to believe that police departments and courts can generally be trusted to administer justice. Where African Americans perceive familiar configurations of abuse, many white Americans see isolated incidents. And while African Americans largely sympathized with (or at least understood) the long simmering anger animating the protests across the country, many white Americans have focused on the damage caused by the riots and looting.

As Figure 5.1 illustrates, public opinion data show that there has been little progress in closing this racial perception gap over the past two decades. In 1992, the same year that riots exploded in Los Angeles following the beating of Rodney King, an unarmed black taxi driver, by a group of white police officers, fewer than one in ten (8 percent) black Americans reported that they believed blacks and other minorities were treated the same as whites in the criminal justice system, while 89 percent disagreed. White Americans, by contrast, were almost evenly divided over whether blacks and whites received equal treatment in the criminal justice (46 percent agreed while 43 percent disagreed). More than two decades later, the racial perception gap stands at more than 30 percentage points: only 14 percent of black Americans, compared to 47 percent of white Americans, agree that the criminal justice system treats minorities the same as whites.[19]

FIGURE 5.1 Blacks and Other Minorities Receive Equal Treatment as Whites in the Criminal Justice System

Percent who agree, by race

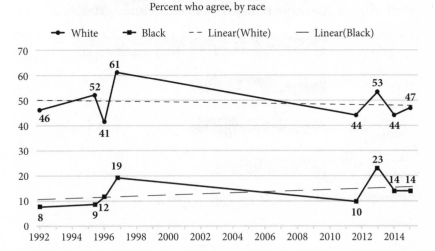

Sources: ABC News/*Washington Post* Surveys, 1992–2012; PRRI Surveys, 2013–2015.

A more specific survey question demonstrates the strength of these different views—and in particular, their power among the descendants of White Christian America (Figure 5.2). Shortly after the April 2015 protests and riots in Baltimore, a PRRI survey asked Americans whether they thought "the recent killings of African American men by police in Ferguson, Missouri, New York City, and Baltimore," were "isolated incidents" or "part of a broader pattern of how police treat African Americans." Nearly three quarters (74 percent) of black Americans said that these incidents were part of a broader pattern.

Among white Americans, only 43 percent saw the men's deaths as part of a larger pattern; roughly the same number (45 percent) saw these events as isolated incidents.

FIGURE 5.2 Recent Killings of African American Men by Police Are Part of a Broader Pattern of How Police Treat African Americans

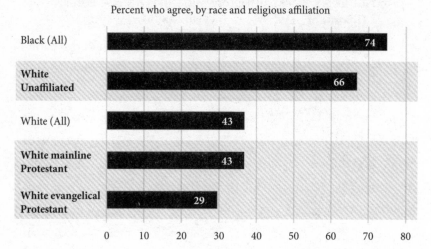

Percent who agree, by race and religious affiliation

Source: PRRI, Religion and Politics Tracking Survey, May 2015.

Within the realm of White Christian America, there are considerable variations between the mainline and evangelical branches, but neither comes close to matching African Americans' levels of concerns. Among mainline Protestants—a white subgroup that one would expect to be more aligned with black perspectives because their denominations have a long history of official support for civil rights—the perception gap is no different from that of whites overall. Only 43 percent of white mainline Protestants see these events as part of a broader pattern, while 47 percent see them as isolated incidents. The racial perception gap between white evangelical Protestants and African Americans is a yawning 45 percentage points. Fewer than three in ten (29 percent) white evangelical Protestants see the recent killings of black men by police as part of a broader pattern, while 57 percent see them as isolated incidents. Among whites, religiously unaffiliated Americans hold the closest views to African Americans: about two thirds (66 percent) of the religiously unaffiliated see these events as signs of a broader problem, compared to 23 percent who see them as isolated incidents.

If there were any lingering hopes that the election of the nation's first black president could move America past its racially fraught history, they died along with Brown, Garner, and Gray. The racial perception gap highlights one of the most powerful—but also least discussed—divisions between Americans on the topic of race: the rift between the descendants of White Christian America and the rest of the country.[20] These stark divides prompt a simple but fundamental question: why can't White Christian America understand how African Americans feel about the black men who have died at the hands of white police officers? To understand the answer, we need to look back at the dynamics of segregation and racial suspicion that have shaped Christian communities and their moral vision over the past century.

Race and American Institutions

America's still-segregated modern life is marked by three realities. First, geographic segregation has meant that—although places like Ferguson and Baltimore may seem like extreme examples—most white Americans continue to live in locales that insulate them from the obstacles facing many majority-black communities.[21] Second, this legacy, compounded by social self-segregation, has led to a stark result: the overwhelming majority of white Americans don't have a single close relationship with a person who isn't white. Third, there are virtually no American institutions positioned to resolve these persistent problems of systemic and social segregation.

Neighborhoods

In May 1911, the mayor of Baltimore signed an ordinance designed to "promote the general welfare of the city" by assigning separate blocks for the city's black and white residents.[22] Schools, churches, and houses would all be formally segregated, in an attempt to keep black neighborhoods—where substandard living conditions provoked the spread of tuberculosis and cholera—from encroaching on white localities. The immediate effect was a sharp drop in the quality of housing in black communities. Unable to move out of crowded tenements, black Baltimoreans now had to contend with rising prices as landlords took advantage of their limited mobility.[23] But the city's white residents were pleased with the ordinance's results. Other cities throughout the country—and especially in the South—followed Baltimore's lead, until the United States Supreme Court struck down a residential segregation ordinance in Louisville, Kentucky, in 1917, effectively gutting the Baltimore law and all others like it.

The spirit of the 1911 ordinance proved difficult to vanquish. Unable to implement de jure segregation, Baltimore city officials—and countless other communities across the country—embarked on an elaborate plan to prevent black residents from moving into white neighborhoods through housing codes and property owners' associations. As African Americans poured into the city in the years after

World War I, an exodus of white Baltimoreans began, leaving a crumbling urban ghetto in the center of the city. Today, Baltimore remains one of the most residentially segregated cities in America, with black residents mostly confined to the inner city and western suburbs—the same part of Baltimore where protesters rioted over Freddie Gray's death.[24]

This historical system of formal and informal segregation continues to be seen in American neighborhoods across the country decades after these practices have been abandoned. As a result, white Americans on average live in neighborhoods with significantly fewer problems than black Americans. A 2012 PRRI survey found that white Americans are, on average, approximately 20 percentage points less likely than black Americans to report experiencing a range of challenges in their communities. While majorities of whites say lack of good jobs (60 percent) and lack of opportunities for young people (52 percent) are major problems in their communities, these numbers rise to eight in ten and nearly seven in ten respectively for black Americans. There are similarly large gaps between white and black Americans on whether other social and economic issues are major problems, such as lack of funding for public schools (45 percent of whites vs. 64 percent of blacks) and crime (28 percent of whites vs. 51 percent of blacks).

These disparities are echoed in findings from the Urban League's *State of Black America* report.[25] The 2015 report finds that the "Equality Index," a composite measure of the well-being of black Americans compared to white Americans, is 72 percent; in other words, black Americans in the aggregate have only 72 percent of the well-being of white Americans—as measured across a number of areas, including economic well-being, health, education, social justice, and civic engagement. The two greatest areas of black-white disparity are economic well-being—which includes joblessness and income inequality—and social justice, which includes factors such as being a victim of violent crime. For 2015, the Equality Index found that blacks had on average only 56 percent of the economic well-being and 61 percent of social justice benefits that whites enjoy.

These numbers come to life in the streets of places like Ferguson and Baltimore, where the police killings of unarmed black men ignited a powder keg of pent-up frustrations rooted in experiences of cumulative injustices, stark inequality, and the historic legacy of residential segregation. In the county surrounding Ferguson, recent statistics show a 20 percentage point employment gap between white and black residents. In 2012, whites had an unemployment rate of 6.2 percent, while the unemployment rate for blacks was 26 percent.[26] Meanwhile, Chris Ingraham, a data journalist at *The Washington Post*, found shocking disparities in life expectancies in different neighborhoods in Baltimore. Ingraham found that an average baby born in 2015 in wealthy, majority-white Roland Park, one of the nation's first planned suburban communities nestled on the northern edge of the city, would have a life expectancy that is nearly twenty years longer than a typical baby born in the impoverished and mostly black Downtown/Seton Hill neighborhood, just three miles away. Map these numbers onto the life expectancies of more than two hundred countries, and the results snap into even starker focus. While Roland Park would rank among the top five longest-living countries in the world, Downtown/Seton Hill ranks 230th, barely edging out Yemen for the lowest life expectancy on the planet. And Downtown/Seton Hill is not alone. As Ingraham notes, "Fourteen Baltimore neighborhoods have lower life expectancies than North Korea. Eight are doing worse than Syria."[27]

Individuals' Social Networks

Jennifer Harvey, a professor of religion, studied white Christian congregations in Baltimore and New York that were struggling to find an appropriate response to the legacy of racism. She concluded that social segregation was one of the biggest impediments, particularly for white Americans, to understanding and engaging racial problems. In *Dear White Christians: For Those Still Longing for Racial Reconciliation*, Harvey notes:

> We have substantial evidence that whites tend to become deeply invested in racial justice and anti-racism work only after they become invested in the lives of people of color through experiencing long-term, meaningful relationships. The power and impact of structural and personal racism, and passive white tolerance of these, become more visceral for whites when we see how real these are in the life of someone for whom we care.[28]

In 2013, a PRRI survey uncovered the staggering levels of segregation within Americans' personal lives. (Figure 5.3.) The survey asked Americans about their core social networks, defined as up to seven people with whom they had discussed important matters in the last six months.[29] The survey found that, on average, the core social networks of white Americans are a remarkable 91 percent white and only one percent black. Moreover, three quarters of white Americans have completely white core social networks.[30] Among white evangelical and white mainline Protestants, these levels of homogeneity are even higher. Fully eight in ten white evangelical Protestants and 85 percent of white mainline Protestants have entirely white core social networks.

FIGURE 5.3 Racial and Ethnic Makeup of Whites' Core Social Networks

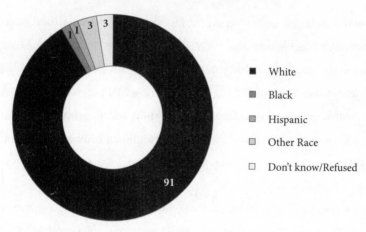

- White
- Black
- Hispanic
- Other Race
- Don't know/Refused

Source: PRRI, American Values Atlas, 2013.

The inhabitants of White Christian America don't understand why African Americans were so angrily protesting in Ferguson, New York, and Baltimore because their communities and experiences are insulated from many of the problems facing black Americans. White Americans' notions of race and fairness are shaped by their everyday experiences (already very different from those of African Americans), which are then reinforced by interactions with neighbors and friends. And these core social networks—the space where meaning is welded onto experience—tend to be extremely segregated. Despite the demise of Jim Crow laws and race-restrictive housing ordinances, and the rise of integrated workplaces, white Americans' most meaningful relationships are almost exclusively with other white people. This effectively closes the door to interactions with people who might challenge what feels like a natural and "common-sense" perspective on the events they see on cable television.

Other Institutions

To make matters worse, America has virtually no large-scale, widely distributed civic institutions that are equipped to nurture strong relationships across racial divides. Today's integrated military, where black and white soldiers live in close proximity and rely on one another in dangerous circumstances, might be the best example of an institution that accomplishes this work, but it can influence only a fraction of the population. In the corporate sector, most Americans continue to work in environments with low or minimal diversity.[31] Even for the one in ten Americans who are employed in high-diversity workplaces, the diversity training offered by most corporations has the more instrumental goal of ensuring an atmosphere that is healthy enough to generate a solid bottom line. Corporate diversity programs encourage respect, inclusion, and fair treatment, but overall the business sector has little interest in tackling more difficult conversations about the roots of racial conflict and injustice. Although the labor movement has had its share of racial strife, in the middle of the twentieth century it seemed that at least some major labor unions could bring black and white workers together in common cause. But labor union membership among U.S. workers peaked at 35 percent in 1954, fell to 20 percent by 1983, and hit 11 percent by 2014.[32]

One of the important purposes of public schools, beyond their educational mission, is to bring together American children—and, more indirectly, their parents—across race and class lines. While children are proportionally represented in public schools in the aggregate, a number of local factors prevent schools from looking like a cross section of the population.[33] The title of a major 2014 study by the Civil

Rights Project at UCLA captures the current state of public schools' work toward desegregation: *Brown at 60: Great Progress, a Long Retreat, and an Uncertain Future.*[34] The report showed that while whites account for only about half of the population of school-age children, the average white student today attends a school that is 73 percent white. The report contained this striking summary of the state of desegregation:

> At the [1988] peak, 44 percent of black southern students were in majority-white schools, the kind of schools that provided strong potential opportunities for diverse learning experiences. By 2011, that number had declined to 23 percent, a drop by nearly half, and the decline has accelerated in recent years. The progress achieved in the last 46 years on this measure of segregation is gone.[35]

Two varieties of "white flight"—each involving the descendants of White Christian America—have fueled the re-segregation of public schools, particularly in the South. The most immediate response to *Brown* was the launching of whites-only private academies—many of them church related—across the South. In Mississippi alone, there are more than 35 "segregation academies," as a 2012 *Atlantic* article dubbed them, each of which were "founded between 1964 and 1972 in response to anticipated or actual desegregation orders, and all of them enroll fewer than two percent black students."[36] In smaller towns like Indianola, these private academies have resulted in dueling, nearly perfectly segregated school systems. In a town with only 10,000 residents, where only 20 percent are white, the private Indianola Academy's enrollment is 99.5 percent white, while the public

Gentry High School is 98 percent black. The leap to private academies provided an immediate mechanism for avoiding mixed race schools in smaller towns, but many whites in larger cities, such as my hometown of Jackson, simply moved out of the city limits to homogeneous suburbs, leaving the city public schools with a declining white student population and a shrinking tax base to support its schools.

Moreover, as books like Robert Putnam's *Bowling Alone* demonstrated, participation in voluntary associations—the sector that includes churches—fell in the closing decades of the twentieth century.[37] All of this leads to the stark conclusion that if Americans are going to bridge the racial divide, we are going to have to build something new—or at the very least, transform existing institutions.

The Most Segregated Hour in America

What role does religion play in segregation? In theory, a central part of the Christian church's mission is to challenge its members to think beyond worldly perspectives and divisions. Churches are supposed to be sacred places where the social distinctions that structure politics or the workplace melt away. This ideal permeates the New Testament scriptures; it's written into the lyrics of popular hymns like "In Christ There Is No East or West." The words of the hymn extol a vision of racial harmony—"Join hands, disciples of the faith, whate'er your race may be. / All children of the living God are surely kin to me"—and its tune was the first African American music to be used in a white mainline North American hymnal.[38] But however deeply the principles of racial equality may be enshrined in theology and liturgy, they have had little impact on the actual racial composition of Christian congregations, past or present.

Nearly a century ago, a leading mainline Protestant theologian H. Richard Niebuhr—brother of Union Seminary's Reinhold Niebuhr—argued in *The Social Sources of Denominationalism* that denominational divisions within the American Protestant churches—which fell along racial, ethnic, and class lines—were a glaring ethical failure.[39] By Niebuhr's lights, the churches of his day had abandoned one of the New Testament's most central themes: the abolition of social distinctions within the walls of religious community. Instead, Niebuhr charged that contemporary churches had accepted "the accommodation of Christianity to the caste-system of human society." He pulled no punches in the opening pages of the book: "The division of the churches closely follows the division of men into the castes of national, racial, and economic groups. It draws the color line in the church of God."[40] Niebuhr noted that nearly 90 percent of all African American Christians in the 1920s were members of churches affiliated exclusively with black denominations, and nearly all of the remainder were restricted to special conferences within white denominations.[41]

Just over three decades later, answering questions after a lecture at Western Michigan University in 1963, Rev. Martin Luther King, Jr. famously testified to the continued reality and effects of these divisions.

We must face the fact that in America, the church is still the most segregated major institution in America. At 11:00 on Sunday morning when we stand and sing, and "Christ has no East or West," we stand at the most segregated hour in this nation. This is tragic. Nobody of honesty can overlook this. Now, I'm sure that if the church had taken a stronger stand all along, we wouldn't have many of the problems that we have. The first way that the church can repent, the first way that it can move out into the arena of social reform, is to remove the yoke of segregation from its own body.[42]

Over the next few years, King returned to this point frequently. He did so for the last time in a sermon at the National Cathedral in Washington, D.C., on March 31, 1968, just five days before his assassination.[43]

During the civil rights movement, some demonstrators tried to expose the hypocrisy of southern churches by sponsoring "kneel-ins," where interracial groups of college students would try to enter large, influential majority-white churches on Sunday mornings, often to find themselves turned away at the door.[44] One white pastor, Rev. Ashton Jones, served six months in jail after leading an interracial group of protesters into Atlanta's First Baptist Church, the largest Protestant church in the city and the twelfth largest in the Southern Baptist Convention. As he stood inside the church's foyer on the day he was arrested, Jones told entering parishioners, "You're going into a segregated church; you must be worshiping a segregated God."[45]

Few churches continue to have overtly discriminatory policies, and there has been some increased integration over the last decade. But today's churches continue to be remarkably segregated. Duke University's National Congregations Study, which has been documenting trends in congregational diversity over the last two decades, found that between 1998 and 2012 the number of churchgoers attending predominantly white congregations *with at least some* black members increased from 57 percent to 69 percent, and the number of churchgoers attending predominantly white congregations *with at least some* Hispanic members increased from 54 percent to 62 percent. Few white Christians today, however, have the experience of attending churches with significant numbers of nonwhite members. For example, the survey makes clear that it's rare to find integration that is more substantive than symbolic. Defining a mono-racial church as one that has more than 80 percent of its membership consisting of a single racial group, nearly nine in ten (86 percent) congregations, which account for 80 percent of churchgoers, remain essentially mono-racial.[46]

White Christian America and Race

The story of White Christian America and race has its roots in the Civil War, when conflicts over slavery and race opened fissures within white Protestant denominations that persist even today. Nearly all of the major white Protestant groups—Episcopalians, Lutherans, Presbyterians, Methodists, and Baptists—were torn apart by disputes over slavery, forcing interdenominational schisms between North and South, Unionist and Confederate, abolitionist and slave-supporting factions.[47] The Episcopalians and Lutherans reunited shortly after the Civil War, as did factions of Presbyterians, while regional divisions lingered among Methodists until 1939.[48] To this day, white Baptists remain fractured, with the smaller denomination, American Baptist Churches USA headquartered in the Northeast, and the much larger Southern Baptist Convention anchored in the South and Midwest. In the 1950s, these groups' divergent reactions to the civil rights movement flowed along familiar channels that had been carved over the course of more than a century by the forces of theology, culture, and politics.

White Evangelical Protestants: From Segregation to Racial Reconciliation

In 1956, the fiery Baptist preacher Rev. W. A. Criswell—pastor of Dallas's First Baptist Church, the largest Baptist church in the world at the time—accepted an invitation from South Carolina State Senator Strom Thurmond to speak on February 22, 1956, to the General Assembly of the South Carolina legislature about the issue of the day: segregation. In his rambling extemporaneous remarks, Criswell defended social segregation within the church *and* in society at large. Marshaling an argument that has long served as a justification for slavery and segregation, Criswell explained that because each race has different physical traits and psychological aptitudes, they flourish best in separate environments. For example, he noted that while his white congregation couldn't sing spirituals, "they can over there at the colored folks church." He had particularly strong words for outsiders who were upsetting what he argued was a mutually beneficial arrangement—those "scantling good-for-nothing fellows who are trying to upset all the things that we love as good old Southern people and good old Southern Baptists." He concluded his remarks by saying: "Don't force me by law, by statute, by Supreme Court decision . . . to cross over in those intimate things where I don't want to go. . . . Let me have my church. Let me have my school. Let me have my friends." [49]

No segment of White Christian America has been more complicit in the nation's fraught racial history than white evangelical Protestants. And no group of white evangelical Protestants bears more responsibility than Southern Baptists, who comprise the overwhelming majority of white evangelicals, particularly in the states of the former Confederacy. As the largest Protestant denomination in the country, and the white

Christian denomination most concentrated in the South, the SBC is an important bellwether for White Christian America's progress on race relations. The SBC was, after all, created in the years before the Civil War as a haven for pro-slavery Southern Christians.[50] In 1845, when the American Baptist Foreign Mission Society declared that any slave owner would be disqualified from consideration for missionary service, Baptist churches in the South seceded and formed the Southern Baptist Convention so that members would not have to choose between their slaves and their calling to be missionaries.

Following the Civil War, Southern Baptists stood by the southern status quo of segregation. Nearly a century after the Confederacy's surrender, they were generally wary or outright hostile to the civil rights movement. In their sweeping *Baptists in America: A History*, historians Thomas Kidd and Barry Hankins summarized Baptists' relationship to the civil rights movement this way: "Typical white Baptists in the South viewed civil rights as at best irrelevant to the Christian faith and at worst a threat to their culture."[51]

The Southern Baptist Convention—known for passing resolutions on even minor matters of concern—largely ignored the early civil rights movement. Their only official race relations resolution during the entire decade of the 1950s—which witnessed the Supreme Court's desegregation of public schools, Rosa Parks and bus boycotts in Alabama, Emmett Till's murder in Mississippi, church bombings in Alabama, and the governor blocking the integration of Little Rock High School in Arkansas—was a resolution issued in 1950 recommending that the denomination officially invite "Negro churches" to participate in simultaneous (but separate) revival meetings.[52] Following the landmark Supreme Court ruling in *Brown v. Board of Education* in 1954, the SBC did urge Baptists to accept the ruling "in harmony with the constitutional guarantee for equal freedom to all citizens, and with the Christian principles of equal justice and love for all men."[53] The report may have landed on the right side of history, but its main appeal was based not on repudiating racism and segregation but on respecting law and order once the matter had been decided.

Criswell's speech to the South Carolina General Assembly was a potent example of the overtly segregationist faction within the Southern Baptist Convention during the civil rights era. Not all of their leaders were so forthright. Others within the SBC were more circumspect, but no less emphatic, in their advocacy for the maintenance of the segregated status quo. In his popular weekly sermons, the Reverend Douglas Hudgins—who presided as pastor of the powerful First Baptist Church in Jackson, Mississippi, from 1946 to 1969—regularly told listeners that Christian faith was exclusively focused on the salvation of individual souls and had nothing to say on political matters. With Sunday services broadcast statewide and a large number of prominent political leaders—such as segregationist governor Ross Barnett—participating in its lay leadership, the church set the tone both within the denomination and in the halls of the Mississippi state capitol just a few blocks away.[54]

Hudgins strenuously avoided the racial tensions roiling all around him, even when the Ku Klux Klan targeted a friend and local rabbi, Perry Nussbaum. In retribution for Nussbaum's outspokenness on civil rights, the KKK bombed first his synagogue and then his home. An exasperated Nussbaum accused Hudgins, on national television, of complicity through his silence. When Hudgins mounted the pulpit the following Sunday, he mentioned the bombing only in passing. As he turned to preach from a text that had nothing to do with racism, he added, "The Lord works in mysterious ways."[55]

Hudgins was certainly not alone in his theological justification of political disengagement on civil rights issues. In the South of the 1950s and 1960s, the widely held gospel of the status quo—what historian John Lee Eighmy described as the "cultural captivity" of southern churches—discouraged a robust Christian voice for racial equality.[56] In 1964, for example, in response to the mobilization of black clergy and churches that drove the civil rights movement, independent Baptist leader Jerry Falwell delivered a famous sermon called "Ministers and Marches," where he justified white clergy inaction on civil rights issues, declaring, "Preachers are not called to be politicians, but soul winners."[57]

To be sure, a vocal minority of Southern Baptists were advocating for civil rights.[58] But in the 1950s and 1960s, the lethal cocktail of resistance and inaction represented by Criswell and Hudgins filled the cup from which most Baptists were drinking. Articles in the leading evangelical magazine, *Christianity Today*, encouraged Christians to root out racism in their own lives, but also criticized integration.[59] Separating people of different races through law was not portrayed as a moral evil—in fact, some argued that it was necessary to maintain peace in the South. One author declared that supporters of integration were espousing a kind of "Christian communism." In sharp contrast to the mainline-oriented *Christian Century*, Martin Luther King, Jr. was barely mentioned in *Christianity Today*'s pages. In January 1964, the editors noted—in two lines—that he had been selected as *Time* magazine's "Man of the Year"; later that year, they mentioned in one sentence that he had won the Nobel Prize.[60]

There is evidence that resistance to racial integration helped rouse Christian conservatives around a political agenda in the late 1970s. The historian Randall Balmer contends that evangelicals were generally reluctant to take up the cause of abortion—which remained primarily a Catholic issue well into the 1970s—until it was linked to a broader conservative agenda, one that revolved around resisting the federal government's crackdown on Christian schools that banned interracial dating, like Bob Jones University. Balmer quotes Paul Weyrich, one of the founders of the Christian Right, reflecting on activist strategy in the early years of the movement. "I was trying to get people interested in [abortion, school prayer, or the proposed Equal Rights Amendment to the Constitution] and I utterly failed," Weyrich said. "What changed their mind was Jimmy Carter's intervention against the Christian schools, trying to deny them tax-exempt status on the basis of so-called de facto segregation. . . . It was not the other things."[61]

By the 1980s, outright public resistance to desegregation had fallen out of favor. But the individualist flavor of Baptist theology, with its tendency to reduce racial problems to individual sin rather than systematic social discrimination, remained, ensuring that most responses to the race problem by groups like the Southern Baptist Convention were fairly shallow. Not until its annual meeting in June 1995 did the SBC adopt a resolution that broke this mold. A month before the convention—which marked the 150th anniversary of the SBC's founding—a group of eight white and eight black leaders drafted a sober apology to African Americans for the role slavery played in the convention's founding and for its consistent failure to support civil rights. Earlier resolutions had gone out of their way to minimize Baptists' complicity in white racism and often simultaneously denounced civil disobedience or destruction of property as legitimate ways to enact social change. But this statement, which the convention-goers adopted, was unambiguous and direct: "We apologize to all African-Americans for condoning and/or perpetuating individual and systemic racism in our lifetime; and we genuinely repent of racism of which we have been guilty."[62]

Given the SBC's racist and segregationist past, this statement was unimaginable even a generation ago. Not surprisingly, however, the sins of the fathers continue to haunt the SBC's attempts to deal with race today as they attempt to move from apology to reconciliation. This struggle was exemplified in the final chapter of the career of Richard Land, the head of the SBC's Ethics and Religious Liberty Commission. Land first came to prominence during the 1980s. As ultraconservatives systematically took control of the SBC, Land was rewarded for his part in the takeover with a position at the head of the agency's lobbying arm. During his early tenure, Land was instrumental in solidifying the SBC's rightward turn and making sure it found expression in the SBC's voice on Capitol Hill and in the media. Although he was best known for his outspoken opposition to abortion and same-sex marriage, Land was also instrumental in organizing and backing the 1995 resolution on racial injustice. But Land was also single-handedly responsible for tainting the most visible signal that the SBC was changing its tune on race issues: the unanimous 2012 election of Rev. Fred Luter as the first black president of the mostly white denomination.[63]

Just months before Luter was slated to take office—and just weeks after the death of Trayvon Martin in Florida, an unarmed teenager who was fatally shot by a neighborhood watch volunteer—Land declared on his nationally broadcast radio show that black leaders were exploiting Martin's case for political gain. When President Obama remarked that if he had a son, he would look like Trayvon Martin, Land accused Obama of "pour[ing] gasoline on the racialist [sic] fires." He called black leaders "racial ambulance chasers," asserting that they were using the tragedy "to gin up the black vote for an African-American president who is in deep, deep, deep trouble for re-election."[64] Land also defended George Zimmerman, the neighborhood watch vigilante who killed the unarmed black teenager. Despite strong criticism from both within and without the SBC—including public remarks from Luter, who said that

Land's comments had hurt efforts to attract nonwhite members—Land stubbornly stood by his words for two weeks, even adding in defense of his remarks that a black man is "statistically more likely to do you harm than a white man."[65]

Land only issued an apology after a graduate student at Baylor University posted evidence on his blog that the bulk of Land's radio show comments—in addition to the insensitivity of their content—were plagiarized from a *Washington Times* editorial. Following that revelation, Land was called to a five-hour meeting with SBC leaders, including several African American pastors. After the meeting Land issued an apology for his "insensitivity," but by then the die had been cast. The SBC canceled his radio show and publicly rebuked his remarks as "hurtful, irresponsible, insensitive, and racially charged."[66] Just five weeks after Luter's historic election, Land announced his retirement.[67]

Land's replacement, Russell Moore, a former professor of Christian theology and ethics at the Southern Baptist Theological Seminary, has struck a decidedly different tone. While Land openly referred to himself as a soldier in the "culture wars" and seemed to relish controversy, Moore has been more circumspect. As we saw in Chapter 4, Moore's position on LGBT rights differs from Land's more in tone than substance, but on the issue of racial equality, Moore is clearly breaking from the past. After a jury declined to indict police in the killing of Eric Garner, Moore released a podcast and the following statement, a striking contrast to Land's remarks:

> I'm stunned speechless by this news. We hear a lot about the rule of law—and rightly so. But a government that can choke a man to death on video for selling cigarettes is not a government living up to a biblical definition of justice or any recognizable definition of justice.[68]

In January 2015, arguing that if black and white Christians could worship together, they would stand up for each other, Moore asked black and white Christians to work to desegregate their churches.[69] Some SBC churches are leading the way. In the same month Moore issued his request, two Florida churches formed an unusual cross-racial union. The predominantly black Shiloh Metropolitan Baptist Church in Jacksonville absorbed Ridgewood Baptist Church, a mostly white congregation. Ridgewood had been struggling for years to keep up its numbers—a familiar story among majority-white churches—but when the merger was complete, the new church boasted eight thousand members. While there were certainly economic incentives in play for the declining Ridgewood Church, the merger was nonetheless a powerful symbol in a state that has long struggled with divisive race relations and was home to Trayvon Martin.[70]

Still, the merger received national attention precisely because of its uniqueness. The latest data indicate that while the number of nonwhite SBC-affiliated congregations grew from 5 percent in 1990 to 20 percent in 2010, this doesn't so much reflect growing diversity *within* churches themselves—rather, the diversification is due to the inclusion of majority-black and Latino churches. Less than one percent of SBC churches are multiethnic.[71]

In March 2015, Moore convened a two-day summit, "The Gospel and Racial Reconciliation." It was ambitious, but it was rife with paradoxes. There were few black leaders from outside the SBC on the program, and only about one fifth of the 550 participants at the conference were nonwhite.[72] One story observed that an afternoon panel dedicated to a discussion about Ferguson and race "veered off into abortion as a social justice issue for African-Americans." *The Atlantic*'s Emma Green noted that in the presentations and discussions, few participants made direct connections between the sin of racism and broader social problems like mass incarceration or poverty. "For the most part," Green concluded at the end of the summit, "Southern Baptists still see the issue of race as a matter of individual hearts and minds, not collective experience and collective policy."[73]

The summit showed the challenges facing Moore, who is arguably the most racially sensitive white voice within the SBC in a generation. One problem is that the SBC has a limited vocabulary for discussing racial issues, and "racial reconciliation" has become the dominant lens.[74] But the concept of reconciliation is easily framed as a problem of the sinful nature of individuals, one that tends to obscure structural injustice and the legacies of past wrongs. A singular emphasis on reconciliation as the end goal has a tendency to be self-undermining. While Southern Baptists, and the evangelical wing of White Christian America generally, show signs of having their hearts in the right place, their individualist theology may block the path that leads to the fulfillment of those aspirations.

White Mainline Protestants and Racial Justice

When it comes to race relations, the northern branch of White Christian America has long been one of its southern neighbors' strongest critics. In 1963, *The Christian Century*, the white mainline Protestant flagship magazine, became the first large-scale media outlet to publish Martin Luther King Jr.'s "Letter from Birmingham Jail." Written on paper smuggled into his cell after King was arrested for leading sit-ins and protests, the open letter refuted a statement made by eight white Alabama clergy—seven Christian pastors and one Jewish rabbi—who were urging King to stand down in the hope of preventing disunity. King's response was at once a scathing denunciation of white Christian apathy in the South and a masterful work of public theology:

I have watched many churches commit themselves to a completely otherworldly religion which makes a strange, unbiblical distinction between body and soul, between the sacred and the secular. We are moving toward the close of the 20th century with a religious community largely adjusted to the status quo—a taillight behind other community agencies rather than a headlight leading men to higher levels of justice.[75]

Over the years, the magazine had been a strong supporter of King's work. After publishing several of King's articles, *The Christian Century* named him an editor-at-large in 1958. By the early 1960s, he was a contributing editor. With the decision to publish the letter, the editors of *The Christian Century* were simultaneously promoting King's civil rights work and castigating the complicity and inaction of their fellow Protestants in the South.

The collaboration between King and white mainline Protestant leaders was bolstered by a long-standing official commitment to racial justice among white mainline Protestant institutions, particularly those above the Mason-Dixon line, in the century since the Civil War.[76] White Christian America's offshoots in the North, while somewhat ambivalent on the question of slavery going into the Civil War, had come out of it staunchly abolitionist. In these northeastern white Christian churches, where members and pastors were more familiar with the problems of urban industrialization than with the cotton economy, a social-justice-oriented Christian theology began to take root.

The cornerstone of this theology was "the social gospel," developed principally by American Baptist pastor Walter Rauschenbusch. Seeing the meager life prospects and dangerous working conditions of his lower-class New York parishioners at the turn of the twentieth century,

Reverend Rauschenbusch powerfully described an inescapable link between Christian theology and social justice work:

> No one shares life with God whose religion does not flow out, naturally and without effort, into all relations of his life. . . . Whoever uncouples the religious and social life has not understood Jesus. Whoever sets any bounds for the reconstructive power of the religious life over the social relations and human institutions, to that extent denies the faith of the Master.[77]

The northern mainline branch of white Christian America was active on civil rights issues through two main institutional arms: the National Council of Churches, the umbrella organization that included participation by some historically black denominations (and which later built the Interchurch Center), and *The Christian Century*, which had grown by midcentury into a national media platform. The magazine didn't just highlight social problems that would interest NCC members—it also covered leaders' efforts to address those issues. The NCC's predecessor, the Federal Council of Churches, made headlines in 1946 when it passed a unanimous resolution supporting "a non-segregated church in a non-segregated society."[78] This broad, influential meeting—which included five hundred Protestant leaders from twenty-five denominations and was addressed by President Truman—signaled that racial equality would be a central goal for the mainline denominations, at least at the institutional level.

Throughout the middle of the twentieth century, the National Council of Churches and *The Christian Century* were pillars of the civil rights movement. In the 1950s, the NCC supported the Montgomery bus boycott. In 1963, it organized the National Conference on Religion and Race in Chicago, which brought together Protestant, Catholic, and Jewish leaders. The meeting was hailed by Martin Luther King, Jr. as "the most significant and historic [convention] ever held for attacking racial injustice."[79] The NCC helped staff the March on Washington—in coordination with leaders at the United Methodist Building, which was used as a meeting and staging area—and the program on August 28, 1963, featured a speech by Rev. Eugene Carson Blake, vice chairman of the NCC's Commission on Religion and Race. The NCC also lobbied extensively and publicly for the 1964 Civil Rights Act.

But these official pronouncements were not always well received or implemented at the local level. Church historian Gardiner H. Shattuck, Jr., documented the struggles the Episcopalian denomination, one of the most liberal among the mainline, faced in its attempts to put its official statements to work on the ground.[80] Like other mainline denominations, the Episcopal Church issued strong statements supporting the *Brown* decision in 1954, championing the court's judgment and calling for "interracial fellowship" within the denomination. But it did little else to support the risky task of dismantling segregation on the local level; it even issued an official statement in 1958 saying that any moves toward integration should be slow.[81] Most tellingly, in 1961 the denomination let stand a decision by an all-white Episcopal private school to deny admission to Martin Luther King Jr.'s son because of his race.[82] This conflicted response was by no means atypical of the major white mainline denominations, whose clarion official statements never dispelled the discomfort and ambivalence within many local institutions and in the pews.

White mainline Protestantism's principal institutions, however, were critical during the civil rights era, and they have remained to this day a consistent voice for racial equality among white Christians. In

2013, NCC president Kathryn Lohre issued a "renewed call for racial justice" after the acquittal of George Zimmerman in the killing of Trayvon Martin, which she characterized as "the shocking impunity granted by a Florida jury to a man who stalked and killed a black child."[83] The NCC issued a statement expressing its "deep disappointment" with the failure to indict the officer who shot Michael Brown in Ferguson, asserting that Brown's death "has helped galvanize across the country a moral will to address the crisis our country faces in the systemic marginalization of young men of color."[84] After a New York grand jury refused to indict the officer who killed Eric Garner, the NCC called for prosecutors "to hold police officers accountable when they kill," and echoed the #BlackLivesMatter theme by asserting that "As a society we must rid ourselves of the notion that one life is worth more than another."[85] Following Freddie Gray's death in Baltimore police custody, the NCC stated flatly, "Too many young African-American men and women are dying at the hands of the police, and the nation must correct this injustice immediately."[86]

But looking back at its goal of bringing about "a non-segregated church in a non-segregated society," one can't help but conclude that the mainline denominations' strength was its ability to be a public Christian voice for racial justice, rather than a force for grassroots cultural or even ecclesial change.

Desegregating Church

The renewed focus on racial injustice that fueled the #BlackLivesMatter movement, coupled with demographic change, has brought White Christian America to a new crossroads. There is, of course, the path of least resistance, which also happens to be the one that will ensure White Christian America's declining relevance: reinforce the current racial isolation that has prevented many white Americans from engaging in meaningful discussions about racial inequality by fortifying the walls around their communities. To be sure, a move to make White Christian America's boundaries more permeable will leave white Christians vulnerable to uncomfortable conversations and even more difficult actions. Such a choice would require critical self-reflection, humility, and—to use a theological term—repentance. But the payoff would be an enormous boost for white Christians' communal health *and* for the country's overall well-being. While such a shift is difficult, it's not an impossible feat. While today's churches mostly reflect the social segregation of the status quo, some are already pioneering a new kind of Christian community that transcends the color line.

Middle Collegiate Church, New York City

In 1628, the Dutch West India Company sent the Reverend Jonas Michaelius to the settlement of New Amsterdam, a fortified trading outpost on the southern tip of the island of Manhattan. From these humble roots grew the oldest continuous Protestant congregation in the United States, anchored by Middle Collegiate Church, one of four congregations that make up the Collegiate Church of New York. In 1696, after the British had taken over New Amsterdam and rechristened it New York, the Collegiate Churches were recognized with a royal charter from King William III, making them the first official corporation in the British colonies.[87] The church interior—clad with dark oak panels, accented with gold leaf, and illuminated by Tiffany windows—is a vivid reminder of the congregation's Old World heritage and long history. Middle

Collegiate Church carried the Protestant tradition across many major events in the nation's history.[88] Its "Liberty Bell" rang for the country's independence on July 9, 1776, and has chimed for the inauguration and death of every American president.

But although Middle Church's neighborhood was changing fast by the end of the twentieth century, the church was not. As *The New York Times*'s Frank Bruni described it: "Time had passed the church by, as German and northern European immigrants were replaced on the Lower East Side by Asians, Latin Americans, artists and young professionals who had never heard of the tiny Reformed church."[89]

By the 1980s, Middle Church was in such bad shape that the Collegiate Corporation considered shuttering it altogether. Membership had dwindled to two dozen older white congregants, many of whom commuted into the city for services. It no longer had a community presence, the building was deteriorating, and the sparse congregation could afford neither the upkeep of the building nor the pastor's salary.

But after surveying the area, the corporation determined that a different kind of church could once again serve the neighborhood. They called Rev. Gordon R. Dragt, who had been serving a church in an artsy community in North Carolina. While Dragt was confident he was well suited for the challenges of ministry in a diverse urban setting, and Collegiate Corporation officers had fully briefed him on the condition of the church and the congregation, he felt overwhelmed to the point of tears as he looked out at the twenty-seven people scattered throughout the pews on his first Sunday in September 1985.[90]

Dragt set to work incorporating the church into its surroundings. He took a gamble by investing in renovations to make the church a more inviting place. He fixed the leaking roof, repaired the plaster, and applied a fresh coat of paint. He made the church more visible and appealing to artists in the neighborhood by providing gallery and performance space. On Sundays, he hired a jazz ensemble to play on the front steps of the church half an hour before the services started. He also organized new community outreach efforts tailored to the needs around the church, like Monday evening meals for people living with HIV/AIDS and affordable after-school child care.

As new kinds of people began to attend church on Sunday morning, Dragt began to adapt the traditional liturgy to their interests. He removed the front row of pews to make more room for performers, and the church started a gospel choir, which turned out to be a vital entry point for many new members. While these rapid changes—and the appearance of "a lot of people with all kinds of earrings," as one of the older members put it—were an uncomfortable departure for some,[91] Dragt managed to balance them with the older liturgy, connecting the newer members with the stalwart supporters. By the mid-1990s, attendance regularly topped two hundred each Sunday, with as many as four hundred on holidays.

Over the next decade, Middle Church strengthened its connections to the neighborhood, and the neighborhood continued to change Middle, too. As it became a larger and more diverse congregation, its success drew the attention of Jacqui Lewis, a PhD candidate at Drew University who was conducting a research project on clergy serving multiracial, multicultural congregations. The choice of research sites turned out to be providential. In 2004, she accepted the invitation to become associate minister, and upon Dragt's retirement in September 2005, she was installed as the first African American and the first woman to serve as a senior minister in the College Churches' nearly four-hundred-year history.[92]

Under the leadership of Reverend Lewis—"Jacqui," as she prefers to be called—the church has continued its commitment to the arts, with services that often include dancing and a gospel choir. Lewis has also encouraged the church to become a stronger voice for racial justice, particularly following the protests in Ferguson, New York, and Baltimore. As Lewis noted, the church's activism on racial justice came not out of guilt or external obligation but because of the very composition of the multiracial group that is now gathered under the century-old Tiffany windows: "We are forced to bump into each other, to pray together, to sing together, and to work for justice together."[93]

After Michael Brown's death in August 2014, Middle Church held a worship service with the theme "Hands Up. In Prayer. For Peace." In November, Joan Baez played at a benefit concert at the church, and all proceeds went to the Ferguson community.[94] On December 7, 2014, following the decision not to indict officers in the death of Eric Garner, Middle hosted an open forum to ask difficult questions around race. Lewis described the forum as fostering needed "conversations with the people we love" and as a way to "make space for deep questions and even the sharing of awkward sentiments."[95] In January 2015, in collaboration with several other faith-based organizations in New York, Lewis led a group of Middle Church members to stage a "die-in" in the U.S. Capitol cafeteria,[96] where participants—many holding signs emblazened with "#BlackLivesMatter"—simultaneously fell to the ground, lying there for more than three minutes. When Capitol police threatened arrests, participants filed out singing the spiritual "Ain't Gonna Let Nobody Turn Me Around."

Following the violence that broke out in Baltimore in 2015, the Middle Church gospel choir performed the song "Glory" from *Selma*, the movie depicting the violent clash between civil rights marchers and police in Selma, Alabama, during a 1965 march for voting rights. On her *Huffington Post* blog, Lewis described the scene this way:

A tall gorgeous Black gay man from our congregation led with, *One day, when the Glory comes, it will be ours, it will be ours,* while his petite white husband played the Hammond organ. The choir—directed by a Mexican American man, accompanied by a lesbian Black woman—filled with the voices of Chinese, Japanese, White, Black, Puerto Rican, married, and single folk who span generations rapped like Common—in unison! They wept, they stomped their feet as though they were stomping out injustice. Our congregation was on fire with deep feelings of both sorrow and hope.[97]

With this blend of tradition, the arts, and social activism, Lewis has accomplished something many Protestant congregations envy—she has managed to build a vibrant group of engaged twenty-somethings who are drawn to Middle's diverse community because of its blend of Christian teaching, social justice, and inclusivity.

Reverend Lewis provides a striking embodiment of Middle Church's transformation from a homogeneous white, elite congregation to an ethnically diverse community comprised of members who are gay and straight, well-off and down-on-their-luck, strait-laced and tattooed. In the halls of the historic main building, there is a portrait gallery featuring the succession of nearly four centuries of white male clergy who have served the church. Reverend Lewis's portrait at the end of the long procession—and her weekly presence in the senior minister's ornately carved Gothic chair—is a vivid symbol of the new kind of church Middle has become, one where hard conversations about race happen not just because of moral commitment but because of the diverse perspectives in the room.

Oakhurst Baptist Church, Atlanta

Oakhurst Baptist Church, in the suburbs of Atlanta, began like many white Baptist churches outside southern cities at the turn of the twentieth century. A new electric trolley line was built from the growing city of Atlanta to the DeKalb County seat in Decatur, and a nascent community sprang up around it. After meeting jointly with Methodists and Presbyterians following successful revival meetings in 1911, Oakhurst Baptist Church was organized officially in 1913. Methodist leaders, who owned the lot on which the combined group was meeting, declared that it was time for each denomination to "strike out on its own." [98]

Oakhurst became a model of church growth during the Southern Baptist Convention's heady expansion in the middle of the twentieth century. The Baptists bought some land nearby, erected their first wooden building in 1922, and hired their first full-time pastor in 1924. By 1959, Oakhurst's growing Sunday school rolls surpassed fourteen hundred, outgrowing an educational space that had only recently been expanded.[99] In 1963, its fiftieth anniversary, Oakhurst Baptist Church was recognized by the SBC Home Mission Board as "the outstanding church in the Southern Baptist Convention for the year 1961–62." [100]

But the demographic wave that had fueled Oakhurst's rapid growth was about to shift, testing Oakhurst's commitment to being a neighborhood church. In the early 1960s, the black population of Atlanta began to expand beyond its historically defined enclaves. Part of this was due to simple population growth, but large-scale civic construction projects were also forcing out black residents by leveling entire traditionally black neighborhoods. African American families moved into the Oakhurst neighborhood, triggering a wave of "white flight" to the suburbs north of Atlanta. By the mid-1960s, what had been an all-white neighborhood was shifting; one fourth of its residents were now African American. Many Oakhurst church members began to leave, and Sunday school attendance dropped by two thirds, down to just over five hundred by 1966.[101]

By the late 1960s, a full-swing racial transformation was under way in the neighborhood. Nearly all of the new residents were black, and self-interested white real estate agents accelerated the exodus of whites with "block busting"—warning entire blocks of white homeowners when a single black family purchased a home. With a significant portion of the all-white membership commuting into the increasingly minority neighborhood, Oakhurst was becoming "a white island in a black sea," as the church historian put it.[102]

Oakhurst had opened its community activities, such as Saturday skating in the church parking lot, to children of both races without much controversy. But when several African American girls showed up at the services of the church that had invited them to skate, the congregation was forced to face the question of full integration. The negative reactions to the presence of the girls prompted Oakhurst pastor John Nichol to pen a bold column in the *Baptist Messenger*, the Georgia Baptist state newspaper, where he concluded: "God will take little pleasure in our building a sanctuary to His Glory if the doors of that building are not open to all His people. Such a building would be little more than a mausoleum in which our vision and concern would be buried." It was such a remarkable statement for its day and place that the story was picked up by *The Atlanta Journal-Constitution*.[103] After much deliberation, and over the objections of some members who threatened to move because they didn't want their children to have to "mix with Negroes," the church officially accepted its first African American members in February 1968.

Two years later, after much discussion about joining the white flight to the suburbs, Oakhurst resolved to remain a neighborhood church, regardless of the racial composition of its surroundings. For the next few years, though, this clarity in mission did not translate into institutional stability. The bold stance attracted some new membership, but Oakhurst lost an estimated 90 percent of its original congregation during these tumultuous years.[104] By the mid-1970s, three of its four ministers were forced to go part-time following sharp decreases in member contributions. But Oakhurst had successfully crossed the color line, and the remnant of the membership, along with some newcomers, began to rebuild as a neighborhood church in the 1980s and 1990s.

Today its membership and finances are stable, and Oakhurst is a lively example of a multiracial, socioeconomically diverse congregation in the heart of the Deep South. The tagline on Oakhurst's website reads: "An inclusive community shining a light in the world." Oakhurst's path to becoming a welcoming neighborhood church broke the mold in many ways. It was one of the first Baptist churches to ordain women in the 1970s and the first to welcome openly gay members and to ordain gay clergy in the 1990s. As a result, the Georgia Baptist Convention voted in 1999 to "withdraw fellowship" from Oakhurst, primarily over its stance on welcoming gay and lesbian members. This decision effectively ended Oakhurst's long-standing association with the Southern Baptist Convention.[105] Oakhurst continues to be affiliated with a number of other Baptist bodies, however, which recognize its mandate for inclusivity.[106] Over the last three decades, Oakhurst has worked to embody the words of a hymn sung often in its services, "Jesus included me, Yes, He included me; When the Lord said, 'Whosoever,' He included me."[107]

Becoming a racially integrated church in the Deep South has certainly not come without its challenges, and in some ways equity is still eluding Oakhurst. As white flight has diminished and weary commuters are looking for neighborhoods closer to a revitalized downtown, the neighborhood is gentrifying. The congregation is becoming more white than black, and the "gospel choir," which sings traditional African American spirituals and other music from the black church tradition, performs much less frequently than the weekly "sanctuary choir." Most notably, the composition of its staff has never quite reflected its commitment to full integration. The Reverend John H. Cross, Jr.—the minister of 16th Street Baptist Church in Birmingham, Alabama, when a bomb planted by white Klansmen took the lives of four black girls in 1963—joined Oakhurst as associate pastor from 1972 to 1977.[108] But beyond this early and important step toward diversifying its leadership, Oakhurst has never had a nonwhite senior minister, and today all three members of the church's full-time ministry staff are white.

Still, the struggle to be a multiracial, "whosoever" church has shaped the congregation in ways that would have been unimaginable had the church followed the white flight to the suburbs. Following the unrest in Ferguson, for example, members from Oakhurst Baptist began meeting with members of Oakhurst Presbyterian—the only other neighborhood church that also chose to stay and adapt with the neighborhood—to discuss the emerging #BlackLivesMatter movement and their own local experiences with racial discrimination. As the movement grew following the protests in Baltimore, the churches co-sponsored a daylong set of events on May 2, 2015, which began with a symbolic funeral processional that wound its way downtown, interrupting Saturday morning traffic. After arriving at Oakhurst Baptist, a mix of nearly four hundred black and white people filled the sanctuary for a service that included testimonies from the family members of two black men recently killed in DeKalb County, alongside music, prayers, and a eulogy. This event—for which multiracial worshippers filled the pews of a historically white Baptist church to listen to black leaders and the family members of those killed tell their stories—is clear evidence that the choice not to leave in the 1960s was a visionary one. It paved the way for something truly rare in twenty-first-century America: a church that is providing an ongoing civic space for black and white Americans to have difficult conversations about race and injustice.

Why Is Desegregating Church So Difficult?

At present, congregations like Middle Collegiate Church, Oakhurst Baptist Church, and Shiloh Metropolitan Baptist Church (the newly merged, multiracial church in Florida) are exceptions to the rule of segregated churches in America. True multicultural, multiethnic congregations are a relatively new phenomenon. Sociologist Michael Emerson described their level of development as equivalent to "the toddler stage." In fact, racially diverse churches are so rare that when Emerson and his colleagues set out in the early 2000s to study four congregations that had been multiracial for more than the tenure of one clergy person, they had difficulty locating them.[109]

As a result, there is no blueprint for becoming a multiracial church. As Jennifer Harvey notes at the end of her study of how churches are trying to bridge the racial divide, "There are no obvious or complete models out there yet for how to do it and see it all the way through."[110] When white congregations set out on this journey, they encounter unexpected pitfalls. Harvey argues that one of the central reasons that so little progress has been made in nearly half a century of real effort is, paradoxically, "the powerful hold that 'reconciliation' has on the white Christian imagination." Many well-meaning white Christians—such as the Southern Baptists following Russell Moore's lead—are eager for racial reconciliation. But Harvey notes that although the "reconciliation paradigm" has laudable theological roots and intentions, it contains subtle assumptions that make it inadequate for our current historical situation.[111] Its central shortcoming is that it encourages white Christians to move too hurriedly toward a healed relationship without fully attending to repentance and—more importantly—to repair. Pausing to contemplate the need for repair, she argues, redirects us from an obsession with the endgame of reconciliation and "requires us not to move so quickly, given the actual situation in which race locates us right now."[112]

A recent example of the racial reconciliation paradigm at work is the #AllLivesMatter retort. In an interview in *The New York Times*, philosopher Judith Butler unpacked the problem:

> If we jump too quickly to the universal formulation, "all lives matter," then we miss the fact that black people have not yet been included in the idea of "all lives." That said, it is true that all lives matter (we can then debate about when life begins or ends). But to make that universal formulation concrete, to make that into a living formulation, one that truly extends to all people, we have to foreground those lives that are not mattering now, to mark that exclusion, and militate against it.[113]

Jennifer Harvey summarizes the unintended consequences of the reconciliation model this way: "If we continue to live in an unacknowledged history of brutal injustice, harm done, white hostility to and violence against communities of color—histories with legacies that are alive and well in the present—then speaking of reconciliation may do more harm than good, may cover more than it discloses."[114] She bluntly concludes that a strategy that is overly reliant on reconciliation has failed White Christian America.

This insight may help explain why white evangelical Protestants' recent efforts aimed at racial reconciliation have been unsuccessful. The move from sincere apology to forgiveness seems logical, because evangelicals' theological individualism tends to obscure the enduring structural injustices that require ongoing, concrete efforts to dismantle. But Harvey also demonstrates that even mainline Protestants, who have an official history of supporting civil rights, are still transfixed by the gleam of reconciliation. The United Church of Christ's "Sacred Conversation on Race" initiative in 2008—which Harvey identifies as one of the most thoughtful mainline Protestant efforts—nonetheless uses language that simultaneously eases the guilt of white participants and raises the expectation that black participants will be able to be "trusting once again."[115] The effect of this framing is to prematurely push reconciliation to center stage, while reparation waits in the wings.

Why is this work so hard? William Faulkner, a Mississippi-born writer who instinctively understood the power of history and culture, captured the essence of the challenge in one of his best-known quotes: "The past is never dead. It's not even past."[116] After the official apologies have been made, the question of what white Christians actually owe African Americans looms uncomfortably large. Especially as White Christian America passes from the scene, it's difficult to recount its full legacy—including unearthing and facing ugly historical events whose consequences live into the present. But even more difficult is repentance, which requires those who have benefited from injustice to enter into relationship with those who have been and continue to be wronged, and to hold their gaze long enough to contemplate the real requirements of repair. Most importantly, repentance requires the beneficiaries of injustice to resist the urge to ask for forgiveness before meaningful action has been taken. If the heirs of White Christian

America do finally embark on this longer, slower, and undoubtedly more hazardous path, they are more likely to realize their goals. Given our still present past, white Christians are more likely to find reconciliation as a *result* of a journey—rather than as a destination that can be reached directly.

The Promise of Desegregated Churches

Despite these daunting challenges, there are two reasons why churches may yet have potential for bridging the racial divide. First, despite their declining membership rates and dwindling social clout, churches remain one of the most omnipresent features of the American civic landscape. Virtually every hamlet in America, no matter how small, has at least one church. According to the latest estimates from the Association of Statisticians of American Religious Bodies, there are approximately 345,000 religious congregations in the country, nearly 78 percent of which are outgrowths of White Christian America, along either its evangelical Protestant (191,000) or mainline Protestant (78,000) branches.[117] To put those numbers into perspective, there are nearly ten times more religious congregations than post offices (35,000).[118] And while churches like Middle Collegiate and Oakhurst Baptist—which are located in urban settings where diversity is a part of everyday life—made active attempts to cross the color line, Michael Emerson found that the country's currently "hypersegregated" churches are actually one fourth as diverse as the neighborhoods in which they reside.[119] In other words, if churches could achieve the simple goal of mirroring their neighborhoods, they could take a big step forward.

Second, forming communities that foster meaningful relationships over time is precisely the kind of thing that churches—at their best—can do. Unlike other institutions where race relations work is a means to other ends, it can be central to the mission of churches. And there is early evidence that forming these communities can be effective. In their national study of pioneering multiracial congregations, Emerson and his colleagues found that they indeed served as "bridge organizations" in their larger communities, breaking down racial barriers and facilitating cross-racial ties. For example, in their study of Wilcrest Baptist Church, a multiracial congregation in Houston, Emerson and his colleagues noted how the church served as an incubator, fostering a friendship between three men: one African American, one Hispanic, and one from the white Cajun culture of south Louisiana. At the time of the study, Emerson and colleagues described their relationship vividly: "These men get together at one another's homes, go to movies together, pray together, support each other during times of stress, eat out together, and babysit each other's children."[120] These experiences changed how congregants participated at church. Even more importantly, it generated considerable "bridging capital" that changed congregants' perspectives on racial inequality issues and carried benefits into other institutions and into other areas of their lives.[121]

The work of desegregating churches will require some trailblazing, both by majority-white congregations and by individual white Christians. At the congregational level, majority-white churches will need to initiate more cultural cross-pollination efforts, such as conducting joint services or initiating regular pulpit exchanges. Beyond Sunday morning, co-sponsoring community service projects, such as taking on a Habitat for Humanity house, could provide a way to build multiracial "sweat equity." And majority-white congregations could look for opportunities to dedicate their resources (meeting space, volunteer power, financial support) to support causes that concern their nonwhite neighbors, even when those causes do not immediately resonate with their own sensibilities.

Ultimately, though, the country will need more multiracial congregations. Moreover, because of the power of dominant cultural white paradigms in the broader culture, these multiracial congregations will need to have significant nonwhite leadership.[122] More white Christians will have to worship in churches with senior leadership that is not white, sit in pews where whites are not the overwhelming majority, and experience the tenor of conversations about the connections between Christian commitment and community problems when they are not driven by white interests. In these multiracial settings, even familiar gospel stories and hymns resonate differently. More than any moral aspiration or religious conviction, this kind of lived experience promises to shrink racial perception gaps and bridge the racial divides.

Despite consistent work by white mainline Protestant leaders and more recent efforts by white evangelical Protestant leaders, the stubborn problem of social segregation remains entrenched within America's churches and the nation as a whole. While not all forms of social separation need be lamented (for example, African American churches have created a vital incubator of community for black Christians in a white-dominated society), the near-absolute homogeneity that currently exists in churches and whites' core social networks hinders our ability to begin to mend racial rifts. Moreover, this homogeneity thwarts our capacity to agree about something as basic as the reality of the problems we face.

White Christians have good reasons to take this myopia seriously. Even for the six in ten evangelicals and nearly half of white mainline Protestants who doubt there is a real racial problem, the country's changing demographics will increasingly mean that the descendants of White Christian America will need nonwhite allies to achieve their political goals, both at the local and national level. As a purely practical matter, white Protestants will have to learn to be less cavalier in dismissing black claims of injustice if they are to transition from unilateral to coalition politics.

Beyond these pragmatic interests, even if white Protestants are not in a position to fully understand black concerns, at least some white leaders are coming around to a newfound humility. This chastened posture is rooted in their recognition of past sins on issues of race, like those that made them the target of King's "Letter from Birmingham Jail." As the SBC's Russell Moore said in a heartfelt statement following the New York grand jury decision, "We may not agree in this country on every particular case and situation, but it's high time we start listening to our African American brothers and sisters in this country when they tell us they are experiencing a problem." [123]

Selma's Edmund Pettus Bridge has now been crossed by the nation's first black president, but fifty years later the ramifications of that "Bloody Sunday" are still with us. Racial reconciliation remains a destination far on the horizon, and there are no shortcuts at hand. The road under White Christian America's descendants' feet must lead first through the uncharted terrain of remembering, repentance, and repair. Given White Christian America's long history of complicity in slavery, segregation, and racism, we are at the beginning, not the end, of the journey across the racial divide.

6

A Eulogy for White Christian America

Stages of Grief Among White Christian America's Descendants

In the aftermath of a death, the passing days and weeks bring mourners face-to-face with the intensity of their loss. This disorienting feeling begins to suffuse the lives of the grieving, as they begin, gradually, to realize what this person's absence means. Whether a positive or negative influence, if a person's presence was meaningful, his or her death is akin to a gravitational force that suddenly retracts, throwing everything within its orbit into disarray. The process of settling back into a world devoid of that person can be heartrending. It's not uncommon to hear, "I just can't imagine the world without her." Ordinary routines seem somehow unfamiliar, workdays blur into dream sequences, and hobbies lose their luster. Even conversations with closest friends and family members can feel like interactions one is watching, rather than having. Life, for a while, is lived at a distance, with each step into the future seeming uncertain.

The nature of this experience of death and loss did not receive systematic attention in the United States until the publication of psychiatrist Elisabeth Kübler-Ross's popular book, *On Death and Dying: What the Dying Have to Teach Doctors, Nurses, Clergy, and Their Own Families,* in 1969.[1] Drawing on her interactions with dying patients and their families, Kübler-Ross identified at least five common "stages" of grief: denial, anger, bargaining, depression, and acceptance. While there is nothing prescriptive about these "stages"—Kübler-Ross emphasized that they were not necessarily sequential and some might be skipped altogether—they have remained compelling enough to keep the book in print for more than four decades. And they provide a useful model for understanding responses to the death of White Christian America among white mainline and evangelical Protestants.

The mainline and evangelical branches of White Christian America have each charted their own course through the grieving process. As the first to grapple with the news of WCA's terminal condition, white mainline Protestants moved the furthest toward acceptance. They have had considerable time to sit both with the loss and the new realities of American demographics, culture, and politics. By contrast, white evangelical Protestants are still struggling to acknowledge their newly diminished status, and few have come to terms with the implications of WCA's death.

Denial and Anger

While each of the stages of grief is interrelated, denial and anger are intimately linked, especially as patients and their families struggle to comprehend the meaning of a terminal diagnosis. While the word "denial" has come to have a particularly pejorative ring in today's pop-psychology-infused culture, Kübler-Ross notes its practical role as "a buffer after unexpected shocking news," which "allows the patient to collect himself and, with time, mobilize other, less radical defenses." In her work, she found that while "the need for denial exists in every patient at times," patients and families tend to rely on it less over time, as they move to at least partial acceptance of their condition.[2]

As denial subsides, it is not uncommon for responses such as anger, rage, and resentment to appear in its wake. Anger often accompanies the realization that plans will not be completed and goals will not be achieved. In the religious realm, anger sometimes materializes when what had been taken as divine promises of future well-being seem to be broken. This stage of grief is also typically messy. Kübler-Ross saw anger "displaced in all directions and projected onto the environment at times almost at random."[3] It is not uncommon for this anger to be directed at fellow family members.

Denial and Anger Among White Mainline Protestants

At the beginning of the twentieth century, white mainline Protestants' aspirations were astronomically high. As historian Elesha Coffman writes in *The Christian Century and the Rise of the Protestant Mainline*, the very "idea of the mainline" was sweeping, aiming for no less than "a unified American Protestantism, socially dominant, socially progressive, fulfilling its obligation as shepherd of the nation's soul."[4] Seeing both Catholicism and secularism as threats—and dismissing the evangelical branch of Protestantism as living "in a kind of cloistered isolation"[5]—leaders like *Christian Century* editor Charles Clayton Morrison understood mainline dominance not just as a social aspiration but as a divine mandate. For these leaders, as Morrison put it at the end of his "Can Protestantism Win America?" series, published in 1946: "It is the will of Christ that it be done."[6]

Against the backdrop of these lofty ambitions, the earliest symptoms of WCA's worsening condition, which began to appear in the mid-1960s, were initially pushed aside. But meticulous record keeping by the largest mainline denominations—which offered tabulated proof of the magnitude of their membership losses—limited the plausibility of denials. By the end of the 1970s, most mainline leaders were forced to acknowledge that the downward trends in the yearly denominational reports represented more than a temporary aberration.[7]

While denial was short-lived, there was plenty of room for anger. Looking across at the apparent vitality among their evangelical kin in the 1970s and 1980s, conservative members of the mainline lashed out at denominational leaders and the National Council of Churches, blaming the decline on theological liberalism and cultural accommodation. The most prominent channel for this anger has been the Institute on Religion and Democracy (IRD), an organization formed in 1981 by theological and political conservatives within the mainline denominations.[8] The IRD's primary mission is to work inside mainline Protestant denominational institutions in order to pull them toward more conservative theological and social positions, or, when that is not possible, to dismantle them altogether. Founded in collaboration with right-leaning evangelical and Catholic activists, the IRD has concentrated its fire on the National Council of Churches and on three of the most influential mainline denominations: the United Methodist Church, the Presbyterian Church (USA), and the Episcopal Church. At the NCC's fiftieth anniversary, the IRD spotlighted the NCC's financial crisis and issued a press release in which IRD president Diane

Knippers quipped, "Rather than a birthday party, the NCC should be given a funeral service."[9]

In a 2010 address to the IRD board of directors, Mark Tooley, president of IRD since 2009,[10] approvingly described the results of the IRD's work as follows: "[IRD founders] almost single-handedly challenged, exposed and ultimately discredited the once formidable and prestigious agencies of mainline Protestantism. The United Methodist Board of Global Ministries is now mostly a defanged nuisance, and the National Council of Churches a virtual non-entity."[11]

While Tooley both overstated the IRD's impact and misdiagnosed the cause—the roots of mainline Protestantism's institutional woes are not to be found primarily in theological soil—the organization continues to provide a platform for the mainline's most prominent internal critics' anger. Recent remarks such as these made at a sympathetic conservative Georgia Methodist church in February 2015 are typical of Tooley's prolific writings, sermons, and speeches: "The decline is indeed deserved and self precipitated. . . . Mainline Protestantism lost its way when it forgot how to balance being American and being Christian, choosing American individualism and self made spirituality over classical Christianity."[12]

Denial and Anger Among White Evangelical Protestants

Until very recently, white evangelical leaders were content to watch their Protestant cousins' decline as a kind of grim spectator sport, waiting with press releases and talking points to emphasize their own health in contrast with the fading mainline's latest vital statistics. As noted in Chapter 2, though, both national data and internal denominational data over the last decade unequivocally show that white evangelicals' numbers are also slipping.

Despite the evidence,[13] denial remains a lively response among white evangelicals, with Richard Land, former president of SBC's Ethics and Religious Liberty Commission,[14] filling the role of denier-in-chief. When a prominent Pew report showed that the proportion of Christians in the general population had declined by roughly 7 percentage points between 2007 and 2014,[15] including a modest one percent drop among evangelicals overall, Land spun the findings this way: "While Evangelicals declined as a percentage of the adult population, they actually grew in real numbers (from 59.8 to 62.2 million)."[16] Researchers at Baptist-affiliated Baylor University countered with their own survey, saying, "There's a story some people want to report—that religion is on life support—but it's just not true."[17] The clear intention of Land's sunny interpretation of the Pew trend numbers was to assert the continued vitality and relevance of white evangelicals, and by extension, the SBC.

But Land overlooked a critical attribute of the Pew data. While most Pew Research Center surveys follow the standard practice in the social sciences of sorting Protestants into distinct racial/ethnic groups— mainly white non-Hispanic, Hispanic, and African American—the Pew Religious Landscape Survey report used a different classification scheme. It separated those belonging to historically African American denominations into a distinct group but left all other white and non-white members of evangelical denominations classified together under the general heading of "evangelicals." This composite classification eclipsed the gloomier reality for white evangelicals, who declined from 21 percent of the population in 2008 to 18 percent of the population in 2014. Virtually all of the numerical growth among this composite evangelical category came not from *white* evangelicals but from *Hispanic* evangelicals.

This distinction is important for two reasons. First, while the SBC has experienced a modest increase in Hispanic membership within its ranks, Hispanic evangelicals are largely organizing their own institutions rather than joining historically white denominations such as the SBC. Second, and most importantly, Hispanic evangelicals have distinctly different political priorities—focused more on economic issues like jobs and access to education and healthcare—than their white brethren, and are unlikely to be animated by the political agenda of White Christian America.

Land, then, was practicing a particularly extreme form of denial— essentially raising the spirits of a dying patient's relatives by reading the medical chart of the healthier patient in the next bed.

Anger has also come naturally to white evangelicals. Throughout their history, white evangelicals have developed a rich lexicon of apocalyptic anger. Evangelical sermons and hymns are infused with martial imagery, and nostalgic "re-" words like "reclaim," "restore," "renew," "repent," and "revive" are staple fare. This vocabulary originates in the evangelical theological emphasis on human sin and divine judgment, but it's bolstered socially by evangelicals' self-perception as an outgunned minority struggling valiantly against outside powers. In the American context, this sensibility has been reinforced time and again over the past 150 years, first in the South's defeat during the Civil War, then during federal occupation and domination during Reconstruction, in the aftermath of the Scopes Trial in the 1920s, and during a second wave of federal interventionism during the civil rights movement.[18]

At midcentury, Rev. Billy Graham's open-handed, inclusive style provided the major exception to these tendencies. Although his wild success might suggest otherwise, Reverend Graham entered the national stage at a deeply uncertain time for evangelicals. In the 1950s, mainline Protestantism was the unchallenged public face of White

Christian America. But the young Billy Graham almost single-handedly reconfigured evangelicalism into a force with the power to shape the national consciousness.

The most prominent example of Graham's influence was his historic crusade in, of all places, New York City. The Big Apple was not only the sophisticated cultural and financial center of the country, but it also housed the headquarters of the mainline Protestant National Council of Churches and its flagship educational institution, Union Theological Seminary. For 110 days in the hot summer of 1957, Graham drew crowds averaging about eighteen thousand people per night to Madison Square Garden. After the first night's success, *The New York Times* devoted nearly three full pages of coverage to the event, even printing Graham's sermon word for word. ABC-TV broadcast fourteen Saturday night services from the Garden, reaching an estimated audience of 96 million viewers. When he preached at Yankee Stadium, Graham set an attendance record of over 100,000 and more than 20,000 people were turned away. On his last weekend in New York City, he preached to an estimated 125,000 in Times Square. By the end, more than two million people had attended his services.[19] What surprised—and captivated—Graham's listeners was that his sermons were not peppered with fire and brimstone, but with invitations to live the Christian life.[20] Graham's broad appeal, along with his nonpartisan posture, set Billy Graham on a path that positioned him as a spiritual advisor to every sitting president from Harry Truman to Barack Obama.[21]

But by the 1980s, Billy Graham's welcoming and largely apolitical appeal was overtaken by a movement built around partisan politics and apocalyptic rhetoric, led in the 1980s by figures such as the Reverend Jerry Falwell and Pat Robertson. As the elder Graham aged and health concerns began to limit his public appearances, his son Franklin—whose temperament and goals resonated more with the Christian Right than with his father—stepped increasingly into the spotlight. It would be difficult to overstate the differences between father and son.

After struggling with his father's long absences during his childhood, Franklin originally had no designs to follow in the elder Graham's footsteps. He was frequently in trouble as a teenager, and described his attitude this way: "I wanted to be a hell raiser that lived my own life. And if it made people mad, tough. If it disappointed people, tough. It's my life, I'm going to live it the way I want to live it, and if you don't like it, get out of my way." [22]

But at twenty-two, he experienced his own religious conversion and began to make changes in his life. Defying expectations, he married and joined the growing family business. In 1979 he became president and CEO of Samaritan's Purse, a nonprofit Christian international aid organization that today has a $400 million budget. In 2000, as his father's health declined, Franklin Graham was appointed CEO of his father's religious organization, the Billy Graham Evangelistic Association (BGEA), which has a budget of over $100 million. [23]

Whereas Billy Graham exuded a relaxed confidence, Franklin became an anxious agitator—more preoccupied with adversaries than invitations, more provocateur than preacher. Unlike his father, Franklin Graham built his career by railing against abortion ("It's a sin against God, okay? It's murder"), [24] gay marriage ("Isn't it sad, though, that America's own morality has fallen so far that on this issue—protecting children from any homosexual agenda or propaganda—[that] Russia's standard is higher than our own?"), [25] and Islam (a "very wicked and evil religion"). [26] While Billy Graham pointedly stopped holding segregated crusade meetings in 1952 and invited Martin Luther King, Jr. to lead a prayer at his New York Crusade in 1957 [27]—his son has failed to heed black Americans' claims about injustice at the hands of police and the courts.

Billy Graham held all American presidents in high esteem, but Franklin Graham harbors particular—and public—antipathy for Barack Obama. Graham has gone as far as to assert that the president is under the thumb of sinister Muslim advisors: "This administration has been heavily influenced by Muslims speaking into and giving advice in various areas of the White House. They are anti-Israel and anti-Semitic— and they are influencing the president who as we all know was raised with a strong Muslim influence in his life." [28] Just days after the 2012 presidential election, Graham declared—without a hint of irony—that Obama's second term would "usher in the largest changes in our society since the Civil War." His reelection, Graham warned, was a sign that Americans have "turned our back on God." In the same interview, Graham lamented waning evangelical influence, declaring, "We need someone like a Jerry Falwell to come back and resurrect the Moral Majority movement." [29]

Bargaining

Bargaining, the third stage of grief described by Kübler-Ross, is a coping mechanism that often emerges when anger has been spent and denial is relinquished. Kübler-Ross summarized its role this way: "If we have been unable to face the sad facts in the first period and have been angry at people and God in the second phase, maybe we can succeed in entering into some sort of an agreement which may postpone the inevitable happening." [30]

In the case of dying patients and their survivors, bargaining often takes place with an entity, such as God or the physician, who is perceived to have power over the outcome. They make an offering—to bury the hatchet with enemies, to spend their remaining days in service to the poor—in exchange, almost universally, for more time. But when it becomes clear that they are not going to be able to secure an extended lease on life, bargaining may shift into a more chastened, desperate form. Even though the reward may seem beyond reach, the patient and her survivors may resort to heroic actions designed to gain the attention of the reluctant divinity; when even this fails, they may exert what power they have by grasping at symbolic victories as the end becomes increasingly inevitable.

Bargaining Among White Mainline Protestants

One example of this kind of end-of-life bargaining among white mainline Protestants came during Rev. Bob Edgar's two terms as the general secretary of the National Council of Churches. Faced with a $5.9 million deficit when he came on board in 2000, Edgar, a former congressman, was clear about his mission, declaring, "I was brought in to do three things: raise money, raise money and raise money."[31] By 2006, Edgar had indeed balanced the budget. But faced with declining numbers and financial resources among mainline member denominations, Edgar had accomplished this feat not with firmer internal commitments but with outside funding from large organizations such as the Ford Foundation and the Sierra Club. Noting that, in the 2005 fiscal year, the NCC received slightly more financial support from outside sources than from member organizations, the Institute on Religion and Democracy in 2006 published an exposé-style report accusing the NCC of abandoning its ecumenical mission in favor of "left-leaning" politics. NCC officials countered by highlighting the sources of IRD's own financial support, which also included considerable backing from large conservative foundations such as the Scaife, Bradley, Coors, and Smith Richardson family charities—major fiscal players behind the conservative political resurgence of the 1980s.

The dispute ended in a draw. It mostly succeeded in highlighting the extent to which the struggle over the symbolic capital of the mainline, within both the NCC and the IRD, was being perpetuated by external funding and political interests. Not surprisingly, the strategy of replacing lost member funding with outside sources turned out to be unsustainable. As the NCC itself noted in a memorial post after Edgar's untimely death in 2013 at the age of sixty-nine, "At the end of his eight-year tenure, the financial emergency had ebbed but the conditions that caused it—including the financial exigency of many of the NCC's contributing communions—were still in place."[32] While Edgar managed to temporarily right the ship, as NCC member denominations continued to struggle financially, his efforts only postponed the inevitable, rather than offering a reprieve.

Bargaining Among White Evangelical Protestants

End-of-life bargaining strategies among white mainline Protestants played out most prominently in their major denominational institutions, but white evangelicals carried out their own bargaining tactics at a broader cultural and societal level. Notably, these bargaining attempts have taken root even in what have historically been WCA's most unassailable strongholds in the South. Two prominent efforts sought to prop up a dying white Christian cultural consensus with the force of law.

In January 2015, two Democratic members of the Mississippi House of Representatives—along with twenty-one co-sponsors—introduced an unusual bill that would designate the Bible as the official state book. The entirety of House Bill 1179 consisted of two sentences: "SECTION 1. The Holy Bible is hereby designated the State Book of Mississippi. SECTION 2. This act shall take effect and be in force from and after July 1, 2015."[33] Not to be outdone, Mississippi Republicans promptly introduced their own separate bill to accomplish these same ends.[34]

To put these events into perspective, no state has an official book.[35] Two states, Michigan and Massachusetts, do have official *children's* books. In 1998, Michigan made *The Legend of Sleeping Bear*—a Native American story of the creation of the Dunes and Islands at Sleeping Bear Dunes National Lakeshore in the northwestern part of the state—its official children's book.[36] And Massachusetts made Robert McCloskey's 1941 classic *Make Way for Ducklings*, set in the Boston Public Garden lagoon, its official children's book in 2003.[37] Neighboring Alabama does not have an official state book, but it does have an official state Bible, an 1853 edition on which Jefferson Davis placed his hand—and also his lips to kiss it according to vivid newspaper reports—when he was sworn in as the president of the Confederate States of America on February 18, 1861. That official Bible has been used for the inauguration of every Alabama state governor since.[38]

Representative Michael Evans, a Democratic co-sponsor of Mississippi's bill, told a reporter that the idea came from interactions with constituents. According to Evans, one particular conversation turned to "all the things going wrong in the world" and "one of them made a comment that people ought to start reading the Bible." When asked about his own motivations, Evans replied simply, "I believe in the Bible."[39] Democratic representative Tom Miles, the other lead sponsor of the bill, told the Associated Press, "The Bible provides a good role model on how to treat people. They could read in there about love and compassion."[40] Miles argued that while he hoped the bill would encourage people to read the Bible, he was "not trying to force religion."[41]

Ultimately, the bills were killed in committee about two weeks after being introduced.[42] But their short lives should eclipse neither their symbolic significance nor their contribution to an emerging pattern of legislation across the South. In 2014–2015, state legislators in Louisiana and Tennessee also filed bills to make the Bible their state's official book.[43]

Mississippi was also home to a more successful symbolic bargaining effort. In April 2014, with the support of Republican governor Phil Bryant, the Mississippi legislature voted to add the words "In God We Trust" to its state seal, modifying it for the first time since its creation in 1818.[44] This provision was attached to Mississippi's Religious Freedom Restoration Act (RFRA), a bill designed to carve out protections for religious individuals and organizations who refuse to comply with laws that might conflict with their religious beliefs,[45] such as the federal contraception mandate or broad nondiscrimination laws that protect gay and lesbian people.[46] Notably, the RFRA bill was introduced by Republican state senator Phillip Gandy,[47] who is also a Baptist pastor with ties to Christian Right leader Tony Perkins, head of the Family Research Council.[48] In a statement accompanying the unveiling of the new seal, Governor Bryant declared, "These words should strengthen our resolve and give us the courage to stand for our principles in our state. I am very proud to see them added to our seal."[49]

How might one explain these curious campaigns? The Bible bill, for example, prompted immediate objections from literary aficionados. Why, in a state that has been home to countless luminaries, would the Bible represent the height of artistic achievement in Mississippi? "What would [William] Faulkner and [Eudora] Welty and Shelby Foote and Richard Wright think?" asked Larry Wells, a local publisher and the widower of Faulkner's niece.[50] But questions about the Bible's relative literary merit perhaps miss the even more perplexing question of why a religion-drenched state like Mississippi would *need* such official symbolic representations in the first place.

In moments of vulnerability, politicians routinely turn to declarations of faith as assertions of American power and unity. Requests to place the motto "In God We Trust" on American coins, for example, first came to the Treasury Department in 1861, during the height of the Civil War. In 1864, the mantra appeared for the first time on a two-cent coin. Nearly a century later, another crisis—anxieties about "godless communism" at the height of the Cold War—produced a similar response. The words "In God We Trust" became the official national motto in 1956 and were added to paper money in 1957.[51] The politics of vulnerability also affected the Pledge of Allegiance. Written in 1892—a more religiously secure time—by Reverend Francis Bellamy, an ordained Baptist minister, the original pledge included no reference to a deity. Even when Congress formally approved the pledge's final language in 1942, there was no suggestion to include a reference to God. But the waves of anticommunist sentiment coursing through the country at midcentury exerted their pull on the pledge; in 1954, Congress voted to insert the words "under God."[52]

When leaders feel it is necessary to state explicitly what has always been assumed, they betray their own cultural insecurity. The twin efforts to ensconce the Bible as Mississippi's state book and recast the state seal were not moves demonstrating White Christian America's vigor. Instead, the flurry of legislative activity is better understood as a last-ditch attempt to resuscitate White Christian America. Even a decade ago, bills like these would have seemed nonsensical. The Bible was the state's official book in everything but name. "The Great Seal of the State of Mississippi" needed no other declaration to express its identity. The need to forcefully elevate their Christian status reflects white Christian lawmakers' fear that for an increasing number of citizens the Bible and God are no longer a guiding cultural force. These efforts amount to little more than bargaining beside the deathbed of White Christian America.

Depression and Acceptance

Most people think of depression as a malady to be treated. But Kübler-Ross argued that among terminally ill patients and their relatives, a kind of "preparatory depression" that looks ahead to the reality of death often functions as a healthy and natural bridge to the final stage of acceptance. Rather than being dismissed or treated as dysfunctional, Kübler-Ross maintained that this type of depression can be a rational, even necessary, component of coming to grips with loss. "The patient is in the process of losing everything and everybody he loves. If he is allowed to express his sorrow he will find a final acceptance much easier, and he will be grateful to those who can sit with him during this stage of depression without constantly telling him not to be sad." [53] One key to moving through depression to acceptance is having the space to process the impending loss. If the patient and family have enough time and help working through previous stages of grief, Kübler-Ross observed, they reach acceptance, where they look toward the end with "a certain degree of quiet expectation." [54]

The final stage of grief—acceptance—is distinct from resignation, which is marked by bitter acquiescence to certain defeat. Acceptance should not be mistaken as a "happy stage." In fact, it's closer to a feeling of equanimity than to any active emotional state. The major ongoing threat to acceptance is the temptation to fight to the end. As Kübler-Ross summed it up, "the harder [terminally patients] struggle to avoid the inevitable death, the more they try to deny it, the more difficult it will be for them to reach this final stage of acceptance with peace and dignity."[55]

Depression and Acceptance Among White Mainline Protestants

Overall, mainline Protestants have accepted the death of white Christian America, although bouts of depression and disillusionment remain. The tough-love pastoral presence of Stanley Hauerwas, a straight-talking Methodist theologian from Texas who moved to center stage at the height of the mainline crisis, helped guide mainline Protestants through this transition. Laying aside the Christian realism of Reinhold Niebuhr in favor of the pacifism of his lesser-known brother H. Richard Niebuhr, Hauerwas excavated a new theological foundation from the grave of a once proud church that now found itself out of power.

His 1989 book, *Resident Aliens: Life in the Christian Colony*, co-written with a prominent Methodist bishop, struck a nerve. It was a pastoral book written to comfort and revitalize depressed mainline Protestants as they headed into the rocky 1990s.[56] In *Resident Aliens*, Hauerwas found a silver lining in a situation that most found lamentable and demoralizing. He unapologetically called for the church to be "a colony of heaven" comprised of Christians who are "resident aliens" in a strange land.[57] Hauerwas emphasized Christianity's function as an institution separate from politics and worldly affairs, not an insider in the halls of power. In Hauerwas's vision, the demise of the "Christian century" aspiration was actually an opportunity for a new, truer Christian faithfulness:

The gradual decline of the notion that the church needs some sort of surrounding "Christian" culture to prop it up and mold its young, is not a death to lament. It is an opportunity to celebrate. The decline of the old, Constantinian synthesis between the church and the world means that we American Christians are at last free to be faithful in a way that makes being Christian today an exciting adventure.[58]

In a short time, *Resident Aliens* became required reading in virtually every white Protestant seminary, while simultaneously attracting a broad audience of lay readers. The book remained in print for more than two decades, and a new edition was published for its twenty-fifth anniversary in 2014. Following the success of this book, and the many others the prolific Hauerwas published in its wake, he was invited to give the prestigious Gifford Lectures at the University of St. Andrews in Scotland in 2001.[59] That same year, *Time* magazine named Hauerwas "America's Best Theologian."[60] Over the years, Hauerwas tackled a wide range of issues, addressing war and pacifism, medical ethics, and the rights of mentally disabled people. But his most lasting role has been that of hospice chaplain, dispensing a critical palliative care theology for a mainline Protestant family struggling toward acceptance as WCA faded from the scene.

Mainline institutions had a few final moments of national impact in the 1990s, such as their leading role in South African divestment over apartheid through their solidarity with the South African Council of Churches, but they have rarely been a major force since. Over the last two decades, following Hauerwas's lead, white mainline Protestants have instead taken an inward, ecclesiastical turn. Rather than crafting strategies for shaping national culture or public policy, most of the contemporary energy within the mainline world has feverishly focused on strategies for stabilizing and revitalizing local churches.

Diana Butler Bass—one of the most astute modern observers of white mainline Protestantism (and a PRRI board member)—identified at least three major competing visions of what the mainline church can and should look like in the long shadow of WCA's loss.[61] A neo-orthodox vision seeks to incarnate a divinely ordained unique institution with a character-shaping liturgy. It takes most seriously Hauerwas's claims about the wrongheadedness of church involvement in politics. Instead, it sees the church's indispensable mission in the world as spiritual formation of distinctively Christian people. In sharp contrast, a panentheist vision sees God infusing not just the church but the world. From this perspective, the chief sin of the mainline was its arrogant assumption that it was the primary vehicle for accomplishing divine purposes. This movement is the most explicit about urging the church to join forces with broader forces—both interfaith and secular—particularly around environmental and global poverty issues. Finally, a liberationist vision seeks to animate the church experience with social justice commitments, connecting particularly with the legacy of Martin Luther King, Jr. and the tradition of black church activism. It is the closest to mainline Protestantism's historical roots, although it is working to build coalitions with churches of color rather than inviting them to participate in projects run by WCA's denominational structures. These ecclesiastical debates—in sparring books, between charismatic personalities, and at pastors' conferences—have preoccupied white mainline Protestant pastors and denominational leaders over the past two decades. Each is offering a distinctive theological and ecclesiastical vision, driven by the need to come to terms with the death of White Christian America.

Depression and Acceptance Among White Evangelical Protestants

With only about a decade of experience with decline, today's white evangelicals have had a relatively short time to reach the later stages of depression and acceptance. So far, perhaps the most prominent insider to express depression over the state of evangelical Christianity was the late David Kuo, deputy director of the White House Office of Faith-Based and Community Initiatives under President George W. Bush. After surviving an initial bout with brain cancer in 2003, Kuo's own grieving process prompted him to reevaluate his professional commitments, and he resigned his White House position. In his best-selling 2006 book, *Tempting Faith: An Inside Story of Political Seduction*, Kuo described Bush's faith-based office as "a sad charade, to provide political cover to a White House that needed compassion and religion as political tools." [62] In the final years before his untimely death in 2013, he challenged evangelicals to take a two-year "fast" from politics, to give themselves time to critically assess whether their public witness was too enmeshed with a partisan agenda. [63]

A sense of depression and disillusionment has also fueled other more radical opt-out movements advocating the formation of small intentional communities, such as the "New Monasticism" movement, where young, primarily progressive evangelicals move to blighted urban areas so they can live among the poor, and the "Benedictine Option," a contemplative rural lifestyle touted by Rod Dreher, a Methodist-turned-Catholic-turned-Eastern-Orthodox author and editor for *The American Conservative*. [64] These models all accept the death of WCA and offer in response a retreat to sectarian enclaves that are disconnected from politics. But these movements are minority movements by design, and none have gained much momentum among rank-and-file white evangelicals.

Two important figures are paving the way toward a partial acceptance of White Christian America's passing, albeit in very different ways: Russell Moore, the relatively new director of the Southern Baptist Convention's Ethics and Religious Liberty Commission, and David Gushee, a professor of Christian ethics at Mercer University's McAfee School of Theology.[65]

The opening paragraph on the dust jacket of Moore's 2015 book, *Onward: Engaging the Culture Without Losing the Gospel*, begins with what seems like a straightforward acceptance of the demise of White Christian America.

> As the culture changes all around us, it is no longer possible to pretend that we are a Moral Majority. That may be bad news for America, but it can be good news for the church. What's needed now, in shifting times, is neither a doubling-down on the status quo nor a pullback into isolation. . . . As Christianity seems increasingly strange, and even subversive, to our culture, we have the opportunity to reclaim the freakishness of the gospel, which is what gives it its power in the first place.[66]

Echoing Stanley Hauerwas, Moore argues that a chastened position is good for the church because Christianity can provide an alternative to the broader culture only when it becomes truly abnormal. In important ways, Moore's stance represents a departure from the posture of his predecessor, Richard Land, who relished his provocative role in the culture wars and still refuses to admit that white evangelicals are declining in numbers and influence. Moore, by contrast, responded to the statistical evidence this way: "This is precisely what several of us have been saying for years. Bible Belt near-Christianity is teetering. I say let it fall." [67]

But Moore still reads the vital signs selectively. Despite these rhetorical flourishes, Moore exudes a confidence that suggests at least a partial denial of WCA's death. When he says "let it fall," he qualifies that statement to apply to "near-Christianity," by which he means merely cultural, rather than authentic, expressions of Christianity. Moreover, he continues to trot out the tired (and inaccurate) theory that mainline churches are losing members because they abandoned their theological principles in favor of being "relevant," while evangelical houses of worship have remained "remarkably steady" thanks to their refusal to compromise. Like a family member who can't quite take in a grim diagnosis, most evangelicals who are following Moore to this stage acknowledge that their vision of a robust white evangelical world will have to be tempered. Still, they continue to resist the full implications of its demise.

Moore's ability to get to acceptance is hindered primarily because he fails to wrestle adequately with White Christian America's history alongside its present situation. While Moore briefly acknowledges that "on many points" such as racism, the broader culture came to hold the right position far earlier than southern Christians, this admission slips by swiftly and does little to mitigate his certainty in evangelicals' ability to occupy the theological and moral high ground. As a result, Moore too readily assumes that the mere state of being in tension with the wider culture is a sign of true faithfulness. Given Southern Baptists' shameful history on slavery and segregation, and Moore's own sensitivity to issues of race, this is a remarkable starting point.

Moore's blind spot is evident from the opening page of his book, which contains an epigraph attributed to Mississippi author Walker Percy:

By remaining faithful to its original commission, by serving its people with love, especially the poor, the lonely, and the dispossessed, and by not surrendering its doctrinal steadfastness, sometimes even the very contradiction of culture by which it serves as a sign, surely the Church serves the culture best.[68]

There are two features of this quote that make it an ironic choice for launching Moore's argument. First, the context of the quote—which Moore does not include—clarifies that Percy, who converted to Catholicism in his early thirties, was speaking specifically about the Roman Catholic Church. The capitalized "Church" is a clue, and reflects the fact that the quote was part of a 1988 address Percy delivered in Rome, where he was one of only fourteen laymen (and the only American) invited to address the Pontifical Council for Culture at the Vatican.[69] Second, while Moore accurately describes the general point Percy is making in that essay, Moore glosses over the fact that, for Percy—even the Percy who took a theologically conservative turn toward becoming a Catholic apologist at the end of his life—*everything* would have hinged on the word "sometimes."

Moore would have been well served to heed the scathing critique, continued throughout Percy's writings, leveled at white southern churches—most prominently represented by Southern Baptists—for their opposition to the civil rights movement. As the broader culture shifted to support civil rights for African Americans, white southern Christians certainly became "countercultural" by staunchly maintaining the southern status quo, confident in their reading of scripture and comfortable in their segregated churches. But for Percy, this particular "contradiction of culture" was nothing to be celebrated. In a 1965 essay entitled "The Failure and the Hope," Percy highlighted the tragic hypocrisy of white Christians in the South, who lived in a region that was more infused with Christian values than any other in the country and yet stubbornly maintained their collusion in the grave sin of racism. As he put it, "A scandal has occurred right enough, but it is not the scandal intended by the gospels."[70] Percy's indictment of Southern Christians is worth quoting at length:

> During the past ten years, the first ten years of the Negro revolution, a good deal was heard about the "good" people of the South, comprising the vast majority, who deplored the violence and who any day would make themselves felt. But these good people are yet to be heard from. If every Christian era has its besetting sin . . . the twentieth century Christian South might well be remembered by its own particular mark: *silence.*[71]

Percy noted that instead of southern Christians, it was ironically "the liberal humanist" who shouldered the burden of working for racial justice. "In the deep South of the 1960s," Percy wrote, "the men who nursed the sick, bound his wounds, taught the ignorant, fed the hungry, went to jail with the imprisoned, were not the Christians of Birmingham or Bogalusa." Rather, they were more likely to be the very people that white Southern Christians denounced: community organizers, "Sarah Lawrence sociology majors," and "agnostic Jewish social workers like Micky Schwerner."[72]

Along the path Moore is marking, it is unclear what might serve as a reliable compass. On the one hand, Moore often demonstrates keen awareness of Southern Baptists' past failures in the area of race relations. As I noted in Chapter 5, Moore has been instrumental in urging his fellow white evangelicals to take the concerns of the #BlackLivesMatter movement seriously, and he has used his position to organize conferences on racial reconciliation. Moreover, he has taken some courageous stands, such as his essay against the public display of the Confederate battle flag, in which he flatly declared, "The cross and the Confederate flag cannot co-exist without one setting the other on fire. White Christians, let's listen to our African-American brothers and sisters. . . . Let's take down that flag."[73]

At the same time, however, Moore seems to stop short of the full measure of humility that consciousness of this scarred history requires. Absent this guidance, Moore's position runs the risk of equating freakishness—a dependent quality that derives its integrity from its referent—with the gospel itself. By confidently asserting that "such freakishness is the power of God unto salvation," Moore leaves little room for the necessary realization that a "countercultural" stance has, in the past, been an expression of the power of white Christians upholding the status quo.[74] Without the serious dose of self-effacement that follows from wrestling with what Percy called "The Great Southern Sin of Silence," it seems likely that those following Moore still have some wondering in the wilderness ahead before they find their way to full acceptance of WCA's death.

David Gushee, a professor of Christian ethics and ordained Baptist minister, has helped chart the way to a more thorough acceptance of White Christian America's death among evangelicals. Gushee is a less well-known figure than Moore, but his work has been instrumental in pushing evangelical elites to reevaluate both the style and substance of their public engagement. Gushee was one of the authors of the 1995 SBC apology on racism, and was the principal drafter of two influential documents, the Evangelical Climate Initiative (2006) and the Evangelical Declaration against Torture (2007).[75]

Gushee's most direct broadside against the evangelical status quo appeared in his sweeping 2008 book, *The Future of Faith in American Politics: The Public Witness of the Evangelical Center.* In the book, Gushee takes the Christian Right to task for being motivated less by the gospel and more by "nostalgia for a less-religiously and morally pluralistic age, when specifically Christian practices dominated American public life in a way that is now impossible and *should be* impossible under our constitutional system."[76] On the other hand, Gushee also criticizes the evangelicals who simply want to retreat into homogeneous enclaves, saying this reaction is immature.[77] Against both dominance and isolationism, Gushee argues that evangelicals should find a middle ground.

The biggest challenge for evangelicals, according to Gushee, is that they have not sufficiently developed an intentional theology of public engagement. Instead, evangelicals have allowed themselves to be thrust half prepared and unreflective into politics, resulting in "a reactive, episodic, boom-and-bust cycle of political engagement."[78] Gushee makes the following appeal to his fellow evangelicals: "We have to grow up— past conspiracy theories, demagoguery, single-issue voting, partisan seductions, mudslinging, and God-and-country conflations and confusions."[79] Gushee contends that "bearing witness" should be the centerpiece of the church in contemporary America. This approach accepts the death of White Christian America and encourages evangelicals to participate fully in a pluralistic society, but avoids the temptations toward domination and sectarianism, each of which is driven by nostalgia for a lost Christian America.

While Gushee's vision of an evangelical middle way seems promising, there are three reasons it is unlikely to win the day. First, it challenges head-on the politics of nostalgia. Given its long-standing presence as part of the DNA of American evangelicalism, abandoning this style of engagement would represent a historic sea change. Second, the success of this approach may also be limited by Gushee's position outside official church structures. While Gushee is a respected professor at a Baptist university and influential in elite evangelical circles, it is Moore who has his hands on the levers of major denominational power. Finally, in his most recent book, *Changing Our Mind*, Gushee explained his own theological journey that led to affirming the full acceptance of LGBT Christians in the life of the church, including an affirmation of the marriages of gay and lesbian couples.[80] While nearly half of younger white evangelical Protestants agree with Gushee on this point, older evangelicals—and particularly the denominational leaders—remain strongly opposed to same-sex marriage and often consider this a litmus test issue for being truly evangelical. Given these challenges, it seems more likely than not that, at least for the foreseeable future, most evangelicals will wander the path Moore is charting, with full acceptance of WCA's death remaining out of reach.

Dancing on the Grave: White Christian America's Critics

Not everyone is grieving. Following the death of any powerful personality, there are inevitably those who will mutter, "Good riddance." Usually, however, these critics keep their satisfaction private, feeling it unseemly to celebrate the end of a human life. While the demise of White Christian America has generated considerable handwringing among its descendants, it has produced a celebratory reaction in other quarters. At times, the response has been surprisingly unabashed.

Two forces in the early 2000s combined to infuse WCA's critics with unprecedented energy: the 9/11 terrorist attacks committed in the name of Islam and the "values voters" campaign that mobilized white evangelicals for President George W. Bush's 2004 reelection bid. Together, these events set off a firestorm of antireligious reactions on the political and cultural left.

Although the Christian Right's mid-2000 critics couldn't yet claim it was dying, they were able to discern its frailty. By identifying the movement as an outlier from America's cultural mainstream, they commandeered the most powerful weapon in the Christian Right's traditional arsenal: its ability to assert itself as "the moral majority." These critics all portrayed White Christian America—seen through the lens of white evangelical Protestantism—as an isolated relic, at best aging and out of touch and at worst bitter and bigoted.

Critiques from the cultural and political left, such as Chuck Thompson's *Better Off Without 'Em: A Northern Manifesto for Southern Secession* and Thomas Schaller's *Whistling Past Dixie*, combined mockery with a realpolitik strategy of cultural and political isolationism. Thompson—a Bronx-based travel writer who toured the South as if it were a foreign country in preparation for the book—singled out southern evangelicals for particular ridicule, describing them as "obstructionists and fanatics who want to conflate biblical law with U.S. law." Exploring a thought experiment that would allow the South to secede from the rest of the country, he wondered aloud: "What would happen if we simply jettisoned the 566,466 square miles and 78,385,623 people responsible for generating so much of the willful ignorance and Jim Crow–style hatred that keeps the rest of the country from moving ahead?"[81] Schaller, a professor of political science at University of Maryland Baltimore County and a weekly political columnist for *The Baltimore Sun*, made a more serious, but similar, argument on political grounds. In national elections,

Schaller argued, Democrats should "forget about recapturing the South in the near term and begin building a national majority that ends, not begins, with restoring their lost southern glory." If the cultural chasm between North and South was so entrenched, Schaller argued that simply bypassing Dixie would be more practical than attempting to "rewind history to re-create a pre–civil rights era Democratic South in post–civil rights America."[82]

Other critics not only celebrated the death of White Christian America but called for the death of all of its kind. During the early 2000s, a group of neo-atheists mounted an offensive, condemning religion itself as a cancerous element of society that "poisons everything."[83] In particular, four prominent authors—Richard Dawkins, Daniel Dennett, Christopher Hitchens, and Sam Harris—developed such a zealous following that they were dubbed "the four horseman" by fans, who created a Twitter feed (@four_horseman) to follow their work. Throughout George W. Bush's second term, these forceful thinkers dominated the best-seller lists. They bluntly declared that "God is not great"[84] and aimed to dispel the "God delusion,"[85] all in the name of saving society from the backwardness of religion.

The backlash from white evangelical Protestants' virtual marriage to the Bush administration, along with the neo-atheist literary explosion, also helped foster the growth of a loose network of secular organizations and bloggers. These organizations successfully established themselves as players in the religious advocacy world.[86] And like the neo-atheist authors and the South's political detractors, they gave voice to those who do not mourn the death of WCA. Responding to important findings from 2014 surveys by PRRI and Pew that found significant decreases in Christian affiliation,[87] David Niose, board member and interim director of the Secular Coalition for America, called the trend a sign of "natural human progress" as people became "less reliant on supernatural explanations."[88] Hemant Mehta, the author of the popular "Friendly Atheist" blog, declared, "It's just incredible news all around. It's also a sign that we need to continue speaking out about the problems with religion—any religion."[89]

While the worst chapters from White Christian America's life have certainly given the neo-atheists, political isolationists, and secularists legitimate reasons to draw some satisfaction at its demise, it is unclear that any of these groups are prepared to offer up promising alternatives. The broadside critique of all religion ultimately runs aground in at least two ways. First, it fails to account for the positive, even noble acts of humanity that are inspired by religious commitment and devotion. While it's impossible to conduct a utilitarian calculus to measure the relative ratio of good versus evil actions that have been inspired by religion, it is at least clear that many of our nation's achievements and critical moments in our history such as the civil rights movement may have been stillborn without their religious DNA. On a practical level, in a nation where nearly eight in ten citizens claim a religious affiliation, any movement that asserts, as a fundamental organizing tenet, that religion is the root of all social problems is bound to founder.

Finally, some prominent neo-atheists have taken their critique of religion in decidedly illiberal directions, focusing their antipathy for religion particularly on Islam. Richard Dawkins, for example, has called Islam "one of the great evils in the world."[90] Sam Harris has asserted that "Islam, more than any other religion human beings have devised, has all the makings of a thoroughgoing cult of death"[91] and wrote on his blog that "we should profile Muslims, or anyone who looks like he or she could conceivably be Muslim, and we should be honest about it."[92] These anti-Muslim rants became so frequent that Nathan Lean of *Salon* concluded that, ironically, "the New Atheists became the new Islamophobes."[93] At the end of the day, the neo-atheist course seems mired in the very bigotry it seeks to extinguish.

Eulogy: Reflections on the Life and Death of White Christian America

The obituary at the beginning of this book sketched the general arc of White Christian America's life. But there is more to say about the meaning of WCA's life and passing. While eulogies typically emphasize the deceased's positive contributions, a more balanced approach is in order here, one that speaks to those survivors and friends of White Christian America who feel a deep sense of loss at its departure but also address those who—confident its presence will not be missed—are already rejoicing at WCA's demise.

As the previous chapters have showed, White Christian America's flaws are all too evident. Surely we should not mourn the disappearance of White Christian America's arrogant assumption that it spoke for the country or its complicity in racism, its mistreatment of LGBT people and mischaracterization of their lives, and its willingness to compromise its theological integrity for partisan ends.

But White Christian America, despite these failings, is also worthy of mourning. As E. J. Dionne—a prominent author and astute commentator on religion and politics—has noted, white Protestantism served as "the civic and moral glue that held American public life together" for most of the United States' history.[94] It spun a coherent national narrative, cultivated a common vocabulary, served as an institutional intermediary between whole sectors of society such as business and government, and curated symbols of national life, all of which created a sense of strong civil solidarity.

Civic integration has presented a perennial challenge for the American experiment. It's the question of how to make good on the dictum that has been with us from the nation's beginnings: *e pluribus unum*, "out of many, one." Although the country has wrestled with these questions before, the passing of White Christian America presents a unique challenge, analogous to the death of the patriarch who served, for good and ill, at the center of family life. Standing beside the resting place of White Christian America, amidst unprecedented diversity and renewed racial tensions, it's unclear what could provide a similar civic glue again.

Saying Goodbye: A Word to White Christian America's Family

Although white mainline and evangelical Protestants are grieving WCA in different ways, they share one common trait. As mainliners bury the dreams of the Christian Century and evangelicals lay to rest the aspirations of the Moral Majority, each has wrestled internally with the crisis of confidence that the loss of White Christian America brought in its wake. Ross Douthat described this "lost world" precisely in these terms:

> The crucial element . . . was a deep and abiding *confidence*: Not just faith alone, but a kind of faith in Christian faith . . . [that] might actually be on the winning side of history. Both institutionally and intellectually, American Christianity at mid-century offered believers a relatively secure position from which to engage society as a whole.[95]

More than anything else, the death of White Christian America has robbed its descendants of their security of their place and beliefs. Peter

Berger, in his classic sociological study of religious life, *The Sacred Canopy*, summarized the presence of a strong cultural world this way:

> The social world intends, as far as possible, to be taken for granted. Socialization achieves success to the degree that this taken-for-granted quality is internalized. It is not enough that the individual look upon the key meanings of the social order as useful, desirable, or right. It is much better (better, that is, in terms of social stability) if he looks upon them as inevitable, as part and parcel of the universal "nature of things."[96]

When a social world succeeds in being taken for granted—as white Protestant Christianity was at the height of its powers—cultural meanings merge with "what are considered to be the fundamental meanings inherent in the universe."[97] Religion, historically and globally, has been one of the most powerful tools for mapping specific cultural worldviews onto ultimate reality. Until its powers failed, WCA served as a kind of ontological cartographer for both mainline and evangelical Protestants, and to some extent for the country as a whole.

Today, White Christian America's faded cultural map is increasingly inaccurate. Like retirees setting out on a trip with their 1950s AAA road atlas, the graying descendants of WCA find themselves frequently pulling off the road in disbelief and frustration as they encounter new routes and cities that are not on their map. The slow death of WCA has left many with a haunting sense of dislocation.

This bewilderment is felt especially along what demographer William Frey has identified as a "cultural generation gap." Today, confronted with a range of shifts—from changing neighborhoods to gay marriage attitudes—the descendants of White Christian America are confronted with a diversity-and-youth-driven country that seems alien to their sense of what it means to be American. For example, nearly two thirds of seniors (age 65 and over) say that "being a Christian" is an important part of "being truly American," while roughly seven in ten young adults (ages 18–29) disagree.[98] Frey notes that this cultural generation gap results in "an older population that does not feel a personal connection with young adults and children who are not 'their' children and grandchildren."[99]

Confronted with the psychic discomfort that results from a lack of cultural confidence and security, the greatest threat to White Christian America's descendants is the siren song of nostalgia. Faced with an unfamiliar cultural landscape, today's white mainline Protestants may find it easier to skip excursions altogether, preferring instead to huddle in their homes and churches around yellowing photo albums of journeys past. Evangelical Protestants, on the other hand, may turn into a homegrown version of the bad American tourist—taking pride in their foreignness while continuing to operate with a sense of entitlement, even though the country no longer belongs to them. But nostalgia is not only unfaithful to the past; it also threatens the integrity of the present.

With regard to WCA's mainline descendants, the culture has moved in the direction of their more socially liberal public agenda but without their banner at the head of the parade. The political and cultural winds are generally friendly to their sensibilities, but there are few recent examples of cultural or political battles where mainline Protestant leadership made an indispensable difference. They risk apathy if they succumb to wistfulness for a powerful past—or perhaps worse, to a kind of autopilot press release activism that mistakes being busy for making real change in the world.

The evangelical branch, closer to WCA's twilight moment, finds itself in the position of having lost much cultural power while still retaining—at least in the southern enclaves—the remnants of significant political clout. Homesickness for a lost parochial world lingers here as well. Evangelicals will feel the lure of safe retreat back into their old enclaves, even if this option is virtually impossible today. Their greatest temptation will be to wield what remaining political power they have as a desperate corrective for their waning cultural influence. If this happens, we may be in for another decade of closing skirmishes in the culture wars, but white evangelical Protestants will mortgage their future in a fight to resurrect the past.

As alluring as turning back the clock may seem to WCA's loyalists, efforts to resurrect the dead are futile at best—and at worst, disrespectful to its memory. Like Mary Shelley's Frankenstein, resurrection by human power rather than divine spirit always produces a monstrosity. If resurrection is not possible, both white evangelicals and white mainline Protestants—each still representing sizable constituencies in the country—will need to choose between sectarian retreat and a new kind of engagement. It seems highly unlikely that the descendants of WCA, having seen themselves at the American center for so long, will find a self-imposed social retreat comfortable. If this option proves ultimately to be unsatisfying, the only other course is a different social arrangement in which white evangelical and white mainline Protestants find their seats at the table alongside Catholics, Jews, Muslims, Hindus, Buddhists, and the religiously unaffiliated. This time, they will be guests rather than hosts.

With Malice Toward None: A Word to the Rest of the Country

White Christian America's critics see in its death a vindication of their long-standing complaints about its excesses and faults. This pivotal moment, however, presents WCA's critics with an opportunity. While WCA's descendants will ultimately bear the responsibility of choosing their own path, its critics' posture during this moment of grief may make one route more inviting than another. As Gushee pleads, "Engaging with us rather than heaping contempt on us simply makes sense. It will prove healthier for us and for American culture." [100]

Lincoln's second inaugural address, given as the Civil War was coming to a close, can serve as a model response for WCA's detractors. As a Union victory seemed more and more likely, Lincoln stubbornly resisted calls to deal with the South in punitive, retributive ways. Lincoln's famous conclusion is instructive at this juncture:

> With malice toward none, with charity for all, with firmness in the right as God gives us to see the right, let us strive on to finish the work we are in . . . to do all which may achieve and cherish a just and lasting peace among ourselves and with all nations. [101]

What would this reaction mean for the nation today? Ross Douthat has fretted that in the aftermath of losing the war on gay marriage, religious conservatives would be left no cultural space for their objections. Douthat pleads, "It's still important for the winning side to recognize its power . . . and for the defeated to find out what settlement the victors will impose." [102]

While Douthat's support for broad exemptions that allow small business owners to opt out of nondiscrimination laws may be more than the winners are likely to concede, and even more than the public supports, the general principle is one that those on the triumphant side could affirm. It seems possible that WCA's critics could, for example, hold to their principles and celebrate their victories on gay rights while simultaneously endorsing local churches' rights to prohibit same-sex marriage ceremonies in their own spaces and local clergy's rights to opt out of performing same-sex marriage ceremonies. Such affirmations would not require gay rights advocates to give up legal ground, and would emphasize a shared understanding of religious liberty.

White Christian America's critics could also stand up for churches when government officials overreach and threaten conservative pastors' freedom to preach openly, as happened in Texas in the fall of 2014. In a case that quickly gained national attention, the office of Houston mayor Annise Parker, the first openly lesbian mayor of a major American city, subpoenaed the sermons of five local pastors as part of a lawsuit related to Houston's Equal Rights Ordinance (HERO), which included protections for LGBT people. The subpoena demanded "all speeches, presentations, or sermons related to HERO, the Petition, Mayor Annise Parker, homosexuality, or gender identity prepared by, delivered by, revised by, or approved by you or in your possession." [103]

Parker ultimately reversed herself after national outcry, but not before providing Christian conservatives and Republican politicians with a case to validate their worst fears. Russell Moore weighed in, declaring, "The separation of church and state means that we will render unto Caesar that which is Caesar's, and we will. But the preaching of the church of God does not belong to Caesar, and we will not hand it over to him. Not now. Not ever." [104] Glenn Beck and Mike Huckabee also excoriated Mayor Parker. But what was missing—and what would have been symbolically very important for the future of the country—were protests from *supporters* of LGBT rights. Few people or organizations who disagreed with the substantive positions of the pastors, but nonetheless supported the rights of pastors to preach freely from their pulpits, spoke up.[105]

For the country to find a way forward, White Christian America's direct descendants and its critics will each need to resist their own temptations—nostalgia on the one hand and callous contempt on the other. Each needs to help the other move toward a sober recognition of the challenges that the death of White Christian America presents. And each will need to help the nation do the work every mourner faces after a death: to come to terms with the loss and to go on.

Life After the Death of White Christian America

The passing of White Christian America may also offer some unprecedented possibilities and opportunities. While neither the United Methodist Building nor the Interchurch Center have fulfilled their founders' visions, the nascent interreligious collaborations happening within their walls—with Catholics, Jews, Muslims, Hindus, Buddhists, Unitarians, and others—are creating a new kind of voice. Rather than providing a platform where White Christian America pretends to speak for all religious people, these buildings today house a diverse array of interests. Instead of interceding as surrogates, they are becoming midwives. Whether these efforts will ultimately be appealing for non-Christian groups and whether they will have influence in the halls of power remain open questions, ones that are perhaps too new to answer. But in the post-WCA world, building new models of interfaith cooperation is vitally important.

The demise of White Christian America also has the potential to reconfigure and revitalize national politics. Given its current makeup, the Republican Party clearly has more at stake here than the Democratic Party, but both parties—and more importantly, the American public—stand to gain from a partisan shake-up. There is strong evidence that the country is more politically polarized today than at any time in recent history. One of the major contributors to this polarization has been the post-Reagan drift of white evangelical Protestants, who now overwhelmingly support Republican candidates. As the GOP's own 2012 autopsy report noted, the party cannot survive as the party of white Christian Americans, or even white Americans. A plan that is mostly tailored to winning supermajorities among a shrinking pool of voters will only lead to obscurity. While Democrats are in a more strategically advantageous place because their core base groups are growing, it's also not healthy for them to become almost exclusively the party of racial minorities and nonreligious whites. This kind of polarized status quo incentivizes each party to stake out ideological positions with little room for compromise. With a two-party system, it may be inevitable that the parties will align along a liberal-conservative spectrum, but the polarization we are currently witnessing is turbocharged by the racial and religious divisions. The death of White Christian America—and the White Christian Strategy that catered to it—provides a rare chance for the development of a new political playbook that will be good for both parties and the democratic process as a whole.

And the decades immediately following White Christian America's demise won't just provide openings for political operatives. White Christian congregations and clergy across the country will be forced to reckon simultaneously with outmoded church growth models and their decentered place in civic life. In some ways, this existential challenge could be a blessing in disguise: it will serve as a solvent to loosen the ties between religious affiliation, race, and partisanship. Free of the strong tug of partisan loyalty, this new arrangement will allow white Christian churches, for the first time in a generation, to reassess theological conclusions that were forged in the fires of partisan conflict.

The death of White Christian America may also provide some opportunities for white Christians to cross the color line in their religious communities. While true multicultural congregations continue to be rare, there are some models for change. Today's upswing in racial tensions makes the emergence of churches that can serve as bridging institutions more important than ever. The data show that whites' attitudes on race mostly change when they rub shoulders and build close relationships with nonwhites. With few institutions poised to play this crucial role, America's churches could be a place where a national, substantive conversation about race finally begins. This dialogue has a much better chance of success if white Christians approach it with a chastened sense of repentance rather than a position of entrenched power that too quickly insists on programs of integration under predominantly white leadership or models focused prematurely on reconciliation.

The work of racial justice and reconciliation may also get a lift from the country's ongoing demographic churn. Rising rates of interracial and interfaith marriage are slowly building more tolerance into families and thus into the country's social fabric—what Putnam and Campbell memorably called the "Aunt Susan effect." [106] As more Americans have the experience of relating to people of different races and religions than their own, this emerging form of social capital will assist in breaking down the interpersonal barriers that have withstood the early stages of White Christian America's decline.

Finally, the death of White Christian America may mark a measurable de-escalation on at least one major front of the culture wars: the battles over LGBT rights. Here, the Millennial generation, which never drank deeply at the well of the culture wars, is already charting a new course. Young adults are generally uncomfortable with politicized religion, and for them, same-sex marriage is not a moral battleground but simply a feature of everyday life. Millennials also came of age during White Christian America's twilight years; even their white evangelical and mainline Protestant members are less likely to cling regretfully to the past. They haven't experienced the same sense of demographic or cultural superiority as their parents and grandparents. As the most diverse generation in American history, Millennials have grown up navigating the kinds of cultural differences that mark the road ahead. All of these characteristics make Millennials—and the generation after them—the carriers of new values and skills that will serve as resources for the nation in the aftermath of White Christian America's demise.

Benediction

More than halfway through the second decade of the twenty-first century, the idea of White Christian America can be difficult to comprehend. From our vantage point, the rhetoric seems jarring, and the great symbols hollow. Grand mottos like "the Christian Century" and "the Moral Majority" feel hopelessly inflated, while scenes of presidents laying cornerstones for imposing religious buildings and millions flocking for weeks on end to un-air-conditioned summer worship services strike contemporary audiences as fantastical. This is a world lost to us today.

As the effects of White Christian America's death ripple outward, the institutions that relied on its fiction of cultural homogeneity are already reorienting themselves to the new realities. In 2010, the 160-year-old Young Men's Christian Association (YMCA) officially changed its name to "The Y" as "a way of being warmer, more genuine, more welcoming." [107] In 2013, the Boy Scouts allowed openly gay youth to participate, and in 2015 it lifted the ban on gay scout leaders. Boy Scout president Robert Gates—former Secretary of Defense for both the George W. Bush and Barack Obama administrations—summed up the situation many civic organizations are facing: "Our oath calls upon us to do our duty to God and our country. The country is changing, and we are increasingly at odds with the legal landscape at both the state and federal levels." For the Boy Scouts, Gates concluded that it was time to put a distracting issue behind the organization in order to "unite behind our shared belief in the extraordinary power of scouting to be a force for good in the community and in the lives of its youth members." [108] The response from the Mormon Church, the largest single sponsor of Boy Scout troops, is representative of the conditional acceptance of the new status quo by at least some religious conservatives. While the Mormon Church initially threatened to sever ties with the Boy Scouts, even with a compromise in place that allowed local troops to make their own decisions about gay scout leaders, it ultimately decided to stay, affirming "the positive contributions scouting has made over the years to thousands of its young men and boys." [109]

Corporate America—which spends billions each year on market research—already understands that White Christian America's heyday has passed, and that the Christian Coalition's white Protestant family at prayer no longer describes the norm. When Franklin Graham recently called for a boycott of gay-friendly companies on his Facebook page, it quickly became apparent that to follow through on his own initiative, he'd need to delete his Facebook account (he didn't), stop using any Microsoft software, and shut down all Apple devices. When he publicly moved the bank accounts of the Billy Graham Evangelistic Association to BB&T Bank in protest of a Wells Fargo ad featuring a lesbian couple and their daughter, it generated this *Miami Herald* headline: "Billy Graham Group Moving Money to BB&T, Sponsor of Miami Beach Gay Pride Fundraiser."[110]

Major companies across the spectrum are demonstrating that they understand the cultural sea change. Coca-Cola's 2012 Super Bowl diversity-affirming declaration, "It's Beautiful," has been accompanied by Honey Maid's "This Is Wholesome," a 2014 ad depicting gay couples, young fathers with tattoos, and interracial families.[111] General Mills has the "Cheerios effect," featuring two gay dads and their adopted daughter,[112] and Tylenol is showing "#HowWeFamily," with a lesbian couple smiling for the camera at the prom and an interracial couple kissing at their wedding.[113] And Chevrolet—a heartland America company if ever there was one—is running ads that connect the dots between traditional family values and contemporary diversity: "While what it means to be a family hasn't changed, what a family looks like has. This is the new us."[114]

The death of White Christian America marks the end of an era in the nation's life. For many, it is a cause for considerable grief; for others, relief or even celebration. But this much is clear: in the soil fertilized by White Christian America's remains, new life is taking root.

Acknowledgments

I dedicate this book to my parents, Pat and Cherry Jones, who raised me in White Christian America. My family, on both my mother's and father's sides, has been rooted in the red clay of middle Georgia for more than two hundred years. My third great-grandfather on my father's side was Rev. James Larry Hobbs, who became the seventh pastor of First Baptist Church in Dublin, Georgia, in 1839 and later founded Mount Carmel Baptist church in Dexter, Georgia, in 1857. On my mother's side, I have inherited the old family Bible, a 1799 King James edition that is inscribed with the name of my maternal fourth great-grandfather, Pleasant Moon, who was born in 1800 in Twiggs County. The Bible's genealogical pages—nestled between the Old and New Testaments—testify to the births, baptisms, marriages, and deaths of three generations of Moon, Andrews, and related families. To my knowledge, it is the oldest existing object in our family, carefully passed down through six generations. There is undoubtedly some irony in dedicating a book about the decline of this world to the people who brought me into it. Like many other white Protestant Americans who share similar family histories, they will not celebrate its loss. But I dedicate this book to them because of the unwavering faith, support, and love they have always provided me, gifts they inherited and passed down from this world.

I was fortunate to have as a research and writing assistant someone who is an outstanding writer. Amelia Thomson-DeVeaux served throughout the project as researcher, drafter, proofreader, and sounding board. Amelia has an investigator's nose, a writer's eye, and an anthropologist's ear. The book as a whole, and the historical narratives in particular, are a better read because of her contributions.

Graphics designer Tim Duffy did an extraordinary job translating complex statistical relationships and trends into clear charts, especially within the constraints of black and white print. Dion Sujatmiko, whom I have never met, answered my request on Facebook through a mutual friend and provided a beautiful photograph of the Interchurch Center in New York City. The leadership of the General Board of Church and Society of the United Methodist Church—General Secretary Susan Henry Crow and Director for Annual Conference Relations Clayton Childers—graciously agreed to be interviewed, opened up their archives, and provided the photo of the United Methodist Building on Capitol Hill in Washington, D.C.

Neither the book nor the data on which it depends would have been possible without generous support from a number of foundations: the Ford Foundation and the Nathan Cummings Foundation for general support of PRRI's work, especially in the areas of economic and racial inequality; the Carnegie Corporation of New York for supporting research on demographic changes and civic integration in the United States; the Evelyn and Walter Haas, Jr. Fund for supporting research on evolving attitudes about LGBT rights; and the Henry Luce Foundation for supporting a long-term survey partnership between Public Religion Research Institute and Religion News Service, now in its fifth year.

I am also deeply indebted to the dedicated board and staff of Public Religion Research Institute. Founding board chair Rabbi David Saperstein has been a friend and mentor to me since I left my faculty position at Missouri State University a decade ago for the think tank world of Washington, D.C. David provided critical guidance during PRRI's first five years of growth and encouraged me to write this book. When he left the board at the end of 2014 to accept an appointment by President Barack Obama as Ambassador-at-Large for International Religious Freedom, Melissa Deckman, chair of the political science department at Washington College, stepped up and has provided fantastic leadership in her first year as board chair. I am grateful to Melissa and the PRRI board for supporting a research leave for several weeks in the summer of 2015, which made completing the book possible amid the day-to-day demands of PRRI's work. Former board member David Gushee read the entire manuscript and provided invaluable criticism from his perspective within the white evangelical Protestant world, and board member Diana Butler Bass offered keen insights from her deep knowledge of and travels within white mainline Protestant circles.

I owe heartfelt thanks to PRRI's research director, Dan Cox, who helped me launch PRRI in 2009, expertly guided the underlying public opinion research for the book, and served as a steady conversation partner as the analysis took shape. The PRRI research team, Betsy Cooper and Rachel Lienesch, provided clarion guidance and assistance in sifting through PRRI's data trove of over 150,000 interviews, and the PRRI communications team, Joanna Piacenza and Charlotte Gendron, helped me keep the prose from being overwhelmed by technical language.

I also owe a special word of thanks to E. J. Dionne, Jr., Bill Galston, and the Governance Studies team at The Brookings Institution, who have served as incredible research and thought partners through an ongoing collaboration between PRRI and Brookings over the last six years. PRRI's research has been richer—and more fun—as a result of this partnership. Many of the survey questions that produced data central to the book were conceived during lively conversations around the Brookings eighth-floor conference table. Additionally, Matt Dorf, Graham Roth, Benny Witovsky, and the rest of the West End Strategy Team have played, since PRRI's inception, an instrumental role in building PRRI's public reach and getting PRRI's data into the hands of journalists. Yoni Appelbaum, Washington bureau chief at *The Atlantic*, David Graham, former editor of the politics channel at *The Atlantic*, and Maureen Fiedler, host of "Interfaith Voices," the nation's leading religion news magazine on public radio, have provided critical opportunities for writing and conversations that have shaped my thinking as I have explored these ideas over the past few years.

As I ventured beyond the world of academic presses, my agent Roger Freet and his colleagues at Foundry Literary + Media were exceptional guides. Roger talked with me about the main ideas for this book over a period of two years over annual rounds of drinks at the American Academy of Religion meeting as the evidence supporting its argument mounted. Those conversations, and especially Roger's confidence that the book's time had come, were instrumental in convincing me to make the space to write it. Roger's expertise also helped this genre-spanning book find the right home. Finally, I am deeply grateful to Bob Bender, vice president and senior editor at Simon & Schuster, who believed in the book and provided valuable insights and advice throughout the writing and editing process.

This book is about the developmental arc of a social world, and my own personal and professional development has been shaped by family, colleagues, friends, and other fellow travelers: my steadfast siblings Ken Jones and Kathy Toomey; my supportive in-laws Arnie and Carol Kanter; influential teachers such as Liz Bounds, the late Nancy Eiesland, Jon Gunnemann, Jim Gustafson, Tim Jackson, Jeff Pool, and Steve Tipton; my seminary-era compatriots Richard Glenn, Brad Hadaway, Ken Hester, Melissa Stewart, and Alan Wright; ongoing friendships from my graduate study days at Emory University with Graham Reside, Chris Scharen, and Ted Smith; my Springfield crew Jody Bilyeu, Brett Miller, Matt Miller, and John Schmalzbauer; and more recent serendipitous connections with Katharine Henderson, Tom Krattenmaker, Rachel Laser, and Eboo Patel. I would also be remiss if I did not thank Sandra Kauffman, owner of the fabulous Highlawn Inn in Berkeley Springs, West Virginia, who provided the perfect writing retreat for several weeks in the summer of 2015. Some of my most productive writing was done in the rocking chair on Highlawn's front porch, looking out over the natural springs in the valley.

Finally, I want to thank my family, who helped give me the space to write this book in addition to my full-time day job at PRRI. My wife and partner Jodi, who is Jewish, believed in the book from its inception and was my first editor for every chapter, even as she was finishing her own book, *Presidential Libraries as Performance: Curating American Character from Herbert Hoover to George W. Bush.* Some of our earliest communications as a couple were about religion and the world of White Christian America, and our now decade-long interfaith conversation has gifted me with a clearer perspective and greater appreciation of its contributions to my own life. My daughter Riley was born in the midst of writing my first book, and it's amazing to see her now as a creative, strong young woman who loves languages and is a beautiful writer herself. My son Jasper has turned into a reader and early writer during the span of this project, and his silly antics and sunny disposition have been a steady source of uplift when my own writing and thinking have felt heavy. As I look beyond the era of White Christian America, my hope is that Riley and Jasper's generation will sift through the best of our past, bringing with them what is beneficial as they live into and help shape a new cultural world.

Appendix

Key Events in the Life of White
Christian America, since 1900

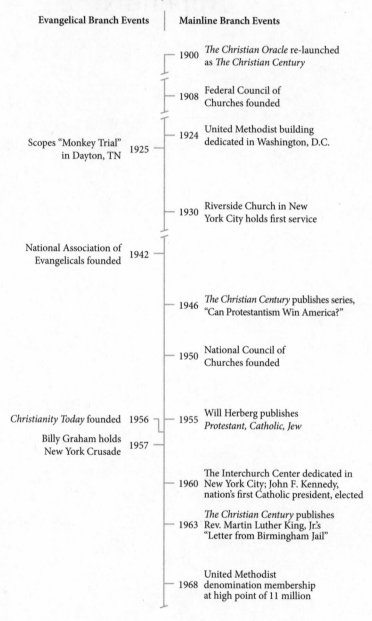

Evangelical Branch Events | Mainline Branch Events

1900   *The Christian Oracle* re-launched as *The Christian Century*

1908   Federal Council of Churches founded

Scopes "Monkey Trial" in Dayton, TN   1925

1924   United Methodist building dedicated in Washington, D.C.

1930   Riverside Church in New York City holds first service

National Association of Evangelicals founded   1942

1946   *The Christian Century* publishes series, "Can Protestantism Win America?"

1950   National Council of Churches founded

Christianity Today founded   1956

1955   Will Herberg publishes *Protestant, Catholic, Jew*

Billy Graham holds New York Crusade   1957

1960   The Interchurch Center dedicated in New York City; John F. Kennedy, nation's first Catholic president, elected

1963   *The Christian Century* publishes Rev. Martin Luther King, Jr.'s "Letter from Birmingham Jail"

1968   United Methodist denomination membership at high point of 11 million

Evangelical Branch Events | Mainline Branch Events

Moral Majority founded
by Rev. Jerry Falwell — 1979

Crystal Cathedral dedicated in
Garden Grove, California — 1980

Moral Majority disbands,
Christian Coalition founded — 1989
by Rev. Pat Robertson

1989 — Stanley Hauerwas and William
Willimon publish *Resident Aliens:
Life in the Christian Colony*

1993 — Last year white Protestant Christians
constitute a majority of Americans

Southern Baptist Convention
apologizes for its complicity — 1995
in slavery and segregation

Southern Baptist Convention
membership at high — 2003
point of 16.3 million

"Values Voter" movement
prominent in re-election of — 2004
President George W. Bush

Christian Coalition effectively
bankrupt, with $2 million in debt — 2006

Southern Baptist Convention reports
negative membership growth rate
for first time since 1950; Jerry — 2007
Falwell, D. James Kennedy die

2008 — Barack Obama, nation's first African
American president, elected

First national Tea Party protest events — 2009

2010 — U.S. Supreme Court has no Protestant
justices for first time in history

Crystal Cathedral bankrupt,
sold to Roman Catholic — 2012
Diocese of Orange County

National Council of Churches, in major
debt, vacates The Interchurch Center
2013 — in New York City, moves into United
Methodist Building in Washington, DC

2015 — U.S. Supreme Court legalizes
same-sex marriage in all 50 states

------ Events affecting
both groups

Notes

Preface

1. Approximately one quarter of President George Washington's first inaugural address was taken up with "fervent supplications to that Almighty Being who rules over the Universe." Washington explicitly justified his religious appeal in his speech by referring to the nation's shared religious culture: "In tendering this homage to the Great Author of every public and private good I assure myself that it expresses your sentiments not less than my own; nor those of my fellow-citizens at large, less than either." National Archives and Records Administration, "Washington's Inaugural Address of 1789," April 30, 1789, http://www.archives.gov/ex hibits/american_originals/inaugtxt.html, accessed June 9, 2015.
2. Sidney Verba, Kay Lehman Schlozman, and Henry Brady, *Voice and Equality: Civic Voluntarism in American Politics* (Cambridge: Harvard University Press, 1995).

Chapter 1: Who Is White Christian America?

1. "New York's Skyline Sits for a Long Portrait," *Life*, August 31, 1942, accessed June 10, 2015.

2. For a fascinating discussion of the decentralization of the western European and American church in relation to other social spheres such as the theater and the market, see Jean Christopher Agnew, *Worlds Apart: The Market and the Theater in Anglo-American Thought, 1550–1750* (Cambridge: Cambridge University Press, 1988).

3. Here and throughout the book, I use the word "white" as shorthand for "non-Hispanic white." E.g., all references to "white evangelical Protestants" can be understood to be "non-Hispanic white evangelical Protestants." In all data analyses, I follow the common practice in the social sciences of classifying respondents who say they are of Hispanic origin as "Hispanic," regardless of their racial identification.

4. "History of the United Methodist Building," http://umc-gbcs.org/about-us/the-united-methodist-building#historic, accessed June 11, 2015.

5. Robert Dean McNeil, *Valiant for Truth: Clarence True Wilson and Prohibition* (Portland: Oregonians Concerned About Addiction Problems, 1992), 47.

6. "History of the United Methodist Building."

7. Daniel Okrent, *Last Call: The Rise and Fall of Prohibition* (New York: Scribner, 2010), 14.

8. Ibid., 19.

9. McNeil, *Valiant for Truth*, 33.

10. Rev. Edmund M. Mills, ed., "Journal of the Twenty-eighth Delegated General Conference of the Methodist Episcopal Church, Held in Des Moines, Iowa May 1–May 27, 1920" (New York: Methodist Book Concern, 1920), 667.

11. McNeil, *Valiant for Truth*, 50.

12. Ibid., 52.

13. Conversation with Rev. Dr. Clayton Childers, Program Director for Annual Conference Relations at the United Methodist General Board of Church and Society, April 17, 2015.

14. McNeil, *Valiant for Truth*, 77.

15. Gary Dorrien, *Social Ethics in the Making: Interpreting an American Tradition* (Hoboken, NJ: Wiley-Blackwell Publishers), 111.

16. McNeil, *Valiant for Truth*, 55.

17. Ibid., 58.

18. *The Christian Century*, March 1931.

19. Conversation with Susan Henry-Crowe, General Secretary, General Board of Church and Society, United Methodist Church, April 30, 2015.

20. *Laying of the Cornerstone of the Interchurch Center* (New York: Interchurch Center, 1958).

21. Francis Stuart Harmon, *The Interchurch Center: Reminiscences of an Incorrigible Promoter* (New York: Harmon, 1972), 205.

22. Ibid., 152.

23. Ibid., 153.

24. Ibid.

25. Ibid., 109.

26. Ibid., 116.

27. The Interchurch Center, "History: The Founding Years," http://www.interchurch-center.org/history.html, accessed June 17, 2015.

28. Harmon, *The Interchurch Center*, 285.

29. James Findley, Jr., *Church People in the Struggle: The National Council of Churches and the Black Freedom Movement, 1950–1970* (New York: Oxford University Press, 1993), 199–255.

30. "Many at Center Support Forman," *New York Times*, June 10, 1969, http://timesmachine.nytimes.com/timesmachine/1969/06/10/78349710.html?pageNumber=35, accessed August 14, 2015.

31. Edwin Sartain Gault, *Ecumenical Adventure: The Interchurch Center, 1970–1990* (New York: Interchurch Center, 1993).

32. Philip E. Jenks, "NCC to Consolidate Operations in Washington, DC," *Special to National Council of Churches News*, February 13, 2013, http://www.pcusa.org/news/2013/2/13/ncc-consolidate-operations-washington-dc/, accessed June 11, 2015.

33. Interchurch Center, "Tenant Agencies," http://www.interchurch-center.org/?q=tenantagencies, accessed June 11, 2015.

34. http://www.interchurch-center.org/, accessed June 17, 2015.

35. Robert Lindsey, "Opening of Crystal Cathedral Is Feast for Eyes and Ears," *New York Times*, May 15, 1980, http://query.nytimes.com/gst/abstract

.html?res=9C05E5D71338E732A25756C1A9639C94619FD6CF, accessed June 11, 2015.

36. David A. Hollinger, "After Cloven Tongues of Fire: Ecumenical Protestantism and the Modern American Encounter with Diversity," *Journal of American History* (June 2011): 21–48. I am grateful to my colleague Sally Steenland for pointing me to this thorough and insightful account.

37. Erik Davis and Michael Rauner, *The Visionary State: A Journey Through California's Spiritual Landscape* (San Francisco: Chronicle Books, 2006), 148.

38. Ibid.

39. Ibid., 149.

40. Robert Lobdell and Mitchell Landsburg, "Rev. Robert H. Schuller, Who Built Crystal Cathedral, Dies at 88," *Los Angeles Times*, April 2, 2015, http://www.latimes.com/local/obituaries/la-me-robert-schuller-20150403-story.html#page=1, accessed June 11, 2015.

41. William Simbro, "Robert Schuller, Iowa Native Televangelist, Dies at 88," *Des Moines Register*, April 2, 2015, http://www.desmoinesregister.com/story/news/2015/04/02/robert-schuller-televangelist-obituary/70823454/, accessed June 11, 2015.

42. Lisa McGirr, *Suburban Warriors: The Origins of the New American Right* (Princeton: Princeton University Press, 2001), 106.

43. Ibid.

44. Ibid., 107.

45. Todd M. Kerstetter, *Inspiration and Innovation: Religion in the American West* (Oxford: Wiley & Sons, 2015), 244.

46. Michelle Vu, "Crystal Cathedral 'Glory of Easter' Celebrates over Two Decades on Stage," *The Christian Post*, March 13, 2006, http://www.christianpost.com/news/crystal-cathedral-glory-of-easter-celebrates-over-two-decades-on-stage-5882/, accessed June 11, 2015.

47. McGirr, *Suburban Warriors*, 105.

48. Ibid.

49. Warren Bird and Scott Thumma, "A New Decade of Megachurches: The 2011 Profile of Large Attendance Churches in the United States," Hartford Institute of Religion Research (November 22, 2011), http://hirr

.hartsem.edu/megachurch/megachurch-2011-summary-report.htm, accessed July 26, 2015.

50. Skye Jethani, "The Megachurch Bubble," *Christianity Today*, November 14, 2011, http://www.christianitytoday.com/parse/2011/november/skye-jethani-megachurch-bubble-part-1.html, accessed June 11, 2015.

51. Megann Cuniff, "Age, Income, Ethnicity: Latest Census Reveals All Facets of O.C.," *Orange County Register*, December 29, 2014, http://www.ocregister.com/articles/percent-646488-county-orange.html, accessed June 11, 2015.

52. Laurie Goodstein, "Dispute over Succession Clouds Megachurch," *New York Times*, October 23, 2010, http://www.nytimes.com/2010/10/24/us/24cathedral.html, accessed June 11, 2015.

53. Rebecca Cathcart, "California's Crystal Cathedral Files for Bankruptcy," *New York Times*, October 18, 2010, http://www.nytimes.com/2010/10/19/us/19crystal.html, accessed June 11, 2015.

54. Ian Lovett, "Ailing Megachurch Is Selling Its Property," *New York Times*, May 27, 2011, http://www.nytimes.com/2011/05/28/us/28crystal.html, accessed June 11, 2015.

55. Kevin Eckstrom and Sally Morrow, "Look Inside: The Transformation of the Crystal Cathedral," Religion News Service, September 25, 2014, http://www.religionnews.com/2014/09/25/look-inside-transformation-crystal-cathedral/, accessed June 11, 2015.

56. Deepa Bharath, "Bobby Schuller Brings Generations Together with New Church," *Orange County Register*, March 12, 2015, http://www.ocregister.com/articles/schuller-654002-cathedral-crystal.html, accessed June 11, 2015.

57. Anh Do, "St. Callistus Catholic Church Moves to Crystal Cathedral Site," *Los Angeles Times*, June 29, 2013, http://www.latimes.com/local/la-me-ff-0630-crystal-cathedral-mass-20130630-story.html, accessed June 11, 2015.

58. Christ Cathedral, "About Us," http://www.christcathedralcalifornia.org/, accessed June 11, 2015.

59. Do, "St. Callistus Catholic Church Moves to Crystal Cathedral Site."

60. Martin E. Marty, *Modern American Religion: The Noise of Conflict, 1919–1941, Volume 2* (Chicago: University of Chicago Press, 1986–96), 155.

61. Ibid., 164.

62. Ibid., 159–60.

63. H. L. Mencken, "The Monkey Trial: A Reporter's Account," University of Missouri-Kansas City Law School, http://law2.umkc.edu/faculty/proj ects/ftrials/scopes/menk.htm, accessed March 4, 2015.

64. Hollinger, "After Cloven Tongues of Fire," 21.

65. Marty, *Modern American Religion: Volume 2*, 214.

66. Hollinger, "After Cloven Tongues of Fire," 35.

67. Ibid., 23.

68. Ibid., 34–35.

69. J. Edgar Hoover, "Communist Propaganda and the Christian Pulpit," *Christianity Today*, October 14, 1960, 5; J. Edgar Hoover, "Soviet Rule or Christian Renewal?," *Christianity Today*, November 7, 1960, 9–11.

70. Will Herberg, *Protestant, Catholic, Jew: An Essay in American Religious Sociology* (Chicago: University of Chicago Press, 1983 [1955]).

71. Dan Gilgoff, "A Supreme Court Without Protestants?", CNN, May 10, 2010, http://www.cnn.com/2010/POLITICS/05/03/supreme.court.prot estants/, accessed July 28, 2015.

72. Nina Totenberg, "Court May Soon Lack Protestant Justices," NPR, April 7, 2010, http://www.npr.org/templates/story/story.php?storyId=125641988, accessed July 28, 2015. Note that there has been some resistance, even in the second half of the twentieth century, to appoint Jews to the Court. When asked by his attorney general when he was going to fill what had traditionally been understood to be a Jewish seat on the Court, President Richard Nixon replied, "Well, how about after I die."

73. "U.S. Interim Projections by Age, Sex, Race, and Hispanic Origin," U.S. Census Bureau, 2004, http://www.census.gov/ipc/www/usinterimproj/, accessed February 20, 2015.

74. Sam Roberts, "Minorities in U.S. Set to Be Majority by 2042," *New York Times*, August 14, 2008, http://www.nytimes.com/2008/08/14/world/ americas/14iht-census.1.15284537.html?_r=0, accessed February 20, 2015.

75. "U.S. Census Bureau Projections Show a Slower Growing, Older, More Diverse Nation a Half Century from Now," U.S. Census Bureau

Newsroom, December 12, 2012, https://www.census.gov/newsroom/releases/archives/population/cb12-243.html, accessed February 20, 2015.

76. Sam Roberts, "In a Generation, Minorities May Be U.S. Majority," *New York Times*, August 13, 2008, accessed February 18, 2015.

77. Michael Hout and colleagues found that lower birth rates, particularly among white mainline Protestants, accounted for most of mainline decline, particularly vis-à-vis conservative white Protestants, whose birth rates remained higher through the 1980s, when their birth rates began to mirror those of mainline Protestants. See Michael Hout, Andrew Greeley, and Melissa J. Wilde, "The Demographic Imperative in Religious Change in the United States," *American Journal of Sociology* 107, no. 2 (September 2001): 468–500.

78. "Does the Census Bureau Have Data for Religion?", U.S. Census Bureau, Frequently Asked Questions, https://ask.census.gov/faq.php?id=5000&faqId=29, accessed February 20, 2015.

79. Nathan Glazer, "Fundamentalism: A Defensive Offensive," in Richard John Neuhaus and Michael Cromartie, eds., *Piety or Politics: Evangelicals and Fundamentalists Confront the World* (Washington, DC: Ethics and Public Policy Center, 1987), 250–51.

Chapter 2: Vital Signs: A Divided and Dying White Christian America

1. "Coca-Cola Faces Social Media Backlash over Super Bowl 'America the Beautiful' Ad," Fox News Latino, February 4, 2014, accessed February 20, 2015.

2. Coca-Cola Company, "It's Beautiful," YouTube video, 1:30, February 2, 2014, https://www.youtube.com/watch?v=ilxRtxqYWt0, accessed February 20, 2015.

3. Ralph Ellis, "Steamrolled: Seattle Seahawks Flatten Denver Broncos 43–8 in Super Bowl," CNN, February 3, 2014, http://www.cnn.com/2014/02/02/us/super-bowl/, accessed February 20, 2015.

4. Allen B. West, "Coca Cola Ad on Super Bowl—America's Brand? Hm," AllenBWest.com, February 2, 2014, http://allenbwest.com/2014/02/coca-cola-ad-super-bowl-americans-brand-hm/, accessed February 20, 2015.

5. "Coca Cola's 'It's Beautiful' Super Bowl Ad Sets Off Twitter Firestorm," *Cedar Posts and Barbed Wire Fences*, February 3, 2014, http://cedarposts .blogspot.com/2014/02/coca-cola-beautiful-super-bowl-ad-sets.html, accessed June 26, 2015.

6. "It's Beautiful: Coke Debuts Inspiring Ad During Big Game," Coca-Cola Company, February 14, 2014, http://www.coca-colacompany.com/sto ries/americaisbeautiful-coke-debuts-inspiring-ad-during-big-game, accessed February 20, 2015.

7. PRRI, American Values Atlas, 2014.

8. Ibid.

9. General Social Survey, 1974.

10. General Social Survey, 2008.

11. PRRI, American Values Atlas, 2014.

12. General Social Survey, 1974–2012; PRRI, American Values Atlas, 2013–2014.

13. Albert Mohler, "When Will They Ever Learn? Mainline Decline in Perspective," December 14, 2005, http://www.albertmohler.com/2005/12/ 14/when-will-they-ever-learn-mainline-decline-in-perspective/, accessed August 15, 2015.

14. General Social Survey, 1988–2012; PRRI, American Values Atlas, 2013–2014. While 4 percentage points is modest, it is a statistically significant decline and is consistent with several other findings that point to an undeniable fall-off among white evangelicals.

15. Robert Putnam and David Campbell, *American Grace: How Religion Unites and Divides Us* (New York: Simon & Schuster, 2012), 141.

16. Ibid., 142.

17. PRRI, American Values Atlas, 2014.

18. General Social Survey, 1972.

19. PRRI, American Values Atlas, 2014.

20. Ibid.

21. Ed Stetzer, "The Southern Baptist Decline Continues—and Accelerates," *Between the Times*, June 11, 2015, http://betweenthetimes.com/index .php/2015/06/11/the-southern-baptist-decline-continues/, accessed June 25, 2015.

22. Carol Pipes, "SBC Reports More Churches, Fewer People," *Baptist Press*, June 10, 2015, http://www.bpnews.net/44914/sbc-reports-more-churches-fewer-people, accessed June 21, 2015.

23. Stetzer, "The Southern Baptist Decline Continues—And Accelerates."

24. PRRI, American Values Atlas, 2014.

25. "History," Hindu Temple Society of Mississippi, http://www.htsm.org/about/history, accessed June 15, 2015.

26. Matthew Frye Jacobson, *Whiteness of a Different Color: European Immigrants and the Alchemy of Race* (Cambridge: Harvard University Press, 1999), 5.

27. Michael E. Parrish, *Anxious Decades: America in Prosperity and Depression, 1920–1941* (New York: W. W. Norton, 1994), 121–22.

28. Robert A. Slayton, *Empire Statesman: The Rise and Redemption of Al Smith* (New York: Free Press, 2001), ix.

29. John T. McGreevy, *Catholicism and American Freedom: A History* (New York: W. W. Norton and Company, 2003), 185.

30. William Clayton Morrison, "Roman Catholicism and Protestantism," *The Christian Century* (May 8, 1946): 585–88.

31. Elesha J. Coffman, *The Christian Century and the Rise of the Protestant Mainline* (Oxford: Oxford University Press, 2013), 150.

32. John Corrigan and Lynn S. Neal, *Religious Intolerance in America: A Documentary History* (Chapel Hill, NC: University of North Carolina Press, 2010), 71.

33. Peter Braestrup, "Protestant Unit Wary on Kennedy," *New York Times*, September 8, 1960, accessed March 4, 2015.

34. "Transcript: JFK's Speech on His Religion," NPR, uploaded December 5, 2007, http://www.npr.org/templates/story/story.php?storyId=16920600, accessed March 4, 2015.

35. Randall Balmer, *God in the White House: A History* (New York: HarperCollins, 2008), 36.

36. Peter Steinfels, "Catholic and Evangelical: Seeking a Middle Ground," *New York Times*, March 30, 1994, http://www.nytimes.com/1994/03/30/us/catholic-and-evangelical-seeking-a-middle-ground.html, accessed March 4, 2015.

37. Daniel K. Williams, *God's Own Party: The Making of the Christian Right* (New York: Oxford University Press, 2010), 63.

38. http://www.ourbodiesourselves.org/health-info/u-s-abortion-history/, accessed June 25, 2015.

39. "Resolution on Abortion," Southern Baptist Convention, St. Louis, Missouri, 1971, http://www.sbc.net/resolutions/13, accessed March 4, 2015.

40. Williams, *God's Own Party*, 130.

41. Seth Dowland, " 'Family Values' and the Formation of a Christian Right Agenda," *Church History* 78, no. 3 (September 2009): 615.

42. Napp Nazworth, "Wheaton College, Catholic University Jointly Sue over Birth Control Mandate," *The Christian Post*, July 18, 2012, http://www.christianpost.com/news/wheaton-college-catholic-university-jointly-sue-over-birth-control-mandate-78491/, accessed March 4, 2015.

43. Evangelicals and Catholics Together, "The Two Shall Become One Flesh: Reclaiming Marriage," *First Things* (March 2015), http://www.firstthings.com/article/2015/03/the-two-shall-become-one-flesh-reclaiming-marriage-2, accessed October 21, 2015.

44. General Social Survey, 1990; PRRI, American Values Atlas, 2014.

45. Robert P. Jones and Daniel Cox, *The "Francis Effect"? U.S. Catholic Attitudes on Pope Francis, the Catholic Church, and American Politics* (Washington, DC: Public Religion Research Institute, August 2015), 2, http://publicreligion.org/research/2015/08/survey-the-francis-effect-u-s-catholic-attitudes-on-pope-francis-the-catholic-church-and-american-politics/, accessed October 21, 2015.

46. *Reynolds v. United States*, Oyez Project at IIT-Chicago Kent School of Law, http://www.oyez.org/cases/1851-1900/1878/1878_0, accessed March 4, 2015.

47. Pew Research Center, "How the Faithful Voted: 2012 Preliminary Analysis" November 7, 2012, http://www.pewforum.org/2012/11/07/how-the-faithful-voted-2012-preliminary-exit-poll-analysis/, accessed June 25, 2015.

48. Jan Shipps, "Mormonism and the Religious Mainstream," in *Minority Faiths and the American Protestant Mainstream*, ed. Jonathan Sarna (Urbana: University of Illinois Press, 1998), 89.

49. Spencer J. Fluhman, *A Peculiar People: Anti-Mormonism and the Making of Religion in Nineteenth-Century America* (Chapel Hill: University of North Carolina Press, 2012), 108.

50. W. Paul Reeve, *Religion of a Different Color: Race and the Mormon Struggle for Whiteness* (Oxford: Oxford University Press, 2015), 163.

51. Ibid., 168.

52. Fluhman, *A Peculiar People*, 161.

53. Martin E. Marty, *The Irony of It All: 1893–1919, Volume 1, Modern American Religion* (Chicago: University of Chicago Press, 1986), 301.

54. "Statistical Report 1963," in "The One Hundred Thirty-fourth Annual Conference of The Church of Jesus Christ of Latter-day Saints," The Church of Jesus Christ of Latter-day Saints, April 1964, 101, https://archive.org/stream/conferencereport1964a#page/n101/mode/2up.

55. J. B. Haws, *The Mormon Image in the American Mind: Fifty Years of Public Perception* (New York: Oxford University Press, 2013), 29.

56. Ibid., 122–23.

57. Susan Friend Harding, *The Book of Jerry Falwell: Fundamentalist Language and Politics* (Princeton: Princeton University Press, 2001), 282.

58. Art Toalston, "Bizarre Theology Does Not Prevent Mormonism's Growth," *SBC Life: Journal of the Southern Baptist Convention*, November 1997, http://www.sbclife.net/Articles/1997/11/sla10, accessed March 4, 2015.

59. Lynn Jones, "Debate Among Southern Baptists and Mormons Continues, Sparked by Video," *Baptist Press*, April 27, 1998, http://www.bpnews.net/4622/debate-among-southern-baptists-and-mormons-continues-sparked-by-video, accessed June 25, 2015.

60. Frank Newport, "Americans' Views of the Mormon Religion," Gallup, March 2, 2007, http://www.gallup.com/poll/26758/americans-views-mormon-religion.aspx, accessed March 4, 2015.

61. Zev Chafets, "The Huckabee Factor," *New York Times Magazine*, December 12, 2007, http://www.nytimes.com/2007/12/12/magazine/16huckabee.html?pagewanted=all, accessed March 4, 2015.

62. "Transcript: Mitt Romney's Faith Speech," NPR, December 6, 2007, http://www.npr.org/templates/story/story.php?storyId=16969460, accessed March 4, 2015.

63. Walter Kirn, "The Mormon Moment," *Newsweek*, June 5, 2011, http://www.newsweek.com/mormon-moment-67951, accessed March 4, 2015.

64. "The Media, Religion and the 2012 Campaign for President," Pew Research Center: Journalism and Media, December 14, 2012, http://www.journalism.org/2012/12/14/media-religion-and-2012-campaign-president/.

65. PRRI/RNS Religion News Survey, May 10, 2012, http://publicreligion.org/research/2012/05/may-rns-2012-research/, accessed March 31, 2015.

66. "Americans Learned Little About the Mormon Faith, but Some Attitudes Have Softened," Pew Forum on Religion and Public Life, December 14, 2012, http://www.pewforum.org/2012/12/14/attitudes-toward-mormon-faith/, accessed March 4, 2015.

67. PRRI, Religion and Politics Tracking Survey, October 27, 2011, http://publicreligion.org/research/2011/10/oct-religion-politics-tracking-romney-cain-perry/#.VXtAbBNVhHw.

68. PRRI/RNS, Religion News Survey, May 10, 2012, http://publicreligion.org/research/2012/05/may-rns-2012-research/.

69. "Americans Learned Little About the Mormon Faith, but Some Attitudes Have Softened."

Chapter 3: Politics: The End of the White Christian Strategy

1. Four presidents were Unitarian (John Adams, John Quincy Adams, Millard Fillmore, and William Howard Taft). Until the twentieth century, Unitarians were typically understood as staking out the left edge of the Christian tradition; today, they are more accurately characterized as a pluralistic denomination that describes itself as having a historical relationship with Christianity, http://vva.org/who-we-are/beliefs/christianity, accessed December 21, 2015.

2. Jodi Kantor, "A President, His Minister, and the Search for Faith," *New York Times*, April 30, 2007, http://www.nytimes.com/2007/04/30/us/politics/30obama.html?pagewanted=all, accessed February 11, 2015.

3. Don Frederick, "Barack Obama Denounces Jeremiah Wright's 'Ridiculous' Notions," *Los Angeles Times*, April 29, 2008, http://latimesblogs .latimes.com/washington/2008/04/barack-obama-cu.html, accessed February 11, 2015.

4. PRRI, "Evangelical Voters Strongly Support Romney Despite Religious Differences," May 10, 2012, http://publicreligion.org/research/2012/05/ may-rns-2012-research/.

5. For a full account of the role of faith in Obama's presidency, see Robert P. Jones and Daniel Cox, "President Barack Obama and His Faith," in Mark J. Rozell and Gleaves Whitney, eds., *Religion and the American Presidency* (New York: Palgrave Macmillan, 2012), 251–61.

6. "Obama Delivers Speech on Faith in America," *New York Times*, July 1, 2008, http://www.nytimes.com/2008/07/01/us/politics/01obama-text .html?pagewanted=all, accessed February 11, 2015.

7. Barack Obama, "Remarks by the President at the National Prayer Breakfast," Washington Hilton, Washington DC, February 3, 2011, http:// www.whitehouse.gov/the-press-office/2011/02/03/remarks-president- national-prayer-breakfast, accessed February 11, 2015.

8. Ben Smith and Byron Tau, "Birtherism: Where It All Began," *Politico*, April 22, 2011, http://www.politico.com/news/stories/0411/53563.html, accessed February 11, 2015.

9. Shannon Travis, "CNN Poll: Quarter Doubt Obama Was Born in US," CNN, August 4, 2010, http://politicalticker.blogs.cnn.com/2010/08/04/ cnn-poll-quarter-doubt-president-was-born-in-u-s/, accessed February 11, 2015.

10. Matthew Hughey, "Show Me Your Papers! Obama's Birth and the Whiteness of Belonging," *Qualitative Sociology* 35, no. 2 (June 2012): 163–81.

11. "A Certificate of Embarrassment," *New York Times*, April 28, 2011, http:// www.nytimes.com/2011/04/28/opinion/28thu1.html, accessed February 15, 2015.

12. Norman Rockwell Museum website, http://www.nrm.org/2013/08/nor man-rockwells-four-freedoms/, accessed February 15, 2015.

13. Pennsylvania State website, http://www.visitpa.com/pennsylvania-facts- history, accessed February 15, 2015.

14. Barack Obama, "Inaugural Address," Washington, DC, January 21, 2013, http://www.whitehouse.gov/the-press-office/2013/01/21/inaugural-ad dress-president-barack-obama.

15. PRRI, Religion, Values, and Immigration Reform Survey, March 21, 2013, http://publicreligion.org/research/2013/03/2013-religion-values-immigration-survey/.

16. Merle Black and Earl Black, *The Rise of Southern Republicans* (Cambridge: Harvard University Press, 2003), 4.

17. Ibid., 4.

18. Ibid., 208.

19. Rick Perlstein, *Nixonland: The Rise of a President and the Fracturing of America* (New York, NY: Simon & Schuster, 2010), 299–300.

20. Black and Black, *The Rise of Southern Republicans*, 210.

21. Ibid., 173.

22. Ibid., 214.

23. Jimmy Carter, "Equal Rights Amendment Letter to Members of the House Judiciary Committee," July 12, 1978, http://www.presidency.ucsb .edu/ws/?pid=31062.

24. *Engel v. Vitale*; *Abington School District v. Schempp*; *Murray v. Curlett*.

25. Jimmy Carter, "Remarks to Members of the Southern Baptist Brotherhood Commission," Atlanta, Georgia, June 16, 1978, http://www.presi dency.ucsb.edu/ws/index.php?pid=30961.

26. Black and Black, *The Rise of Southern Republicans*, 214.

27. In 1976, *Newsweek* published a cover story declaring the "Year of the Evangelical," http://www.newsweek.com/editors-desk-106637. The same year, a widely reported Gallup poll found that 34 percent of Americans said they were "born again" Christians. James Dobson's Focus on the Family was founded in 1977 (http://www.focusonthefamily.com/about_us/james-dobson.aspx); its first radio broadcast aired that year. A fuller discussion of the "evangelical moment" in the 1970s can be found in Steven P. Miller, *The Age of Evangelicalism: America's Born-Again Years* (New York: Oxford University Press, 2014), 9–32.

28. Daniel Williams, *God's Own Party: The Making of the Christian Right* (New York: Oxford University Press, 2010), 2.

29. Ibid., 171.

30. Ibid., 187.

31. Ibid., 188.

32. Jimmy Carter, *White House Diary* (New York: Farrar, Straus & Giroux, 2010), 469.

33. Black and Black, *The Rise of Southern Republicans*, 218.

34. Ibid., 208.

35. Peter B. Levy, *Encyclopedia of the Reagan-Bush Years* (New York: Greenwood, 1996), 249.

36. Black and Black, *The Rise of Southern Republicans*, 217.

37. Peter Steinfels, "Moral Majority to Dissolve, Says Mission Accomplished," *New York Times*, June 12, 1989, http://www.nytimes.com/1989/06/12/us/moral-majority-to-dissolve-says-mission-accomplished.html, accessed February 10, 2015.

38. Williams, *God's Own Party*, 244.

39. Brian Knowlton, "Republican Says Bush Panders to 'Agents of Intolerance': McCain Takes Aim at Religious Right," *New York Times*, February 29, 2000, http://www.nytimes.com/2000/02/29/news/29iht-bush.2.t_9.html, accessed February 10, 2015.

40. John C. Green and Kimberly H. Conger, "Spreading Out and Digging In: Christian Conservatives and State Republican Parties" (*Campaigns & Elections*, 2002), 58.

41. Williams, *God's Own Party*, 257.

42. Robert P. Jones, *Progressive and Religious* (New York: Rowman & Littlefield, 2008), 4.

43. John Green, *The Values Campaign? The Christian Right and the 2004 Elections* (Washington, DC: Georgetown University Press, 2006), 13–14, 99.

44. National Exit Poll, 2004.

45. Jennifer Riley, "Focus on the Family Cuts More Jobs," *Christian Post*, August 2, 2010, http://www.christianpost.com/news/focus-on-the-family-cuts-more-jobs-46133/, accessed February 10, 2015.

46. Electa Draper, "Focus on the Family Announces More Layoffs," *Denver Post*, September 16, 2011, http://www.denverpost.com/ci_18912132, accessed February 10, 2015.

47. Neela Banerjee and Laurie Goodstein, "Pastor Dismissed for 'Sexually Immoral Conduct,'" *The New York Times*, November 5, 2006.

48. Steven Tomma, "The religious right's political power ebbs," McClatchy Newspapers, September 30, 2007, http://www.mcclatchydc.com/2007/09/30/20062/the-religious-rights-political.html, accessed June 18, 2015.

49. David Kirkpatrick, "Christian Right Labors to Find '08 Candidate," *The New York Times*, February 25, 2007.

50. Barbara Bradley Haggerty, "Evangelicals Struggle to Crown a Candidate," NPR, January 13, 2012, http://www.npr.org/2012/01/13/145121706/evangelical-leaders-struggle-to-crown-a-candidate, accessed August 15, 2015. Erik Eckholm and Jeff Zeleny, "Evangelicals, Seeking Unity, Back Santorum for Nomination," *New York Times*, January 14, 2012, http://www.nytimes.com/2012/01/15/us/politics/conservative-religious-leaders-seeking-unity-vote-to-back-rick-santorum.html?_r=0, accessed August 15, 2015.

51. Liz Robbins, "Tax Day Is Met with Tea Parties," *New York Times*, April 16, 2009, http://www.nytimes.com/2009/04/16/us/politics/16taxday.html, accessed February 11, 2015.

52. Eric Etheridge, "Rick Santelli: Tea Party Time," *New York Times*, February 20, 2009, http://opinionator.blogs.nytimes.com/2009/02/20/rick-santelli-tea-party-time/, accessed February 11, 2015.

53. Robbins, "Tax Day Is Met with Tea Partiers."

54. Jim Spellman, "Tea Party Has Anger, No Dominant Leaders," CNN, September 12, 2009, http://www.cnn.com/2009/POLITICS/09/12/tea.party.express/index.html?eref=rss_us, accessed February 11, 2015.

55. "Thousands of Anti-Tax Tea Party Protesters Turn Out in US Cities," Fox News, April 15, 2009, http://www.foxnews.com/politics/2009/04/15/thousands-anti-tax-tea-party-protesters-turn-cities/, accessed February 11, 2015.

56. Michael Cooper, "GOP Senate Victory Stuns Democrats," *New York Times*, January 20, 2010, http://www.nytimes.com/2010/01/20/us/politics/20election.html, accessed February 11, 2015.

57. PRRI, "Religion and the Tea Party in the 2010 Elections," October 5, 2010, http://publicreligion.org/research/2010/10/religion-tea-party-2010/.

58. Kate Zernike, "Shaping Tea Party Passion into a Campaign Force," *New York Times*, April 26, 2010, http://www.nytimes.com/2010/08/26/us/politics/26freedom.html, accessed February 11, 2015.

59. Ashley Fantz, "Obama as Witch Doctor: Racist or Satirical?," CNN, September 17, 2009, http://www.cnn.com/2009/POLITICS/09/17/obama.witchdoctor.teaparty/, accessed February 11, 2015; Philip Kennicott, "Image of 'Socialist Joker' Obama Image," *Washington Post*, August 5, 2009, http://www.washingtonpost.com/wp-dyn/content/discussion/2009/08/05/DI2009080503252.html, accessed February 11, 2015. "10 Most Offensive Tea Party Signs and Extensive Photo Coverage from Tax Day Protests," *Huffington Post*, April 16, 2009, http://www.huffingtonpost.com/2009/04/16/10-most-offensive-tea-par_n_187554.html, accessed June 15, 2015.

60. Susan Davis, "Rand Paul Taking Heat for Civil Rights Comments," *Wall Street Journal*, May 20, 2010, http://blogs.wsj.com/washwire/2010/05/20/rand-paul-taking-heat-for-civil-rights-act-comments/, accessed February 11, 2015.

61. Shannon Travis, "NAACP Passes Resolution Blasting Tea Party 'Racism,'" CNN, July 16, 2010, http://www.cnn.com/2010/POLITICS/07/14/naacp.tea.party/, accessed February 11, 2015.

62. PRRI, "Religion and the Tea Party in the 2010 Elections."

63. PRRI, "2013 American Values Survey: In Search of Libertarians in America," October 29, 2013, http://publicreligion.org/research/2013/10/2013-american-values-survey/.

64. PRRI, "A Shifting Landscape: A Decade of Change in American Attitudes About Same-sex Marriage and LGBT Issues," February 26, 2014. http://publicreligion.org/research/2014/02/2014-lgbt-survey/.

65. PRRI, "2014 Pre-Election American Values Survey: Economic Insecurity, Rising Inequality, and Doubts About the Future," September 23, 2014, http://publicreligion.org/research/2014/09/survey-economic-insecurity-rising-inequality-and-doubts-about-the-future-findings-from-the-2014-american-values-survey/.

66. PRRI, "Beyond Guns and God: Understanding the Complexities of the White Working Class in America," September 20, 2012, http://publicre ligion.org/research/2012/09/race-class-culture-survey-2012/.

67. David Freelander, "Mitt Romney's Victory Party a Bust," *The Daily Beast*, November 7, 2012, http://www.thedailybeast.com/articles/2012/11/07/mitt-romney-s-victory-party-a-bust.html, accessed February 11, 2015.

68. "Where Barack Obama and Mitt Romney Are on Election Night," *Washington Post*, November 6, 2012, http://www.washingtonpost.com/politics/decision2012/where-barack-obama-and-mitt-romney-are-on-election-night/2012/11/06/dd2310d8-287d-11e2-96b6-8e6a7524553f_story.html, accessed February 11, 2015.

69. Elspeth Reeve, "The Whole Romney Ticket Believed in Unskewed Polls?" *The Atlantic*, November 8, 2012, http://www.thewire.com/poli tics/2012/11/whole-romney-ticket-believed-unskewed-polls/58852/, accessed February 15, 2015.

70. Mackenzie Weinger, "Karl Rove: Fox News Call 'Premature,'" *Politico*, November 6, 2012, http://www.politico.com/blogs/media/2012/11/karl-rove-fox-news-ohio-call-premature-148745.html, accessed February 11, 2015.

71. http://elections.nytimes.com/2012/results/president/exit-polls; http://elections.nbcnews.com/ns/politics/2012/ohio/president/, accessed June 1, 2015.

72. Pew Forum on Religion and Public Life, "How the Faithful Voted in 2012: A Preliminary Exit Poll Analysis," November 7, 2012, http://www .pewforum.org/2012/11/07/how-the-faithful-voted-2012-preliminary-exit-poll-analysis/.

73. Chris Cillizza, "How Many More White Votes Did Mitt Romney Need to Get Elected in 2012? A Lot," *Washington Post*, August 4, 2014, http://www.washingtonpost.com/blogs/the-fix/wp/2014/08/04/how-many-more-white-votes-did-mitt-romney-need-to-get-elected-in-2012-a-lot/, accessed February 11, 2015.

74. Thomas B. Edsall, "How Democrats Can Compete for the White Working Class," *New York Times*, March 12, 2014, http://www.nytimes

.com/2014/03/12/opinion/edsall-how-democrats-can-compete-for-the-white-working-class.html, accessed February 11, 2015.

75. Rachel Weiner, "Black Voters Turned Out at a Higher Rate than White Voters in 2012 and 2008," *Washington Post*, April 29, 2013, http://www .washingtonpost.com/blogs/the-fix/wp/2013/04/29/black-turnout-was-higher-than-white-turnout-in-2012-and-2008/, accessed February 11, 2015.

76. Mark Hugo Lopez and Ana Gonzalez-Barrera, "Inside the 2012 Latino Electorate," Pew Hispanic Center, June 3, 2013, http://www.pewhispanic .org/2013/06/03/inside-the-2012-latino-elelectorate/.

77. Hope Yen, "In a First, Black Voter Turnout Rate Passes Whites," Associated Press/Yahoo News, April 29, 2013, http://news.yahoo.com/first-black-voter-turnout-rate-passes-whites-115957314.html, accessed June 15, 2015.

78. Karen Tumulty, "As Republicans Ponder 2012 Defeat, Party's Philosophy Hangs in the Balance," *Washington Post*, December 15, 2012, http://www.washingtonpost.com/politics/as-republicans-ponder-2012-defeat-partys-philosophy-hangs-in-the-balance/2012/12/15/ca030ab4-449b-11e2-8e70-e1993528222d_story.html, accessed February 11, 2015.

79. Henry Barbour, Sally Bradshaw, Ari Fleischer, Glenn McCall, and Zori Fonalledas, "Growth and Opportunity Project," March 2013, https://go project.gop.com/RNC_Growth_Opportunity_Book_2013.pdf.

80. Ibid., 1.

81. Ibid., 6.

82. Ibid., 15–17.

83. Robert Jones, Daniel Cox, and Juhem Navarro-Rivera, "The Hispanic Values Survey: How Shifting Religious Identities and Experiences Are Influencing Hispanic Approaches to Politics," Washington, DC: Public Religion Research Institute, September 27, 2013, http://publicreligion. org/2013/09/hispanic-values-survey-2013/, accessed June 11, 2015.

84. Barbour et al., "Growth and Opportunity Project," 97.

85. Thomas B. Edsall, "The Republican Autopsy Report," *New York Times*,

March 20, 2013, http://opinionator.blogs.nytimes.com/2013/03/20/the-republican-autopsy-report/, accessed February 11, 2015.

86. Jennifer Rubin, "GOP Autopsy Report Goes Bold," *Washington Post*, March 18, 2013, http://www.washingtonpost.com/blogs/right-turn/wp/2013/03/18/gop-autopsy-report-goes-bold/, accessed February 11, 2015.

87. Aaron Blake, "Conservatives Balk at RNC's Ideas on Immigration, Presidential Primary," *Washington Post*, March 18, 2013, http://www.washingtonpost.com/blogs/post-politics/wp/2013/03/18/as-gop-leaders-praise-priebus-report-some-conservatives-balk/, accessed February 11, 2015.

88. Alexandra Jaffe, "Tea Party Groups Warn Grassroots Activism at Risk in RNC Proposals," *The Hill*, March 18, 2013, http://thehill.com/blogs/ballot-box/presidential-races/288829-tea-party-groups-warns-grassroots-activism-at-risk-in-rnc-proposals, accessed February 11, 2015.

89. Rush Limbaugh, "Message to GOP: The Problem Isn't Who You Are, It's What People Say About You," *Rush Limbaugh Show*, March 19, 2013, http://www.rushlimbaugh.com/daily/2013/03/19/message_to_gop_the_problem_isn_t_who_you_are_it_s_what_people_say_about_you, accessed February 11, 2015.

90. Katie Glueck, "Reince Priebus Predicts 2014 GOP 'Tsunami,'" *Politico*, March 18, 2014, http://www.politico.com/story/2014/03/reince-priebus-2014-prediction-104762.html, accessed February 11, 2015.

91. Ben Jacobs, "Democrats Attack GOP's Rebranding Effort on Its One-Year Anniversary," *The Daily Beast*, March 18, 2014, http://www.thedailybeast.com/articles/2014/03/18/dems-criticize-gop-rebrand.html, accessed February 11, 2015.

92. Molly Ball, "The Republican Wave Sweeps the Midterm Elections," *The Atlantic*, November 5, 2014, http://www.theatlantic.com/politics/archive/2014/11/republicans-sweep-the-midterm-elections/382394/, accessed February 11, 2015.

93. Charlotte Alter, "Voter Turnout in Midterm Elections Hits 72-Year Low," *Time*, November 10, 2014, http://time.com/3576090/midterm-elections-turnout-world-war-two/, accessed February 11, 2015.

Chapter 4: Family: Gay Marriage and White Christian America

1. Casey McNerthney, "Mary Lambert: The Voice Behind Macklemore's 'Same Love,'" *Seattle Post-Intelligencer*, April 10, 2013, http://www.seattlepi.com/local/article/Mary-Lambert-The-voice-behind-Macklemores-Same-4422552.php, accessed August 16, 2015.

2. Lynn Neary, "Some TV Networks Refuse to Run Church Ad," NPR, December 4, 2004, http://www.npr.org/templates/story/story.php?storyId=4197277, accessed March 21, 2015.

3. "Gay Dating Ad Sacked Before Super Bowl," CBS News, January 29, 2010, http://www.cbsnews.com/news/gay-dating-ad-sacked-before-super-bowl, accessed March 21, 2015.

4. "GLAAD Releases 14th Annual Where We Are on TV Ad," GLAAD, press release, October 1, 2009, http://www.glaad.org/2009/10/01/glaad-releases-14th-annual-where-we-are-on-tv-study, http://www.glaad.org/publications/nri2010/, accessed March 21, 2015.

5. James Hibberd, "CBS Adding Three Gay Characters to Shows," *Hollywood Reporter*, July 28, 2010, http://www.hollywoodreporter.com/news/cbs-adding-three-gay-characters-26017, accessed March 21, 2015.

6. "2014 Where We Are on TV Report," GLAAD, https://www.glaad.org/files/GLAAD-2014-WWAT.pdf, accessed March 5, 2015.

7. Ryan Reed, "Grammys Draw Second-Highest Ratings in Over 20 Years," *Rolling Stone*, January 27, 2014, http://www.rollingstone.com/tv/news/grammys-draw-second-highestratings-in-over-20-years-20140127, accessed March 5, 2015.

8. "Macklemore, Queen Latifah, Turn 'Same Love' into Mass Grammy Wedding," *Rolling Stone*, January 26, 2014, http://www.rollingstone.com/music/news/macklemore-queen-latifah-turn-same-love-into-mass-grammy-wedding-20140126, accessed March 5, 2015.

9. James Nichols, "Anti-Gay Pundits Freak Out Over Grammys Gay Wedding Ceremony," *Huffington Post*, January 27, 2014, http://www.huffingtonpost.com/2014/01/27/same-sex-weddinggrammys_n_4674469.html.

10. Ed Stetzer, "The Grammys, Grace, and the Gospel: 3 Things the Grammys Can Remind Christians," *Christianity Today*, January 28, 2014, http://www.christianitytoday.com/edstetzer/2014/january/grammys.html.

11. David K. Johnson, *The Cold War Persecution of Gays and Lesbians in the Federal Government* (Chicago: University of Chicago Press, 2009).

12. Gregory B. Lewis, "Lifting the Ban on Gays in the Civil Service: Federal Policy Toward Gay and Lesbian Employees Since the Cold War," *Public Administration Review* 57, no. 5 (September/October 1997): 387–95.

13. Williams, *God's Own Party*, 147–48.

14. Ibid., 148–49.

15. Lillian Faderman, *The Gay Revolution: The Story of the Struggle* (New York: Simon & Schuster, 2015), 354.

16. Williams, *God's Own Party*, 150–51.

17. Dudley Clendinen and Adam Nagourney, *Out for Good: The Struggle to Build a Gay Rights Movement in America* (New York: Simon & Schuster, 1999), 378.

18. "School Employees. Homosexuality," California Proposition 6 (1978), http://repository.uchastings.edu/ca_ballot_props/838/, accessed October 21, 2015.

19. Williams, *God's Own Party*, 151.

20. Anthony M. Petro, *After the Wrath of God: AIDS, Sexuality, and American Religion* (New York: Oxford University Press, 2015), 187.

21. Katharine Q. Seeyle, "Helms Puts the Breaks to Bill Financing AIDS Treatment," *New York Times*, July 5, 1995, http://www.nytimes.com/1995/07/05/us/helms-puts-the-brakes-to-a-bill-financing-aids-treatment.html, accessed October 21, 2015.

22. PSRA/*Times Mirror Poll*, June 1992 (N=3,517).

23. Jeffrey Schmalz, "In Hawaii, Step Toward Legalized Gay Marriage," *New York Times*, May 7, 1993, http://www.nytimes.com/1993/05/07/us/in-hawaii-step-toward-legalized-gay-marriage.html, accessed October 21, 2015.

24. Paul F. Horvitz, "Don't Ask, Don't Tell, Don't Pursue is White House's Compromise Solution: New U.S. Military Policy Tolerates Homosexuals," *New York Times*, July 20, 1993, http://www.nytimes.com/1993/07/20/news/20iht-gay_1.html, accessed October 21, 2015.

25. Eric Schmitt, "Senators Reject Both Job-Bias Ban and Gay Marriage," *New York Times*, September 11, 1996, http://www.nytimes.com/1996/09/11/us/senators-reject-both-job-bias-ban-and-gay-marriage.html, accessed October 21, 2015.

26. "Falwell Apologies for Placing Blame," ABC News, http://abcnews.go.com/GMA/story?id=126698&page=1, accessed October 21, 2015.

27. Michael Klarman, *From the Closet to the Altar: Courts, Backlash and the Struggle for Gay Marriage* (New York: Oxford University Press, 2013), 187.

28. Pew Research Center, "State Policies on Same-sex Marriage Over Time," June 26, 2015, http://www.pewforum.org/2015/06/26/same-sex-marriage-state-by-state/, accessed October 21, 2015.

29. Ibid.

30. David W. Chen, "New Jersey Court Backs Full Rights for Gay Couples," *New York Times*, October 26, 2006, http://www.nytimes.com/2006/10/26/nyregion/26marriage.html?pagewanted=all, accessed February 10, 2015.

31. The ban reappeared on the ballot in 2008, when it passed. Jesse McKinley, "Same-Sex Marriage on the Ballot in Arizona, a Second Time," *New York Times*, October 29, 2008, http://www.nytimes.com/2008/10/30/us/politics/30marriage.html, accessed February 10, 2015.

32. Anthony Faiola, "N.H. Lawmakers Approve Civil Unions," *Washington Post*, April 26, 2007, http://www.washingtonpost.com/wp-dyn/content/article/2007/04/26/AR2007042601192.html, accessed February 10, 2015.

33. Robert D. McFadden, "Gay Marriage Ruled as Legal in Connecticut," *New York Times*, October 10, 2008, http://www.nytimes.com/2008/10/11/nyregion/11marriage.html?pagewanted=all, accessed February 10, 2015.

34. Jill Tucker, "Schwarzenegger Vetoes Same-Sex Marriage Bill Again," *San Francisco Chronicle*, October 12, 2007, http://www.sfgate.com/bayarea/article/Schwarzenegger-vetoes-same-sex-marriage-bill-again-2497886.php, accessed February 10, 2015.

35. Adam Liptak, "California Supreme Court Overturns Same-Sex Marriage Ban," *New York Times*, May 16, 2008, http://www.nytimes.com/2008/05/16/us/16marriage.html?pagewanted=all, accessed February 10, 2015.

36. *Obergefell v. Hodges* (2015), http://www.supremecourt.gov/opinions/14pdf/14-556_3204.pdf, accessed July 31, 2015.

37. "Religious Beliefs Underpin Opposition to Homosexuality," Pew Research Center, 2003, http://www.pewforum.org/2003/11/18/religious-beliefs-underpin-opposition-to-homosexuality/, accessed December 21, 2015.

38. Gallup (53 percent), CNN (51 percent), ABC News and *The Washington Post* (53 percent), and PRRI (51 percent) all found majority support for same-sex marriage in the spring of 2011.

39. "American Values Atlas," PRRI, http://ava.publicreligion.org/#lgbt/2014/States/lgbt_ssm/2, accessed March 25, 2014.

40. See Robert P. Jones, Daniel Cox, and Juhem Navarro Rivera, *A Shifting Landscape: A Decade of Change in American Attitudes about Same-sex Marriage and LGBT Issues* (Washington, DC: Public Religion Research Institute, 2014), http://publicreligion.org/research/2014/02/2014-lgbt-survey/, accessed October 21, 2015.

41. See http://publicreligion.org/2015/04/map-every-states-opinion-on-same-sex-marriage/, accessed October 21, 2015.

42. It is likely that Jewish Americans were also among the most supportive groups in 2003, but there are no surveys from the early 2000s with reliable Jewish subsamples.

43. Pew Research Center, October 2003, http://www.pewforum.org/2003/11/18/religious-beliefs-underpin-opposition-to-homosexuality/, accessed on October 21, 2015.

44. All results are from PRRI, American Values Atlas, 2014. Because the survey was conducted in English and Spanish only, results for smaller religious subgroups in which other language preferences are significant—such as Hindus, Buddhists, and Muslims—should be interpreted with some caution.

45. PRRI, LGBT Issues and Trends Survey, February 2014, http://publicreligion.org/research/2014/02/2014-lgbt-survey/, accessed July 31, 2015.

46. The 2012 American Values Survey found the top three reasons Americans cited for leaving their childhood faith were that they no longer believed in God or the teachings of their former faith, they disliked organized religion or believed it caused problems, or because of personal experiences—they grew out of it.

47. Even a decade ago, Michael Hout and Claude Fischer found that the conservative stance some religious organizations took on gay and lesbian issues was an important reason why some Americans were disaffiliating. Michael Hout and Claude S. Fischer, "Why More Americans Have No Religious Preference: Politics and Generations," *American Sociological Review* 67, no. 2 (2002): 165–90.

48. David Kinnaman, *UnChristian: What a New Generation Really Things About Christianity . . . And Why It Matters* (Grand Rapids: Baker, 2007), 17, 28.

49. Putnam and Campbell, *American Grace: How Religion Divides and Unites Us,* 130.

50. Robert P. Jones, Daniel Cox, and Juhem Navarro-Rivera, "A Shifting Landscape: A Decade of Change in American Attitudes About Same-Sex Marriage and LGBT Issues," Washington, DC: Public Religion Research Institute, February 2014, http://publicreligion.org/research/2014/02/2014-lgbt-survey/, accessed March 25, 2015.

51. Note that this survey was not large enough to break out responses of Mormons separately.

52. David Masci and Michael Lipka, "Where Christian churches, other religions stand on Gay Marriage," Fact Tank: News in the Numbers, Pew Research Center, July 2, 2015, http://www.pewresearch.org/fact-tank/2015/07/02/where-christian-churches-stand-on-gay-marriage/, accessed July 31, 2015.

53. General Assembly of the Disciples of Christ, "GA-1327—Becoming a People of Grace and Welcome to All," July 2013, http://disciples.org/Portals/0/PDF/ga/2013/resolutions/GA1327-BecomingAPeopleOfGraceAndWelcomeToAll-Final.pdf, accessed July 31, 2015.

54. Diane Degnan, "General Conference 2016 Delegates Allotted, with U.S. at 58.3 and Africa at 30 percent," UMC Connections, November 14, 2013, http://umcconnections.org/2013/11/14/general-conference-2016-delegates-allotted/, accessed August 16, 2015.

55. Robert P. Jones, "Attitudes on Same-Sex Marriage by Religious Affiliation and Denominational Family," PRRI, April 22, 2015, http://publicreligion.org/2015/04/attitudes-on-same-sex-marriage-by-religious-affiliation-and-denominational-family/, accessed July 31, 2015; PRRI, American Values Atlas, 2014.

56. Sarah Pulliam, "Richard Cizik Resigns from the National Association of Evangelicals," *Christianity Today*, December 11, 2008, http://www .christianitytoday.com/ct/2008/decemberweb-only/150-42.0.html, accessed July 31, 2015.

57. "Evangelicals Respond to SCOTUS Ruling for Equality," RISE Network, June 29, 2015, http://www.evangelicalresponse.com/, accessed July 31, 2015.

58. David P. Gushee, *Changing Our Mind* (Canton, MI: Read the Spirit Books, 2014). Disclosure: David Gushee is a former PRRI board member.

59. Matthew Vines, *God and the Gay Christian: The Biblical Case in Support of Same-Sex Relationships* (New York: Convergent Books, 2014).

60. Sarah Pulliam Bailey, "From Franklin Graham to Tony Campolo, Some Evangelical Leaders Are Splitting over Gay Marriage," *Washington Post*, June 9, 2015, http://www.washingtonpost.com/news/acts-of-faith/wp/2015/ 06/09/from-franklin-graham-to-tony-campolo-some-evangelical-leaders-are-dividing-over-gay-marriage/, accessed August 16, 2015.

61. http://www.drjamesdobson.org/news/commentaries/marriage_under_ fire, accessed March 8, 2015.

62. James Dobson, *Marriage Under Fire: Why We Must Win this Battle* (Colorado Springs, CO: Multnomah Books, 2004); "Manhattan Declaration: A Call Of Christian Conscience," *First Things*, November 20, 2009, http:// www.firstthings.com/web-exclusives/2009/11/manhattan-declaration-a-call-of-christian-conscience, accessed October 21, 2015.

63. Evangelicals and Catholics Together, "The Two Shall Become One Flesh: Reclaiming Marriage," *First Things*, March 2015, http://www.firstth ings.com/article/2015/03/the-two-shall-become-one-flesh-reclaiming-marriage-2, accessed March 15, 2015.

64. Ibid.

65. Jonathan Merritt, "Manhattan Declaration Unlikely to Inspire Young Christians," *Newsweek/Washington Post*, November 24, 2009, http:// www.faithstreet.com/onfaith/2009/11/24/manhattan-declaration-unlikely-to-inspire-young-christians/2203, accessed March 25, 2015.

66. Dan Gilgoff, "Can a Culture War Manifesto Reach a New Generation of Evangelicals and Catholics?," *U.S. News & World Report*, November 20, 2009, http://www.usnews.com/news/blogs/god-and-

country/2009/11/20/can-a-culture-war-manifesto-reach-a-new-genera tion-of-evangelicals-and-catholics, accessed March 25, 2015.

67. Russell Moore, "The Supreme Court and Same-Sex Marriage: Why This Matters for the Church," January 16, 2015, http://www.russellmoore .com/2015/01/16/the-supreme-court-and-same-sex-marriage-why-this-matters-for-the-church/, accessed March 30, 2015.

68. Russell Moore, "Same-Sex Marriage and the Future," April 5, 2014, http://www.russellmoore.com/2014/04/15/same-sex-marriage-and-the-future/, accessed March 30, 2015.

69. Russell Moore, *Onward: Engaging the Culture without Losing the Gospel* (Nashville, TN: B&H Books, 2015).

70. Ross Douthat, "The Terms of Our Surrender," *New York Times*, March 1, 2014, http://www.nytimes.com/2014/03/02/opinion/sunday/the-terms-of-our-surrender.html?_r=0, accessed March 25, 2015.

71. PRRI, Religion and Politics Tracking Survey, June 2015, http://publicreligion .org/research/2015/06/survey-majority-favor-same-sex-marriage-two-thirds-believe-supreme-court-will-rule-to-legalize/, accessed July 31, 2015.

Chapter 5: Race: Desegregating
White Christian America

1. Emily Brown, "Timeline: Michael Brown Shooting in Ferguson, MO," *USA Today*, December 2, 2014, http://www.usatoday.com/story/news/na tion/2014/08/14/michael-brown-ferguson-missouri-timeline/14051827/, accessed June 9, 2015.

2. Monica Davey and Julie Bosman, "Protests Flare After Ferguson Police Officer Is Not Indicted," *New York Times*, November 24, 2014, http:// www.nytimes.com/2014/11/25/us/ferguson-darren-wilson-shooting-michael-brown-grand-jury.html, accessed June 9, 2015.

3. J. David Goodman and Al Baker, "Wave of Protests After Grand Jury Doesn't Indict Officer in Eric Garner Chokehold Case," *New York Times*, December 4, 2014, http://www.nytimes.com/2014/12/04/nyregion/grand-jury-said-to-bring-no-charges-in-staten-island-chokehold-death-of-eric-garner.html, accessed June 9, 2015.

4. Nancy Scola, "Watch as Twitter shifts from "#BlackLivesMatter" to "#ICantBreathe"—and back again," *Washington Post*, December 5, 2014, http://www.washingtonpost.com/blogs/the-switch/wp/2014/12/05/watch-as-twitter-shifts-from-blacklivesmatter-to-icantbreathe-and-back-again/, accessed on April 23, 2015.

5. Eliott McLaughlin and Holly Yan, "Ferguson: Man Admits Shooting, Denies He Aimed for Officers," *CNN*, March 16, 2015, http://www.cnn.com/2015/03/16/us/ferguson-police-shot-arrest/ accessed June 9, 2015.

6. For the full post with comments, see https://www.facebook.com/franklingraham/posts/883361438386705/, accessed on April 23, 2015.

7. Bob Smietana, "Obeying Police is Not Enough, Group of Diverse Religious Leaders Tell Franklin Graham," *Christianity Today*, March 21, 2015, http://www.christianitytoday.com/gleanings/2015/march/obeying-police-franklin-graham-sojourners-ferguson.html, accessed April 23, 2015.

8. Ross Douthat, "God and Politics," *New York Times*, April 18, 2009, http://www.nytimes.com/2009/04/19/books/review/Douthat-t.html?pagewanted=all&_r=0, accessed June 9, 2015.

9. Michael Chapman, "Rev. Franklin Graham: Islam is a Religion of War," *CNS*, December 10, 2014, http://www.cnsnews.com/blog/michael-w-chapman/rev-franklin-graham-islam-religion-war, accessed June 9, 2015.

10. Lisa Sharon Harper, "An Open Letter to Franklin Graham," March 19, 2015, http://sojo.net/blogs/2015/03/19/open-letter-franklin-graham, accessed April 23, 2015.

11. Email to the author from Betsy Shirley, associate editor, *Sojourner's*, April 23, 2015.

12. *The New York Times* notes that in the prime adult years of 25–64, nearly one in twelve black men are behind bars. See Justin Wolfers, David Leonhardt, and Kevin Quealy, "1.5 Million Missing Black Men," *New York Times*, April 20, 2015, http://www.nytimes.com/interactive/2015/04/20/upshot/missing-black-men.html?abt=0002&abg=0, accessed August 17, 2015.

13. James Gerken, "Time Magazine Cover Harkens Back to 1968," *Huffington Post*, April 30, 2015, http://www.huffingtonpost.com/2015/04/30/time-magazine-cover-baltimore_n_7180698.html, accessed June 9, 2015.

14. https://twitter.com/RickWarren/status/631761407105634304, accessed August 17, 2015.

15. Perry Stein, " 'Black Lives Matter' Sign at a Maryland Church Defaced a Second Time," *Huffington Post*, August 11, 2015, http://www.washing tonpost.com/news/local/wp/2015/08/11/black-lives-matter-sign-at-a-maryland-church-defaced-a-second-time/, accessed August 17, 2015.

16. Chris Moody, "O'Malley Apologizes for Saying 'All Lives Matter' at Liberal Conference," CNN, July 19, 2015, http://www.cnn.com/2015/07/18/politics/martin-omalley-all-lives-matter/, accessed August 17, 2015.

17. Michael Wines and Sarah Cohen, "Police Killings Rise Slightly, Though Increased Focus May Suggest Otherwise," *New York Times*, April 30, 2015.

18. Julie Hirschfeld Davis and Matt Apuzzo, "President Obama Condemns Both the Baltimore Riots and the Nation's 'Slow-Rolling Crisis,'" *New York Times*, April 28, 2015.

19. ABC News/*Washington Post* Surveys, 1992–2012; PRRI Surveys, 2013–2015.

20. Franklin Graham's eruption on Facebook was hardly an aberration; as the national debate about race relations unfolded, Dinesh D'Souza, a Christian conservative firebrand, compared the looting of stores in Ferguson to the beheading of Christians by Islamic extremists in Syria and Iraq. See Jay Wang, "Conservative Firebrand Compares Ferguson Protestors to ISIS," August 23, 2014, http://www.msnbc.com/conservative-fire brand-compares-ferguson-protestors-to-isis/, accessed June 16, 2015.

21. For a more in-depth take on these issues, see my column in *The Atlantic*. Robert P. Jones, "Self-Segregation: Why It's So Hard for Whites to Understand Ferguson," *The Atlantic*, August 21, 2014, http://www.the atlantic.com/national/archive/2014/08/self-segregation-why-its-hard-for-whites-to-understand-ferguson/378928/, accessed May 30, 2015. See also Robert P. Jones, Daniel Cox, and Juhem Navarro-Rivera, "Beyond Guns and God: Understanding the Complexities of the White Working Class in America," Washington, DC: Public Religion Research Institute, September 2012, http://publicreligion.org/research/2012/09/race-class-culture-survey-2012/, accessed May 30, 2015.

22. Garrett Power, "Apartheid Baltimore Style: The Residential Segregation Ordinances of 1910–1913," 42 *Maryland Law Review* 289 (1983), http://digitalcommons.law.umaryland.edu/mlr/vol42/iss2/4.

23. Antero Pietila, *Not My Neighborhood: How Bigotry Shaped a Great American City* (New York: Ivan R. Dee, 2010).

24. Alissa Scheller, "6 Maps That Show How Deeply Segregated Baltimore Is," *Huffington Post*, April 28, 2015, http://www.huffingtonpost.com/2015/04/28/baltimore-segregated-maps-riots_n_7163248.html, accessed June 9, 2015.

25. Marc H. Morial et al., *2015 State of Black America* (Washington, DC: National Urban League, 2015).

26. Stephen Gandel, "The Economic Imbalance Fueling Ferguson's Unrest," *Fortune Magazine*, August 15, 2014.

27. Christopher Ingraham, "14 Baltimore Neighborhoods Have Lower Life Expectancies than North Korea," *Washington Post*, April 30, 2015, http://www.washingtonpost.com/blogs/wonkblog/wp/2015/04/30/baltimores-poorest-residents-die-20-years-earlier-than-its-richest/, accessed May 1, 2015.

28. Jennifer Harvey, *Dear White Christians: For Those Still Longing for Racial Reconciliation* (Grand Rapids: William B. Eerdmans, 2014), 78–79.

29. For more on the methodology of analyzing core social networks, see Robert P. Jones, "Race and Americans' Core Social Networks," PRRI blog, August 28, 2014, http://publicreligion.org/research/2014/08/analysis-social-network/, accessed April 30, 2015.

30. Robert P. Jones, "Self-Segregation."

31. *What American Workers Really Think About Religion: Tanenbaum's 2013 Survey of American Workers and Religion* (Boston: Tanenbaum Center for Religious Understanding, 2013). The underlying national survey of American workers was conducted by PRRI. Report available at https://tanenbaum.org/publications/2013-survey/, accessed May 21, 2015.

32. Bureau of Labor Statistics, United States Department of Labor, January 23, 2015, http://www.bls.gov/news.release/union2.nr0.htm, accessed May 21, 2015.

33. U.S. Department of Education, National Center for Education Statistics, Common Core of Data (CCD), "State Nonfiscal Survey of Public Elementary and Secondary Education," 2001–02 and 2011–12, https://nces .ed.gov/programs/coe/indicator_cge.asp, accessed May 21, 2015.

34. Gary Orfield and Erica Frankenberg, with Jongyeon Ee and John Kuscera, *Brown at 60: Great Progess, a Long Retreat, and an Uncertain Future*, white paper by the UCLA Civil Rights Project, May 2014, http:// civilrightsproject.ucla.edu/reseach/k-12-education/integration-and-diversity/brown-at-60-great-progress-a-long-retreat-and-an-uncertain-future/Brown-at-60-051814.pdf, accessed May 25, 2014.

35. Ibid., 10.

36. Sarah Carr, "In Southern Towns, 'Segregation Academies' Are Still Going Strong," *The Atlantic*, December 13, 2012, http://www.theatlantic.com/ national/archive/2012/12/in-southern-towns-segregation-academies-are-still-going-strong/266207/, accessed October 20, 2015.

37. Robert Putnam, *Bowling Alone: The Collapse and Revival of American Community* (New York: Simon & Schuster, 2000).

38. Hymn #317, *Glory to God—The Presbyterian Hymnal* (Louisville: Presbyterian Publishing, 2013). Full lyrics are online here: http://www.hym nary.org/hymn/GG2013/317, accessed April 30, 2015.

39. Niebuhr wrote *The Social Sources of Denominationalism* in 1929 after finding his attempts to explain to his students the differences between Christian denominations by referring to doctrine alone an "artificial and fruitless" approach. Although church insiders often articulated and justified schisms in theological terms, Niebuhr concluded that secular social dynamics, not principled theological squabbles, were the real drivers of Christian factionalism. H. Richard Niebuhr, *The Social Sources of Denominationalism* (Gloucester, MA: Peter Smith, 1987 [1929]).

40. Ibid., 6.

41. Ibid., 239. Niebuhr relied here on the U.S. Religious Census of 1926, a tabulation of nationwide data on religious bodies conducted by the U.S. Census Department, and on the *Negro Year Book, 1925–26*, complied by sociologist Monroe Work at the Tuskegee Institute.

42. For a full transcript of King's Western Michigan University speech and the Q&A following it, see http://www.wmich.edu/sites/default/files/attach ments/MLK.pdf, accessed April 17, 2105. Although King is often credited with coining the idea of Sunday morning as the most segregated hour in American life, this insight was expressed a decade earlier by Helen Kenyon, a moderator of the Congregational Christian Churches and board member of the National Council of Churches. See "Worship Hour Found Time of Segregation," *New York Times*, November 4, 1952, p. 26.

43. Joseph Barndt, *Becoming an Anti-Racist Church: Journeying Toward Wholeness* (Minneapolis, MN Fortress Press, 2011).

44. Stephen R. Haynes, *The Last Segregated Hour: The Memphis Kneel-ins and the Campaign for Southern Church Desegregation* (New York: Oxford University Press, 2012).

45. Charles Brown, "The Epic of Ashton Jones: Dixie-Born White Minister Leads One-Man Crusade for Interracial Brotherhood," *Ebony*, October 1965, accessed June 9, 2015.

46. Mark Chaves and Shawna Anderson, "Changing American Congregations: Findings from the Third Wave of the National Congregations Study," *Journal for the Scientific Study of Religion* 53 (2014): 676–86.

47. C. C. Goen, *Broken Churches, Broken Nation: Denominational Schisms and the Coming of the Civil War* (Macon, GA: Mercer University Press, 1997).

48. Ibid. The Presbyterian case is more complicated, involving deep theological differences over what constitutes conversion and over the legitimacy of revival methods. While full reunification did not occur until the 1983 creation of the Presbyterian Church (USA), the northern and southern groups of each respective theological faction reunited shortly after the Civil War.

49. L. Tuffly Ellis, ed., Texas State Historical Association, *The Southwestern Historical Quarterly* 83 (July 1979–April 1980), http://texashistory.unt .edu/ark:/67531/metapth101207/, accessed May 06, 2015, 34–35.

50. Barry Hankins and Thomas Kidd, "Southern Baptists Cleanse Past," *USA Today*, June 24, 2012, http://usatoday30.usatoday.com/news/opinion/

forum/story/2012-06-24/religion-southern-baptist-luter-slavery/
55796742/1, accessed June 9, 2015.

51. Thomas S. Kidd and Barry Hankins, *Baptists in America: A History* (Oxford: Oxford University Press, 2015), 224.

52. Ibid., 226–27.

53. Andrew Michael Manis, *Southern Civil Religions in Conflict: Civil Rights and the Culture Wars* (Macon, GA: Mercer University Press, 2002), 96.

54. Hudgins was one of the most influential men in the state during the civil rights years. He served as chaplain of the Mississippi Highway Safety Patrol, director of the Jackson Chamber of Commerce, member of both the Masonic Order and the Chamber of Commerce, and president of the Jackson Rotary Club. See University of Virginia, Lived Theology Project, http://archives.livedtheology.org/node/2383, accessed May 30, 2015.

55. Kidd and Hankins, *Baptists in America*, 221.

56. John Lee Eighmy, *Churches in Cultural Captivity: A History of the Social Attitudes of Southern Baptists* (Knoxville: University of Tennessee Press, 1988).

57. Peter Applebome, "Jerry Falwell, Moral Majority Founder, Dies at 73," *New York Times*, May 16, 2007, http://www.nytimes.com/2007/05/16/obituaries/16falwell.html?pagewanted=print&_r=0, accessed February 9, 2015.

58. Will Campbell, T. B. Maston, Clarence Jordan, and Foy Valentine were all voices for racial equality within the Southern Baptist world.

59. Matthew Avery Sutton, *American Apocalypse: A History of Modern Evangelicalism* (Cambridge: Harvard University Press, 2014), 334.

60. Curtis J. Evans, White Evangelical Protestant Responses to the Civil Rights Movement, *Harvard Theological Review* 102 (2009): 245–73; Mark G. Toulouse, *God in Public: Four Ways American Christianity and Public Life Relate* (Louisville: Westminster John Knox Press, 2006), 93.

61. Randall Balmer, *Thy Kingdom Come: How the Religious Right Distorts the Faith and Threatens America* (New York: Basic Books, 2006), 15. As Balmer notes, Weyrich was also a Republican political operative whose activism went back as far as the 1964 Goldwater campaign. Weyrich's

account linked both the *Green* decision of 1973 and the IRS action against Bob Jones University in 1975 to Jimmy Carter, although they predated his presidency.

62. Southern Baptist Convention, "Resolution on Racial Reconciliation on the 150th Anniversary of the Southern Baptist Convention," resolution adopted at annual meeting, Atlanta, June 1995, http://www.sbc.net/reso lutions/899/resolution-on-racial-reconciliation-on-the-150th-anniver sary-of-the-southern-baptist-convention, accessed May 7, 2015.

63. Karen Willoughby, "Historic: Fred Luter Elected SBC President," Associated Baptist Press, June 19, 2012, http://www.bpnews.net/38081, accessed June 9, 2015.

64. Amy Sullivan, "Richard Land Goes Out on the Bottom," *The New Republic*, August 7, 2012, http://www.newrepublic.com/article/105852/amy-sullivan-richard-land-goes-out-bottom, accessed May 10, 2015.

65. Travis Loller, "Southern Baptist Convention's Leader Criticizes Trayvon Martin Support," The Associated Press, in *Kingsport Times-News*, April 14, 2012, http://www.timesnews.net/article/9045307/southern-baptist-convention39s-leader-criticizes-trayvon-martin-support, accessed May 10, 2015.

66. David Gibson, "Southern Baptists' Richard Land Loses Show, Keeps Job," *Washington Post*, June 3, 2012, http://www.washingtonpost.com/national/on-faith/southern-baptists-richard-land-loses-show-keeps-job/2012/06/01/gJQARgQf7U_story.html, accessed May 10, 2015.

67. Adele Banks, "Richard Land to Retire: Southern Baptist Leader Will Step Down Following Ethics Probe," Religion News Service, August 1, 2012, http://www.huffingtonpost.com/2012/08/01/richard-land-retire-southern-baptist-leader-step-down-after-ethics-probe_n_1730636.html, accessed June 9, 2015.

68. SBC Ethics and Religious Liberty Commission, "ERLC's Russell Moore Responds to Eric Garner Case," press release, December 3, 2014, http://erlc.com/article/erlcs-russell-moore-responds-to-eric-garner-case, accessed May 10, 2015.

69. Staff Writer, "Southern Baptist Leaders Call for Integration Within Churches," *Christianity Today*, January 27, 2015.

70. Lilly Workneh, "Two Florida Churches Merge with the Hope of Bridging the Racial Divide," *Huffington Post*, November 30, 2014, http://www.huff ingtonpost.com/2014/11/30/church-merger-racial-divide_n_6204244 .html, accessed June 9, 2015.

71. "Southern Baptists Meet During Challenging Times," Associated Press, June 19, 2012, http://accesswdun.com/print/2012/6/249806, accessed May 10, 2015.

72. Heidi Hall, "Southern Baptist Race Summit Calls for Focus on Reconciliation," Religion News Service, March 26, 2015, http://www.religionnews .com/2015/03/26/southern-baptist-race-summit-calls-focus-reconcilia tion/, accessed June 9, 2015.

73. Emma Green, "Southern Baptists and the Sin of Racism," *The Atlantic*, April 7, 2015, http://www.theatlantic.com/politics/archive/2015/04/southern-baptists-wrestle-with-the-sin-of-racism/389808/, accessed June 9, 2015.

74. Hall, "Southern Baptist Summit Calls for Focus on Reconciliation," accessed June 9, 2015.

75. Martin Luther King, Jr., "Letter from Birmingham Jail," *The Christian Century*, June 12, 1963, http://www.christiancentury.org/sites/default/ files/downloads/resources/mlk-letter.pdf, accessed May 10, 2015.

76. Robert Westbrook, "MLK's Manifesto," *The Christian Century*, April 8, 2013, http://www.christiancentury.org/article/2013-03/mlk-s-manifesto, accessed June 9, 20115.

77. Walter Rauschenbusch, *Christianity and the Social Crisis* (Louisville: Westminster John Knox Press, 1992 [1907]). Rauschenbusch's words above are still cited prominently as the theological cornerstone of the National Council of Churches on its website today. See http://national councilofchurches.us/about/history.php, accessed May 10, 2015.

78. W. E. Orser, "Racial Attitudes in Wartime: The Protestant Churches During the Second World War," *Church History* 41, no. 3 (September 1972): 337–53.

79. Stanley Pieza, "Rev. King Urges Boycott by Churches to Fight Bias," *Chicago's American*, January 16, 1963.

80. Gardiner H. Shattuck, Jr., *Episcopalians and Race: Civil War to Civil Rights* (Lexington: University of Kentucky Press, 2000), 67.

81. Ibid., 95–98.

82. Ibid., 136.

83. National Council of Churches, "In Wake of Zimmerman Acquittal, NCC Calls for Racial Justice," press release, July 15, 2013, http://www.national councilofchurches.us/news/zimmermanjuly2013.php, accessed May 10, 2015.

84. National Council of Churches, "National Council of Churches Statement on the Grand Jury Action in Ferguson, Mo.," press release, November 2014, http://www.nationalcouncilofchurches.us/news/2014-11ferguson noindictment.php, accessed May 21, 2015.

85. National Council of Churches, "National Council of Churches Calls for Accountability," press release December 2014, http://www.nationalcouncilof churches.us/news/2014-12ericgarnerstatement.php, accessed May 21, 2015.

86. National Council of Churches, "NCC Calls for Justice, End to Violence in Baltimore," press release, April 2015, http://nationalcouncilofchurches .us/news/2015-4_Baltimore.php, accessed May 21, 2015.

87. For a full historical timeline, see http://www.collegiatechurch.org/ ?q=content/historical-timeline, accessed May 1, 2015.

88. Middle's current location in the East Village, completed in 1892, represents its third location.

89. Frank Bruni, "An Old-Time Religion Gets Some New Twists; Child Care, Unisex Prayers and More Attract Parishioners to Failing Church," *New York Times*, November 8, 1996.

90. For Reverend Dragt's first-person account of the transformation of the church, see Gordon R. Dragt, *One Foot Planted in the Center, the Other Dangling Off the Edge: How Intentional Leadership Can Transform Your Church* (Salt Lake City: American Book Publishing, 2009), 23.

91. Bruni, "An Old-Time Religion Gets Some New Twists."

92. Albert Amateaux, "Pastor Is Breaking New Ground at Middle Collegiate," *The Villager* 75, no. 17, September 14–20, 2005.

93. Jacqueline Lewis, "Cracked Wide Open Around Race," *Huffington Post*, December 3, 2014, http://www.huffingtonpost.com/the-rev-jacqueline-j-lewis-phd/cracked-wide-open-around-race_b_6265242.html, accessed May 1, 2015.

94. "Standing with Ferguson: A Benefit for Youth Activists," http://www
.middlechurch.org/about/calendar/2014/11/19/standing-with-fergu-
son-benefit-for-youth-activists, accessed June 9, 2015.

95. Lewis, "Cracked Wide Open Around Race."

96. Jacqueline Lewis, "The Longest Four Minutes of My Life," http://www.
middlechurch.org/about/blogs/jacquis-blog/the-longest-four-minutes-
of-my-life, accessed May 1, 2015. See also Wesley Lowery, " 'Black Lives
Matter' Protesters Stage 'Die-in' in Capitol Hill Cafeteria," *Washington
Post,* January 21, 2015.

97. Jacqueline Lewis, "One Day, When the Glory Comes, It Will Be Ours,"
Huffington Post, April 28, 2015, http://www.huffingtonpost.com/the-
rev-jacqueline-j-lewis-phd/one-day-when-the-glory-comes-it-will-be-
ours_b_7164160.html, accessed May 1, 2015.

98. Alverta Wright, *Not Here by Chance: The Story of Oakhurst Baptist
Church* (Decatur, GA: Oakhurst Baptist Church, 1988), p. 87. One of
the other churches that was created from this early collaboration was
Oakhurst Presbyterian Church, a church with its own remarkable journey of moving from being a white southern church to an integrated multicultural church. See Nibs Stroupe and Caroline Leach, *O Lord, Hold
Our Hands: How a Church Thrives in a Multicultural World—The Story
of Oakhurst Presbyterian Church* (Louisville, Westminster John Knox
Press, 2003).

99. Wright, *Not Here by Chance,* 194.

100. Ibid., 200.

101. Ibid., 213.

102. Ibid., 226.

103. Ibid., 226–227.

104. Walker L. Knight, *Struggle for Integrity* (Waco: Word, 1969).

105. Bob Allen, "Oakhurst Baptist Church Celebrates 100 Years," Baptist News
Global, September 20, 2013, http://baptistnews.com/ministry/congre
gations/item/8867-oakhurst-baptist-church-celebrates-100-years, accessed
May 1, 2015.

106. Oakhurst has also launched a number of programs to address issues in
its neighborhood and congregation. In the 1990s, Oakhurst established

programs for people struggling with addiction. It also embarked on accessibility and engagement plans for those with mental and physical disabilities. In 2010, Oakhurst entered into a space-sharing arrangement with Georgia Chin Baptist Church, a church of approximately one hundred members, primarily recent immigrants from Myanmar. By 2015, the group had grown to nearly three hundred.

107. "He Included Me," http://www.hymnary.org/media/fetch/146621, accessed May 1, 2015.

108. "Obituary: John Cross Jr., Pastor of Church Bombed in Civil Rights Clashes," *Boston Globe*, November 18, 2007, http://www.boston.com/bostonglobe/obituaries/articles/2007/11/18/john_cross_jr_pastor_of_church_bombed_in_civil_rights_clashes/, accessed May 1, 2015.

109. Michael O. Emerson with Rodney M. Woo, *People of the Dream: Multiracial Congregations in the United States* (Princeton: Princeton University Press, 2006).

110. Harvey, *Dear White Christians*, 250.

111. Ibid., 2–3.

112. Ibid., 5.

113. George Yancey and Judith Butler, "What's Wrong with 'All Lives Matter,'" *New York Times*, January 12, 2015, http://opinionator.blogs.nytimes.com/2015/01/12/whats-wrong-with-all-lives-matter/?_r=1, accessed August 17, 2015.

114. Harvey, *Dear White Christians*, 5.

115. Ibid., 72.

116. William Faulkner, *Requiem for a Nun* (New York: Vintage, 2012 [1951]).

117. Clifford Grammich et al., "U.S. Religion Census: Religious Congregations and Membership Study," Association of Statisticians of American Religious Bodies (2010), http://www.rcms2010.org/, accessed May 21, 2015.

118. Kevin R. Kosar, "The U.S. Postal Service: Common Questions About Post Office Closures," Congressional Research Service, June 13, 2012, https://fas.org/sgp/crs/misc/R41950.pdf, accessed May 21, 2015.

119. Emerson with Woo, *People of the Dream*, 43–44.

120. Emerson et al., 95.

121. Ibid., 162–63.

122. There is some evidence that congregational racial diversity alone may not be enough to shift attitudes of white congregants. Drawing on data from the 1998 and 2006 waves of the General Social Survey and the 2012 National Congregations Study, Samuel L. Perry and colleagues found that at least at the aggregate level and on one composite measure— affirming structural explanations for racial inequality—attendance at a multiracial congregation alone had no impact on white congregants' attitudes. See Samuel Perry, Ryan J. Cobb, Kevin D. Dougherty, "United by Faith? Race/Ethnicity, Congregational Diversity, and Explanations of Racial Inequality," *Sociology of Religion* 76:2 (January 2015): 177–198.

123. Elizabeth Bristow, "Russell Moore Responds to Eric Garner Case," SBC Ethics and Religious Liberty Commission blog, December 3, 2014, http://erlc.com/article/erlcs-russell-moore-responds-to-eric-garner-case, accessed May 22, 2015.

Chapter 6: A Eulogy for White Christian America

1. Elisabeth Kübler-Ross, *On Death and Dying: What the Dying Have to Teach Doctors, Nurses, Clergy, and Their Own Families* (New York: Macmillan, 1969).

2. Ibid., 52–53.

3. Ibid., 64.

4. Elesha Coffman, *The Christian Century and the Rise of the Protestant Mainline* (Oxford: Oxford University Press, 2013).

5. Charles Clayton Morrison, quoted in "Religion: Protestant Prescription," *Time*, July 8, 1946.

6. Ibid. Morrison's full series was subsequently published in a book. See Charles Clayton Morrison, *Can Protestantism Win America?* (New York: Harper, 1948).

7. David Roozen noted that a combination of the suddenness of the losses and a lack of solid data created a decade-long lag before the trends that began in 1965 were unequivocally accepted: "Unlike the immediate awareness and

response typically related to an earthquake, it was not until the mid-1970s that the mainline decline was widely accepted as a 'new' reality that demanded attention." David A. Roozen, "Denominations Grow as Individuals Join Congregations," in David A Roozen and C. Kirk Hadaway, *Church and Denominational Growth* (Nashville: Abingdon, 1993), 15.

8. The Institute on Religion and Democracy, "Our History," https://theird .org/about/our-history/, accessed June 24, 2015.

9. "'Mainline' Reform Leaders Call for Dissolution of the National Council of Churches," press release, Institute on Religion and Democracy, November 21, 1999, http://listserv.virtueonline.org/pipermail/virtue online_listserv.virtueonline.org/1999-November/000874.html, accessed May 29, 2015.

10. The Institute on Religion and Democracy, "Our Team," https://theird .org/about/our-team/, accessed June 24, 2015.

11. Mark Tooley, "Remarks to the IRD Board," March 14, 2010, https:// theird.org/about/our-history/mark-tooley-remarks-to-the-ird-board-march-14/, accessed May 28, 2015.

12. Mark Tooley, "Mainline Protestant Decline and Hope," speech delivered at Mount Bethel United Methodist Church, Marietta, Georgia, February 18, 2015, http://juicyecumenism.com/2015/02/19/mainline-protestant-decline-and-hope/, accessed May 29, 2015.

13. Ed Stetzer, "The Southern Baptist Decline Continues—And Accelerates," June, 11, 2015, http://betweenthetimes.com/index.php/2015/06/11/the-southern-baptist-decline-continues/, accessed June 15, 2015; Travis Loller, "Southern Baptist Convention Membership Declined for Seventh Year," Associated Press/*Huffington Post*, May 29, 2014, http://www.huffing tonpost.com/2014/05/29/southern-baptist-convention-membership-decline_n_5411695.html, accessed May 29, 2014.

14. "About Dr. Richard Land," https://www.google.com/webhp?sourceid= chrome-instant&ion=1&espv=2&ie=UTF-8#q=richard%20land, accessed June 24, 2015.

15. Pew Forum on Religion and Public Life, "America's Changing Religious Landscape," May 12, 2015, http://www.pewforum.org/2015/05/ 12/americas-changing-religious-landscape/, accessed June 24, 2015.

16. Richard Land, "Cultural Christianity vs. Convictional Christianity," May 26, 2015, http://www.drrichardland.com/press/entry/cultural-christianity-vs.-convictional-christianity, accessed June 24, 2015.

17. Vincent Funaro, "Christianity Is Not Dying; Reports Pointing to Decline of Church Are Skewing Data, Says Baylor University Scholars," *The Christian Post*, May 13, 2015, http://www.christianpost.com/news/christianity-is-not-dying-reports-pointing-to-decline-of-church-are-skewing-data-says-baylor-university-scholars-139069/, accessed May 30, 2015.

18. Christian Smith, *American Evangelicalism: Embattled and Thriving* (Chicago: University of Chicago Press, 1998).

19. Curtis Mitchell, *God in the Garden: The Story of the 1957 Billy Graham New York Crusade* (Garden City: Doubleday, 1957).

20. Ross Douthat recently summarized the appeal of Graham's approach as being "ecumenical, openhanded, confident, American." See Ross Douthat, *Bad Religion: How We Became a Nation of Heretics* (New York: Free Press, 2012), 35.

21. "Billy Graham, Pastor to Presidents," Billy Graham Evangelistic Association, http://billygraham.org/story/billy-graham-pastor-to-presidents-2/, accessed May 30, 2015.

22. "Franklin Graham, The Hell-Raising Evangelist's Son," CBS News, April 20, 2012, http://www.cbsnews.com/news/franklin-graham-the-hell-raising-evangelists-son/, accessed September 3, 2015.

23. Todd Sumlin, "Franklin Graham Takes Pay He Once Gave Up," *Charlotte Observer*, August 5, 2015, http://www.charlotteobserver.com/living/religion/article30505932.html, accessed September 3, 2015.

24. Miranda Blue, "Franklin Graham Exhorts Pastors: 'Don't Shut Up' About Homosexuality and Abortion," *Right Wing Watch*, March 16, 2015, http://www.rightwingwatch.org/content/franklin-graham-exhorts-pastors-dont-shut-about-homosexuality-and-abortion, accessed June 24, 2015.

25. Kevin Eckstrom, "Franklin Graham: Putin Is Better on Gay Issues than Obama," Religion News Service, March 14, 2014, http://www.religionnews.com/2014/03/14/franklin-graham-putin-better-gay-issues-obama/, accessed May 30, 2015.

26. Ruth Gledhill, "Franklin Graham: 'Islam Is a Religion of War,'" *Christianity Today*, December 6, 2014, http://www.christiantoday.com/article/franklin .graham.islam.is.a.religion.of.war/43986.htm, accessed May 30, 2015.

27. David L. Chappell, *A Stone of Hope: Prophetic Religion and the Death of Jim Crow* (Chapel Hill: University of North Carolina Press, 2005), 144.

28. Brian Tashman, "Franklin Graham: Muslims Who 'Hate Israel and Hate Christians' Run the White House," *Right Wing Watch*, March 2, 2015, http://www.rightwingwatch.org/content/franklin-graham-muslims- who-hate-israel-and-hate-christians-run-white-house#sthash.EHM157Qk .dpuf, accessed May 29, 2015.

29. Brian Tashman, "Franklin Graham: Americans 'Turned Our Back on God' by Re-Electing Obama; Marriage Equality 'Takes the Family Away,'" *Right Wing Watch*, November 16, 2012, http://www.rightwingwatch.org/ content/franklin-graham-americans-turned-back-marriage-equality- family, accessed June 24, 2015.

30. Kübler-Ross, *On Death and Dying*, p. 93.

31. Alan Cooperman, "Christian Groups Trade Barbs on Their Sources of Funding," *Washington Post*, January 11, 2007, http://www.washington post.com/wp-dyn/content/article/2007/01/10/AR2007011002074.html, accessed September 8, 2015.

32. "National Council of Churches Remembers Bob Edgar," Episcopal News Service, April 24, 2013, http://www.episcopalchurch.org/library/article/ national-council-churches-remembers-bob-edgar, accessed September 8, 2015.

33. http://index.ls.state.ms.us/isysnative/UzpcRG9jdW1lbnRzXDIwMTVc cGRmXGhiXDExMDAtMTE5OVxoYjExNzlpbi5wZGY=/hb1179in .pdf#xml=http://10.240.72.35/isysquery/irl99a0/1/hilite, accessed June 24, 2015.

34. Michael Schaub, "Will the Bible Become the Official State Book of Mississippi?", *Los Angeles Times*, January 13, 2015, http://www.latimes.com/ books/jacketcopy/la-et-jc-will-the-bible-become-the-official-state- book-of-mississippi-20150113-story.html, accessed May 13, 2015.

35. State Symbols USA, http://www.statesymbolsusa.org/, accessed June 24, 2015.

36. State Symbols USA, http://www.statesymbolsusa.org/symbol-official-item/michigan/state-arts-drama-symbol-state-award-recognition/leg end-sleeping-bear, accessed June 24, 2015.

37. Secretary of the Commonwealth of Massachusetts, "State Symbols," http://www.sec.state.ma.us/, accessed June 24, 2015.

38. Alabama Department of Archives and History, "Official Symbols and Emblems of Alabama: Official Alabama State Bible," http://www.ar chives.alabama.gov/emblems/st_bible.html, accessed June 24, 2015.

39. Cassie Fambro, "Two Mississippi Democrats Propose Making Bible the State Book," AL.com, January 12, 2015, http://www.al.com/news/mo bile/index.ssf/2015/01/two_mississippi_democrats_prop.html, accessed May 13, 2015.

40. Emily Wagster Pettus, "Mississippi Lawmakers Want to Make the Bible the State Book," Associated Press/*Huffington Post*, January 13, 2015, http://www.huffingtonpost.com/2015/01/13/mississippi-bible-state-book_n_6462982.html, accessed May 14, 2015.

41. Fambro, "Two Mississippi Democrats Propose Making Bible the State Book."

42. Mississippi Legislature 2015 Regular Session, House Bill 1179, http://bill status.ls.state.ms.us/2015/pdf/history/HB/HB1179.xml, accessed June 24, 2015.

43. Michael Schaub, "Tennessee Senate Kills Proposal to Make the Bible Official State Book," *Los Angeles Times*, April 20, 2015, http://www.lat imes.com/books/jacketcopy/la-et-jc-tennessee-kills-bible-proposal-20150420-story.html, accessed June 24, 2015. Julia O'Donoughue, "Law-maker pulls bill to make Holy Bible Louisiana's official state book," *The Times-Picayune*, April 21, 2014. http://www.nola.com/politics/index .ssf/2014/04/louisiana_bible_state_book.html, accessed December 18, 2015.

44. Cassie Fambro, " 'In God We Trust' Added to Mississippi State Seal with Passage of Religious Freedom Act," AL.com, July 2, 2014, http://www .al.com/news/mobile/index.ssf/2014/07/in_god_we_trust_added_to_ missi.html, accessed June 24, 2015; Jonathan Kaminsky, "Mississippi Law-makers Want to Make Bible State's Official Book," Reuters, January 12,

2015, http://www.reuters.com/article/2015/01/13/us-usa-mississippi-bible-idUSKBN0KM03020150113, accessed May 14, 2015.

45. Mississippi Legislature 2014 Regular Session, Senate Bill 2681, http://billstatus.ls.state.ms.us/documents/2014/html/SB/2600-2699/SB2681SG.htm, accessed May 14, 2015.

46. Paresh Dave, "Miss. Governor Signs Religious Freedom Bill; Civil Rights Groups Dismayed," *Los Angeles Times*, April 4, 2014, http://articles.latimes.com/2014/apr/04/nation/la-na-nn-mississippi-governor-signs-religious-freedom-bill-20140404, accessed June 24, 2015.

47. Mississippi Legislature 2014 Regular Session, Senate Bill 2681, http://billstatus.ls.state.ms.us/2014/pdf/history/SB/SB2681.xml, accessed June 24, 2015.

48. The "About the Senator" page on Gandy's official website is dominated by a large color photo of him shaking hands with Tony Perkins at the Family Research Council award banquet where Gandy received the 2014 "John Witherspoon Award for Defending Faith, Family, and Freedom" for his work in introducing and passing the RFRA legislation; http://www.senatorphillipgandy.com/about.php, accessed May 14, 2015.

49. Governor Phil Bryant, "Mississippi Unveils New State Seal," press release, July 1, 2014, http://www.governorbryant.com/mississippi-unveils-new-state-seal/, accessed May 14, 2015.

50. Pettus, "Mississippi Lawmakers Want to Make the Bible the State Book."

51. U.S. Department of the Treasury, "History of 'In God We Trust,'" http://www.treasury.gov/about/education/Pages/in-god-we-trust.aspx, accessed May 30, 2015.

52. Jeffrey Owen Jones, "The Man Who Wrote the Pledge of Allegiance," *Smithsonian Magazine*, November 2003, http://www.smithsonianmag.com/history/the-man-who-wrote-the-pledge-of-allegiance-93907224/#XR5WxKFyWZoLEKKp.99, accessed May 30, 2015. Jones notes that although Bellamy wrote extensively about his role in creating the pledge, there is no indication in any of his papers that he ever considered adding a reference to God.

53. Kübler-Ross, *On Death and Dying*, 99.

54. Ibid., 123–24.

55. Ibid., 125.

56. Stanley Hauerwas and William H. Willimon, *Resident Aliens: Life in the Christian Colony*, 25th anniversary edition (Nashville: Abingdon, 2014).

57. Ibid., 10.

58. Ibid., 11.

59. The Gifford Lectures, "The Grain of the Universe," http://www.gif fordlectures.org/lectures/grain-universe, accessed June 24, 2015.

60. Jean Bethke Elshtain, "Theologian: Christian Contrarian," *Time* (September 17, 2001), http://content.time.com/time/magazine/arti cle/0,9171,1000859,00.html, accessed June 24, 2015.

61. I am grateful for an insightful conversation with Diana Butler Bass, in which she articulated these three contemporary responses among white mainline Protestants. Her *Christianity After Religion: The End of Church and the Birth of a New Spiritual Awakening* (New York: HarperOne, 2012) is one of the most insightful treatments of mainline struggles over the future of the church.

62. David Kuo, *Tempting Faith: An Inside Story of Political Seduction* (New York: Free Press, 2006), 242.

63. Ibid., 265.

64. Rod Dreher, "The Benedict Option: A Medieval Model Inspires Christian Community Today," *American Conservative*, December 12, 2013, http://www.theamericanconservative.com/articles/benedict-option/, accessed June 24, 2015.

65. Disclosure: David Gushee is a former board member of PRRI.

66. Russell Moore, *Onward: Engaging the Culture Without Losing the Gospel* (Nashville: B&H, 2015).

67. Russell Moore, "Is Christianity Dying?," "Moore to the Point" blog, May 15, 2015, http://www.russellmoore.com/2015/05/12/is-christianity-dying/, accessed May 30, 2015.

68. Moore, *Onward*, vii.

69. In the collection of Percy's papers, the manuscript is entitled "Some Random Thoughts About Culture, the Church, and Evangelization." See Walker Percy Papers, Circa 1910–1996, University of North Carolina, http://www2.lib.unc.edu/mss/inv/p/Percy.Walker.html#d1e2615, accessed

September 11, 2015. The remarks remained unpublished until appearing in the collection of essays following his death. See "Culture, the Church, and Evangelization," in *Signposts in a Strange Land: Essays* (New York: Picador, 2000), 295–303.

70. Walker Percy, "The Failure and the Hope," *Signposts in a Strange Land*, 328.
71. Ibid., 329.
72. Ibid.
73. Russell Moore, "The Cross and the Confederate Flag" (June 19, 2015), https://www.russellmoore.com/2015/06/19/the-cross-and-the-confederate-flag/, accessed December 18, 2015.
74. Moore, *Onward*, 221.
75. http://davidpgushee.com/, accessed June 15, 2015.
76. David P. Gushee, *The Future of Faith in American Politics: The Public Witness of the Evangelical Center* (Waco: Baylor University Press, 2008), 6.
77. Ibid., 14.
78. Ibid., 15.
79. Ibid., 221.
80. David P. Gushee, *Changing Our Mind* (Canton, MI: David Crumm Media, 2014).
81. Chuck Thompson, *Better Off Without 'Em: A Northern Manifesto for Southern Secession* (New York: Simon & Schuster, 2012), xviii.
82. Thomas Schaller, *Whistling Past Dixie: How Democrats Can Win Without the South* (New York: Simon & Schuster, 2006), 2–3.
83. Christopher Hitchens, *God Is Not Great: How Religion Poisons Everything*, (New York: Twelve, 2007).
84. Ibid.
85. Richard Dawkins, *The God Delusion* (Boston: Houghton Mifflin, 2006); Daniel Dennett, *Breaking the Spell: Religion as a Natural Phenomenon* (New York: Penguin, 2007); Sam Harris, *The End of Faith: Religion, Terror, and the Future of Reason* (New York: W. W. Norton, 2004); Sam Harris, *Letter to a Christian Nation* (New York: Alfred A. Knopf, 2006).
86. The Secular Coalition for America, for example, was founded in 2002 and opened its first office in Washington, D.C., in 2005 with a staff of one. By 2015, it had grown to six full-time staff, seventeen member

organizations, and fifty state chapters. It also counts Dawkins, Dennett, and Harris as advisory board members.

87. PRRI, American Values Atlas, 2014, http://ava.publicreligion.org/#religious/2014/States/religion/16, accessed May 28, 2015. See also Pew Research Center, http://www.pewresearch.org/fact-tank/2015/05/12/5-key-findings-u-s-religious-landscape/, accessed May 28, 2015.

88. *Huffington Post Live*, May 15, 2015, http://live.huffingtonpost.com/r/segment/rise-of-secularism-in-america/50f575d902a76015b900004f, accessed May 28, 2015.

89. Hemant Mehta, "Landmark Study Shows Remarkable Growth of Non-Religious Americans," "Friendly Atheist" blog, *Patheos*, May 12, 2015, http://www.patheos.com/blogs/friendlyatheist/2015/05/12/landmark-study-shows-remarkable-growth-of-non-religious-americans/, accessed May 28, 2015.

90. Abby Ohlheiser, "A Short History of Richard Dawkins vs. the Internet," *The Atlantic*, August 8, 2013, http://www.thewire.com/national/2013/08/short-history-richard-dawkins-vs-internet/68149/, accessed December 18, 2015.

91. Sam Harris, *The End of Faith: Religion, Terror, and the Future of Reason* (New York: W. W. Norton, 2005), 113.

92. Sam Harris, "In Defense of Profiling," April 28, 2012, http://www.samharris.org/blog/item/in-defense-of-profiling, accessed December 18, 2015.

93. Nathan Lean, "Dawkins, Harris, Hitchens: New Atheists flirt with Islamophobia," *Salon*, March 30, 2013, http://www.salon.com/2013/03/30/dawkins_harris_hitchens_new_atheists_flirt_with_islamophobia/, accessed December 18, 2015.

94. E. J. Dionne, *Souled Out: Reclaiming Faith and Politics After the Religious Right* (Princeton: Princeton University Press, 2008), 21.

95. Douthat, *Bad Religion*, 53.

96. Peter Berger, *The Sacred Canopy: Elements of a Sociological Theory of Religion* (New York: Anchor, 1967), 24.

97. Ibid., 25.

98. PRRI/RNS Religion News Survey, June 2015, http://publicreligion.org/research/2015/06/survey-americans-believe-protests-make-country-

better-support-decreases-dramatically-protesters-identified-black/, accessed September 13, 2015.

99. William H. Frey, *Diversity Explosion: How New Racial Demographics Are Remaking America* (Washington, DC: Brookings Institution Press, 2014).

100. Gushee, *The Future of Faith in American Politics*, 4.

101. Abraham Lincoln, "Second Inaugural Address," in Joint Congressional Committee on Inaugural Ceremonies, *Inaugural Addresses of the Presidents of the United States* (Washington, DC: U.S. Government Printing Office, 2001).

102. Ross Douthat, "The Terms of Our Surrender," *New York Times*, March 1, 2014, accessed March 25, 2015.

103. Katherine Driessen, "City Subpoenas Pastors' Sermons in Equal Rights Ordinance Case," *Houston Chronicle*, October 14, 2014, http://www .chron.com/news/politics/houston/article/City-subpoenas-pastors-sermons-in-equal-rights-5822403.php, accessed September 10, 2015.

104. Sarah Pulliam Bailey, "Houston Subpoenas Pastors' Sermons in Gay Rights Ordinance Case," *Washington Post*, October 14, 2014, https:// www.washingtonpost.com/national/religion/houston-subpoenas-pas tors-sermons-in-gay-rights-ordinance-case/2014/10/15/9b848ff0-549d-11e4-b86d-184ac281388d_story.html, accessed September 9, 2015.

105. The ACLU of Texas issued a statement supporting the withdrawal of the subpoenas demanding the sermons: "We are glad that Mayor Parker has acknowledged that subpoenas issued in ongoing litigation were too broad and that there is no need to intrude on matters of faith to have equal rights in Houston." But this statement was only issued after the request had been withdrawn. http://www.aclutx.org/2014/10/17/city-of-houston-subpoenas-of-sermons-statement-from-the-aclu-of-texas/, accessed September 13, 2015.

106. Putnam and Campbell, *American Grace: How Religion Divides and Unites Us*, 526–27.

107. Stephanie Strom, "Y.M.C.A. Is Downsizing to a Single Letter," *New York Times*, July 11, 2010, http://www.nytimes.com/2010/07/12/us/12Y .html?_r=0, accessed September 10, 2015.

108. Todd Leopold, "Boy Scouts Change Policy on Gay Leaders," CNN, July 28, 2015, http://www.cnn.com/2015/07/27/us/boy-scouts-gay-leaders-feat/, accessed September 9, 2015.

109. Erik Eckholm, "Mormon Church Will Keep Ties With Boy Scouts Despite Objecting to Gay Leaders," *New York Times*, August 26, 2015, http://www.nytimes.com/2015/08/27/us/mormon-church-to-keep-ties-with-boy-scouts-despite-concern-over-gay-leaders.html?_r=0, accessed December 21, 2015.

110. Steve Rothaus, "Billy Graham Group Moving Money to BB&T, Sponsor of Miami Beach Gay Pride Fundraiser," *Miami Herald*, June 9, 2015, http://www.miamiherald.com/news/local/community/gay-south-flor ida/article23615095.html#storylink=cpy, accessed September 13, 2015.

111. Noreen O'Leary, "Honey Maid Didn't Test Its 'This Is Wholesome' Campaign Before It Launched. 'It's Reality' Says Brand Leader," *Adweek*, September 24, 2014, http://www.adweek.com/news/advertising-branding/honey-maiddidnt-test-its-wholesome-campaign-it-launched-160256, accessed June 28, 2015.

112. Michelle Castillo, "Cheerios Just Made One of the Sweetest Ads Ever with a Gay Family," *Adweek*, October 6, 2014, http://www.adweek.com/news/advertising-branding/ad-day-cheeriosjust-made-one-sweetest-ads-ever-gay-family-160587, accessed June 28, 2015.

113. Curtis M. Wong, "Tylenol's #HowWeFamily Campaign Uses LGBT Couples to Portray the Changing Face of the Family," *Huffington Post*, June 11, 2015, http://www.huffingtonpost.com/2015/06/12/tylenol-how-we-familycommercial-n_7561768.html, accessed June 28, 2015.

114. Mae Anderson, "Chevrolet Ads Feature Gay Couples During Olympics Broadcast," Associated Press, February 8, 2014, http://www.huffingtonpost.com/2014/02/08/chevrolet-adsgay_n_4749547.html, accessed June 28, 2015.

INDEX

Page numbers in *italics* refer to figures.

abortion, 60, 66–67, 96, 170
acceptance (stage of grief), 212–23
Affordable Care Act, 68, 95–96
African American Protestants, 17, 39, 51, *51*, 60, 87, 127, 133, 135, 202–3
African Americans, *see* black men; racial injustice; segregation; slavery
African Methodist Episcopal Church, 135
AIDS/HIV, 119, 182
"Ain't Gonna Let Nobody Turn Me Around" (song), 183
Alabama, 58, 62, 126, 129, 168, 175, 209
#AllLivesMatter, 151, 190
American Baptist Churches USA, 135, 166, 168, 176–77
American Civil Liberties Union (ACLU), 32, 120, 296*n*
American Family Association, 115
American Grace (Putnam and Campbell), 53–54, 132
"America the Beautiful" (song), 45–46
Anderson, Leith, 136
anger, *see* denial and anger
Arkansas, 32, 58, 126, 168
Asian Americans, 27, 41, 61
atheists, atheism, 225–27
Atlanta, Ga., 185
    First Baptist Church in, 165
    Oakhurst Baptist Church in, 185–89, 192, 285*n*-86*n*
Atlantic, The, 162, 174–75
Auburn Theological Seminary, 30

Balmer, Randall, 170–71, 281*n*-82*n*
Baltimore, Md., 152, 159
    Freddie Gray killing in, 150, 153, 155, 157, 179

protests in, 42–43, 150, 151, 153, 157, 160, 183, 188
    segregation in, 156–57, 158
Baptists, 10, 31, 32, 74, 89, 90, 94, 118, 135, 166, 167–71, 175, 176–77, 185–89, 202, 210, 211, 218, 221, 223
    see also American Baptist Churches USA; Southern Baptist Convention
Baptists in America: A History (Kidd and Hankins), 168
bargaining (stage of grief), 206–12
Barnett, Ross, 169
Bass, Diana Butler, 215
Bauer, Gary, 91, 139
Baylor University, 173, 202
Bayne, Katie, 46
Beck, Glenn, 233
Bell, L. Nelson, 36
Bellamy, Francis, 211, 292*n*
Berger, Peter, 228–29
Better Off Without 'Em (Thompson), 224
Bible, 9, 16, 33, 84, 136, 137, 141, 163, 164
    as historical document, 31–32, 77
    Southern legislation on, 208–12
Billy Graham Evangelistic Association (BGEA), 205, 238–39
Birmingham, Ala., 62, 188
birth rates, 42, 48, 255*n*
Black, Hugo, 62, 63
#BlackLivesMatter movement, 148, 151, 179, 183, 188, 220–21
"Black Manifesto" (Forman), 19
black men:
    mass incarceration of, 150, 276*n*
    police killings of, 42–43, 147–50, 155, 157, 158, 173, 179, 183–84

Blake, Eugene Carson, 178
Bob Jones University, 171, 282n
Boggs, Lilburn, 70
Bowling Alone (Putnam), 163
Boy Scouts, 2, 38, 238
Bozell, Brent, 103
Bradley Foundation, 208
Brandon, Miss., 59
Briggs, John, 118–19
Brookings Institution, 96
Brown, Michael, 147, 155, 179, 183
Brown, Scott, 95
Brown at 60, 162
Brown v. Board of Education, 162, 168, 178
Bruni, Frank, 181
Bryan, William Jennings, 9, 32–33
Bryant, Anita, 117–18
Bryant, Phil, 210
Buddhists, Buddhism, 27, 127, 231, 234
Bush, George H. W., 107
Bush, George W., 41, 76, 92, 93, 100, 120, 216,
        224, 225, 238, 247
Butler, Judith, 190

California, 90, 112, 118–19, 121–22
California, University of, Los Angeles, Civil
        Rights Project at, 161–62
California Supreme Court, 122
Campbell, David, 53–54, 132, 236
Campolo, Tony, 137
"Can Catholicism Win America?" (Fey), 63
"Can Protestantism Win America?"
        (Morrison), 63, 200, 246
Carter, Jimmy, 89, 90, 171, 282n
Catholic Relief Services, 14
Catholics, Catholicism, 9, 27, 37, 38, 41, 43,
        47n, 49, 50, 60, 61–65, 71, 94, 100, 127,
        128, 143, 144, 145, 170, 178, 199, 200,
        216, 219, 231, 234, 246
    abortion opposed by, 66–67
    cultural change as viewed by, 87
    evangelicals' alliances with, 65–69
    gay rights supported by, 133
    Hispanic, 69, 87
    mainline Protestant alliances with, 65
    multiculturalism and, 28–29, 30
    prejudice against, 61–66, 79
    public funding of parochial schools sought
        by, 66
    religious liberty as redefined by, 144–45
    same-sex marriage opposed by, 138–41
    as threat to WCA, 12–13, 18, 63, 199

    WCA alliances with, 77
    white, declining numbers of, 69
Catholic University of America, 68
CBS, gays and, 114–15
Census Bureau, U.S., 41, 42, 101
Changing Our Mind (Gushee), 137, 223
Chicago, University of, 42
Christ Cathedral (Orange County, Calif.), 28–29
Christian Broadcasting Network, 120
"Christian Century," 34, 37, 213–14, 228, 237
Christian Century (magazine), 13, 34, 36, 63,
        73, 170, 175–76, 177, 199, 246
Christian Century and the Rise of the Protestant
        Mainline, The (Coffman), 63, 199
Christian Coalition of America, 82–84, 83, 85,
        91, 92, 238, 247
Christian Community Development
        Association, 150
Christianity Today, 36, 116, 137, 170, 246
Christian Right, 1, 60, 72, 82, 89–90, 91, 92,
        132, 171, 205, 210, 222, 230–31
    critics of, 224
    gay rights opposed by, 116–22, 133, 139
    goals of, 22–23
    Republican Party and, 26, 77, 94, 235
    Tea Party and, 96–98
Christians, declining numbers of, 1–2, 39,
        42, 47–56, 51, 53, 54, 55–56, 56, 69, 77,
        105–10, 106, 107, 200, 201–2, 217–18,
        255n, 256n
Christian Scientists, 73
churches:
    as "bridge organizations," 193, 236
    desegregation of, 179–95, 236, 287n
    social segregation and, 163–66, 194
    steeples of, 6–7, 39
civic integration, WCA and, 227–28
civil rights, 88, 171, 177–78
Civil Rights Act (1964), 79, 88, 96, 178
civil rights movement, 14, 168–69, 203, 219
Civil Rights Project (UCLA), 161–62
Civil War, U.S., 2, 3, 31, 79, 88, 166, 168, 176,
        203, 206, 211, 232, 280n
Cizik, Richard, 135–36, 137
Clinton, Bill, 65, 105, 107, 108, 116, 119, 120
Clinton, Hillary, 81
Coca-Cola, 45–47, 239
Coffman, Elesha, 63, 199
Cold War, 117, 211
Coleman, Sheila Schuller, 28
Collegiate Church of New York, 180–84, 189,
        192

Colson, Charles, 66, 139
Columbia University, 19
communists, communism, 36, 211
Confederacy, Confederates, 166, 167, 168, 209, 221
Congress, U.S., 14, 71, 104, 120, 211
Constitution, U.S., 36, 64, 69, 84, 122, 144, 171
consumer culture, evangelicals and, 23–24, 26
Coors Foundation, 208
Corinthians, 112–13
Council for National Policy, 94
Covey, Stephen, 75–76
Coyle, James, 62, 63
Criswell, W. A., 167, 169, 170
Cross, John H., Jr., 188
Crystal Cathedral (Garden Grove), 7, 21–23, 22, 24, 25, 30, 247
    Catholic Church's purchase of, 28–29, 30
cultural change, 1–2, 200, 237–39
    generation gap and, 229–30
    public opinion on, 85–87, 86

Dallas, Tex., First Baptist Church in, 167
Darrow, Clarence, 32–33
Darwinism, 32
Davis, Jefferson, 209
Dawkins, Richard, 225, 226, 295n
Dayton, Tenn., 33, 246
Dear White Christians (Harvey), 159
Decatur, Ga., 185
Declaration of Independence, 84
Deep South, 58, 59, 187–88
Defense of Marriage Act, 120
DeKalb County, Ga., 185, 188
Democratic Party, Democrats, 33, 62, 64, 67, 80, 88, 89, 90–91, 103, 104, 108, 109, 151, 208, 209, 225, 234–35
demographic change, 1, 41–42, 179, 195, 236
denial and anger (stages of grief), 198–206
Dennett, Daniel, 225, 295n
depression and acceptance (stages of grief), 212–23
desegregation, 160, 161
    of churches, 179–95, 236, 287n
Dionne, E. J., 227
Disciples of Christ, 134–35
Dobson, James, 91, 92–93, 138, 139, 262n
"Don't Ask, Don't Tell" policy, 119
Douglas, William O., 63
Douthat, Ross, 145, 228, 289n
Dragt, Gordon R., 181–82
Dreher, Rod, 216

Drew University, 182
D'Souza, Dinesh, 277n
Duke University, National Congregations Study of, 165–66
Dulles, John Foster, 34
Dutch West India Company, 180

Eastern Orthodox Churches, 16, 17, 18, 37, 47n, 60, 127, 216
Eastern University, 137
Edgar, Bob, 207, 208
Edsall, Thomas B., 103
Eighmy, John Lee, 170
Eighteenth Amendment, 10, 11, 13
Eisenhower, Dwight D., 15–16, 34, 117
elections, U.S.:
    of 1960, 64–65
    of 1980, 90
    of 1992, 107–8
    of 2000, 92
    of 2004, 120–21
    of 2008, 80, 94
    of 2012, 70, 75, 76–77, 82, 98–101
    of 2014, 104
    of 2016, 107
    midterm demographics of, 104–5
Emerson, Michael, 189, 192, 193
Episcopal Church, Episcopalians, 6, 10, 134, 166, 178, 200
Equality Index, 157–58
Equal Rights Amendment, 14, 89, 171
Evangelical Climate Initiative (2006), 221
Evangelical Declaration against Torture (2007), 221
Evangelical Lutheran Church in America, 134
Evangelicals and Catholics Together coalition, 65–66, 68, 140, 142
evangelical white Protestants, 3
    abortion opposed by, 60, 67, 170–71
    in bargaining at end of WCA, 208–12
    Catholic alliances with, 65–69
    consumer culture and, 23–24, 26
    declining numbers of, 47, 51–56, 53, 54, 56, 77, 201–2, 217–18, 256n
    in denial and anger at end of WCA, 201–6
    in depression and acceptance at end of WCA, 216–23
    gay rights and, 26, 115–22, 134, 223
    mainline Protestants' feuds with, 40, 52, 60, 68
    media as used by, 21, 23, 24–25, 36
    in mid-twentieth century, 36

evangelical white Protestants (*cont.*)
  Mormons attacked by, 72–73
  1980s expansion of, 7, 21–29, 35, 37, 77
  nostalgia and, 222–23, 230
  Obama presidency and, 81
  political influence of, *see* Christian Right
  racial injustice and, 167–75
  religious liberty as redefined by, 144–45
  same-sex marriage opposed by, 43, 60, 93,
    113–14, 115–16, *130,* 138–39, 223
  same-sex marriage support among, 135–38,
    141–42, 223
  social and cultural influence of, 22–23,
    203–4, 230
  social segregation among, 159
  South as base of, 31
  tent-broadening efforts of, 37
  women's rights and, 26
  young adult, 136, 141–42
Evans, Michael, 209

Facebook, 137, 148, 149, 238, 277*n*
"Failure and the Hope, The" (Percy), 219–20
Fairbanks, Charles, 12
Faith and Freedom Coalition, 93
faith-based organizations, 2, 14
Falwell, Jerry, 67, 72, 90, 91, 93, 118, 119, 120,
    170, 204, 206, 247
Family Research Council, 91, 210, 292*n*
Faulkner, William, 191
FBI, 117
Federal Council of Churches (FCC), 17, 34–35,
    36, 177, 246
  see also National Council of Churches
Federal District Court, San Francisco, 122
Ferguson, Mo., 153, 158, 174, 277*n*
  Michael Brown killing in, 147, 153, 155,
    179, 183
  protests in, 42–43, 148, 160, 183, 188
Fey, Harold, 63
Findlay, James F., Jr., 16
First Amendment, 144
First Baptist Church (Atlanta), 165
First Baptist Church (Dallas), 167
First Things, 66
Fischer, Bryan, 115
Fischer, Claude, 272*n*
Florida, 93, 94, 117, 129, 172, 174, 179, 189
Focus on the Family, 91, 92, 93, 138, 262*n*
ForAmerica, 104
Ford Foundation, 207
Forman, James, 19
Fox News, 95, 98, 99

"Freedom from Want" (Rockwell), 84
FreedomWorks, 95
Frey, William, 229, 230
"Friendly Athiest" blog, 226
Fuller Theological Seminary, 36
Fullmer, Gene, 72
Fundamentalists, 31, 32, 33–34
Future of Faith in American Politics, The
    (Gushee), 222

Gallup poll, 73–74, 123, *123,* 262*n*
Gandy, Phillip, 210, 292*n*
Garden Grove, Calif., 7, 21, *22,* 25–26, 28, 247
Garden Grove Community Church, *see* Crystal
    Cathedral
Garner, Eric, 147–48, 155, 173, 179, 183
Gates, Robert, 238
gay, lesbian, bisexual, and transgender people,
    114–15
  as church members and clergy, 187
  discrimination against, 116–19
gay rights, 3, 42, 106, 232–33
  evangelicals' opposition to, 26, 115–22,
    133, 223
  legalization of, 66
  marriage and, *see* same-sex marriage
  military and, 119
  Millennials' support of, 236–37
  public support for, 146
  religious liberty and, 144–46
General Social Survey, 42, 53, 123
George H. W. Bush Presidential Library, 74
Georgia Baptist Convention, 186, 187
Gifford Lectures, 214
Gilgoff, Dan, 142
Gilliard, Dominique, 150
Gingrich, Newt, 106
Girl Scouts, 2
GLAAD, 114–15
Glazer, Nathan, 44
"Glory" (song), 183
Goldwater, Barry, 36, 88, 89, 281*n*
Gore, Al, 92
"Gospel and Racial Reconciliation, The" (2015
    summit), 174–75
Graham, Billy, 24, 36, 39, 148, 149, 203–6, 246
Graham, Franklin, 148–50, 204–6, 238–39,
    277*n*
Grammy Awards, 111–16
Gray, Freddie, 150, 155, 157, 179
Great Depression, 13, 105
Green, Emma, 174–75
Green, John, 92

grief, stages of, 197–98
and end of WCA, 198–223
Gross, Terry, 135–36
Gushee, David, 137, 217, 221–23, 232

Haggard, Ted, 93
Hankins, Barry, 168
Harmon, Francis Stuart, 18
Harris, Sam, 225, 226, 295n
Harvey, Jennifer, 159, 189–90, 191
Hauerwas, Stanley, 213–14, 215, 217, 247
Hawaii State Supreme Court, 119
Helms, Jesse, 119
Henry, Carl F. H., 36
Henry-Crowe, Susan, 14–15
Herberg, Will, 39, 246
Hindus, Hinduism, 59, 127, 231, 234
Hines, Thomas, 24
Hispanic Americans, 41, 47n, 100–101, 102,
165, 193, 202, 203
Catholic, 69, 87, 127
evangelical, 202–3
Protestant, 51, 51, 127, 202–3
Republican Party as viewed by, 102
and 2012 election, 100–101
Hitchens, Christopher, 225
HIV/AIDS, 119, 182
Hollinger, David A., 33, 35
Hoover, Herbert, 62
Hoover, J. Edgar, 36
Hour of Power (broadcasts), 21, 24, 26
House of Representatives, U.S., 71, 104, 120
Houston, Tex., 64, 193, 233, 296n
Houston's Equal Rights Ordinance (HERO),
233
Hout, Michael, 255n, 272n
Huckabee, Mike, 74, 75, 94, 233
Hudgins, Douglas, 169–70, 281n
Hughey, Matthew, 82
Humphrey, Hubert, 64
Huntsman, Jon, 75

"I Love America" rallies, 90
immigrants, immigration, 27, 42, 48, 61
immigration reform, 106
"In Christ There Is No East or West" (hymn),
163, 164
Indianola, Miss., 162–63
Ingraham, Chris, 158
Institute on Religion and Democracy (IRD),
200–201, 207–8
Interchurch Center (New York City), 7, 15–21,
15, 30, 34, 37, 177, 234, 246, 247

interfaith organizations, 20–21, 30, 60, 234–35
International Center for Possibility Thinking,
28
Iowa, 58, 75, 121, 129
Irish immigrants, 61
Islam, Muslims, 27, 30, 71, 72, 80, 81, 127, 205,
206, 224, 226–27, 231, 234, 277n
critics of, 226–27
Islamic Society of North America, 14
Israel, 206
"It's Beautiful" ad, 45–47, 239

Jackson, Miss., 59, 163, 169
Jacobson, Matthew Frye, 61
Jehovah's Witnesses, 73
Jesus Christ, 24, 32, 36, 71, 74, 114, 136, 142,
177, 187, 200
Jews, Judaism, 21, 30, 38, 41, 43, 49, 127, 133,
143, 175, 178, 231, 234, 254n, 272n
Jim Crow laws, 149, 160, 224
Johnson, Lyndon B., 72
Johnson, Philip, 25
Jones, Ashton, 165
Jones, Bob, Jr., 67

Kagan, Elena, 41
Kelly, Megyn, 99
Kennedy, Anthony, 122
Kennedy, D. James, 93, 247
Kennedy, Edward, 95
Kennedy, John F., 64–65, 74, 79, 246
Kentucky, 58, 96, 126
Kidd, Thomas, 168
King, Martin Luther, Jr., 2, 84, 164–65, 170,
175–76, 178, 195, 205, 215, 246, 279n–
80n
King, Rodney, 152
Kinnaman, David, 131–32
Kirn, Walter, 75–76
Knippers, Diane, 200–201
Kübler-Ross, Elisabeth, 198, 199, 206, 212–13
Ku Klux Klan, 62–63, 169, 188
Kuo, David, 216

Lambert, Mary, 111, 113, 115
Land, Richard, 142, 172–73, 202, 203, 217
Latifah, Queen, 111, 112
Laws, Curtis Lee, 32
Lean, Nathan, 226–27
"Letter from Birmingham Jail" (King), 2,
175–76, 195, 246
Lewis, Jacqui, 182–84
Lewis, Ryan, 111, 115

LGBT rights, *see* gay rights
liberalism, 67, 200, 220, 230
libertarians, 96–97, 98
life expectancy, 158
Limbaugh, Rush, 104
Lincoln, Abraham, 2, 232
Lohre, Kathryn, 20, 179
Los Angeles, Calif., 24, 117, 152
Louisiana, 193, 210
Louisville, Ky., 156
Luce, Henry R., 34–35
Luter, Fred, 172–73
Lutherans, 134, 166
Lyon, Caleb, 71

McCain, John, 92, 94, 100
McClaren, Brian, 137
Macklemore, 111–12, 113, 115
Madonna, 112, 113
"Manhattan Declaration, The" (2009
    manifesto), 138–39, 140, 141–42
March on Washington (1963), 178
marriage, 236
    same-sex, *see* same-sex marriage
Marriage Under Fire (Dobson), 138, 139
Mars Hill Church (Seattle), 113
Martin, Trayvon, 172, 174, 179
Marty, Martin, 33–34, 72
Maryland, University of, Baltimore County,
    224
Massachusetts, 74, 95, 121, 122, 124, 126, 209
Mather, Mark, 41
Mayo, Paul, 21
media, evangelicals' use of, 21, 23, 24–25, 36
megachurches, 21–22, 26–27, 39
Mehta, Hermant, 226
Mencken, H. L., 33
Mercer University, McAfee School of Theology
    at, 217
Merritt, Jonathan, 141–42
Methodist Episcopal Church, 8–10
Methodists, 9, 10, 11, 12, 13–15, 16, 31, 35, 62,
    135, 166, 185, 213, 216
    African American, 135
    1907 statement of moral principles of, 12
    political influence of, 11, 13–14, 16
    same-sex marriage debate among, 135
    temperance movement and, 9–10, 11–12,
        13–14
    see also United Methodist Church
Meyer, Stephenie, 76
Miami, Fla., 117, 118
Michaelius, Jonas, 180

Michigan, 72, 99, 209
Middle Collegiate Church (New York City),
    180–84, 189, 192
Midwest, 3, 31, 39, 58, 91, 126, 166
Miles, Tom, 209–10
military, U.S.:
    gay rights and, 119
    integration of, 161
Millennials, 102, 108, 132–33, 142, 236–37
    gay rights supported by, 102, 124, 129,
        131–33, 136, 141–42, 223, 236–37
    religious affiliation of, 48
    religious disaffiliation among, 1–2, 132–33
    Republican Party as viewed by, 102
    2012 election and, 108–9, *109*
    white evangelical, 136
Minnesota, 58, 99, 118
Mississippi, 32, 58, 59, 126, 129, 150, 162–63,
    168, 169, 191
    Bible bills in, 208–12
Mississippi State University, 82
Missouri, 70, 147
Mitt (documentary), 99
Modernists, 31–32, 33–34
Mohler, Albert, 52
Montgomery bus boycott, 177
"Moonies" (Unification Church), 73
Moore, Russell, 142–44, 145, 146, 173–75, 190,
    195, 217–19, 220–21, 223, 233
Moral Majority (concept), 37, 206, 217, 228, 237
Moral Majority (political organization), 37, 67,
    90, 91, 92, 93, 206, 228, 247
Mormonism Unmasked (SBC book), 73
Mormon Puzzle, The (SBC video), 73
Mormons, Mormonism, 37, 71–73, 75–76, 94,
    127, 238
    polygamy and, 69–70, 71, 73–74, 75
    same-sex marriage opposed by, 127,
        128–31, *130*
    WCA and, 70–77
Morrison, Charles Clayton, 63, 199–200
Mott, John R., 35
Muhammad, Prophet, 72
multiculturalism, 28–29, 30, 236

NASA, 19
National Association of Evangelicals (NAE),
    36, 43, 93, 135, 246
National Cathedral (Washington, D.C.), 165
National Conference on Religion and Race
    (1963), 177–78
National Congregations Study (Duke
    University), 165–66

National Council of Churches (NCC), 17–18, 19, 20, 29, 34, 36, 93, 177–79, 200–201, 204, 207–8, 246, 247, 283*n*
National Opinion Research Center, 42
National Prayer Breakfast, 81
Neeleman, David, 75
Neff, David, 137–38
neo-atheists, 226–27
Neuhaus, Richard John, 66
New Amsterdam, 5, 180
New England, 31, 58, 121, 125
New Evangelical Partnership for The Common Good, 137
New Hampshire, 99, 121, 129
New Hope Covenant Church (Oakland), 150
New Jersey, 63, 121, 128
"New Monasticism" movement, 216–17
New York, N.Y., 159, 176
   Billy Graham crusade in, 204, 205, 246
   Eric Garner killing in, 147–48, 153, 155, 173, 179, 183
   Interchurch Center in, 7, 15–21, *15*, 30, 34, 37, 177, 234, 246, 247
   Middle Collegiate Church in, 180–84, 189, 192
   1964 World's Fair in, 17
   One World Trade Center in, 5–6
   protests in, 42–43, 160, 183
   Riverside Church in, *15*, 19, 246
   World Trade Center in, 5, 120
New York State, 62, 70, 71, 121, 128, 138, 139, 179, 195
   same-sex marriage legalized in, 138–39
New York Supreme Court, 19
Nichol, John, 186
Niebuhr, H. Richard, 164, 213, 279*n*
Niebuhr, Reinhold, 64, 164, 213
Niose, David, 225–26
Nixon, Richard, 65, 66, 72, 88–89, 254*n*
nongovernmental organizations, 2, 14, 20–21
North, 31, 166, 176, 225
Northeast, 3, 125, 128, 166
nostalgia:
   evangelicals and, 222–23, 230
   Tea Party and, 97
   in White Christian Strategy, 82–88, 91–92, 222–23
Nussbaum, Perry, 169

Oakhurst Baptist Church (Atlanta), 185–89, 192, 285*n*-86*n*
Oakhurst Presbyterian Church, 188, 285*n*
Oakland, Calif., 150

Obama, Barack, 67, 76, 97, 100, 101, 116, 121, 149, 152, 172, 204, 206, 238, 247
   attacks on, 80–82, 96, 206
   second inaugural address of, 84–85
   in 2012 election, 99, 108, 109, *109*
   WCA and, 40–41, 80–82, 94–96
Obama administration, 68, 95, 206, 238
Obergefell v. Hodges, 122
O'Connell, Edward, 67
Ohio, 99, 100, 129
O'Malley, Martin, 151
On Death and Dying (Kübler-Ross), 198, 199, 206, 212–13
One World Trade Center, 5–6
Onward (Moore), 142–44, 217–19, 220–21
"Open Your Heart to Me" (song), 112
Orange County, Calif., 21, 24, 25–26, 27
Orthodox Christians, *see* Eastern Orthodox Churches
Osteen, Joel, 24

Parker, Annise, 233, 296*n*
Parks, Rosa, 168
Pasadena, Calif., 36
Paul, Rand, 96
Paul, Ron, 96
Paul, Saint, 16
Peale, Norman Vincent, 23, 39, 64
Pearl Harbor, Japanese attack on, 84
Pennsylvania, 82, 84, 99
People for the American Way, 120
Percy, Walker, 218–20, 221
Perkins, Tony, 91, 93, 210, 292*n*
Perry, Samuel L., 287*n*
Pew, J. Howard, 36
Pew Charitable Trusts, 36
Pew Religious Landscape Survey, 202
Pew Research Center, 123, *123*, 202, 225
Pittsburgh, Pa., 98
Pledge of Allegiance, 211
pluralism, 91, 260*n*
police, killing of black men by, 42–43, 147–50, 155, 157, 158, 173, 179, 183–84
politics, polarization of, 235
Pollard, Ramsey, 65
polygamy, 69–70, 71, 73–74, 75
Pontifical Council for Culture, 219
Population Reference Bureau, 41
Populists, 33
Possibility Thinker's Creed, 26
Presbyterian Church (USA), Presbyterians, 19–20, 30, 31, 32, 34, 36, 134, 166, 185, 200, 280*n*

Priebus, Reince, 101, 104
Prison Fellowship, 66
Prohibition, 10, 11, 14
Proposition 8, 122
"prosperity gospel," 24
Protestant, Catholic, Jew (Herberg), 39, 246
Protestant Reformation, 66
Protestants:
    African American, 17, 39, 51, *51*, 60, 87,
        127, 133, 135, 202–3
    Fundamentalist-Modernist split in, 31–34
    Hispanic, 51, *51*, 127
    white, *see* White Christian America
    white evangelical, *see* evangelical white
        Protestants
Protestants, white mainline, 3
    in bargaining at end of WCA, 207–8
    Catholic alliances with, 65
    Catholicism as threat to, 12–13, 18, 63, 199
    civil rights and, 177–78
    conflicting visions of future of, 215
    declining numbers of, 1, 47, 51–54, *53*, *54*,
        56, 77, 200, 255*n*
    in denial and anger at end of WCA, 199–201
    in depression and acceptance at end of
        WCA, 213–15
    ecumenism of, 7, 15–21, 37, 60
    evangelicals' feuds with, 40, 52, 60, 68
    gay rights supported by, 133, 134–35
    interfaith organizations and, 20–21, 30, 60
    liberal social agenda of, 230
    Methodists' political activity decried by,
        13–14
    New England and Midwestern base of, 31
    optimism of, 7, 8–15, 34
    racial injustice and, 175–79
    same-sex marriage supported by, 43
    slavery and, 176
    social and cultural influence of, 6–7, 16–17,
        22, 34–35, 60, 77, 203–4
    social segregation among, 159
protests, against police violence, 42–43, 148,
    150, 151, 160, 183, 188
public opinion:
    on cultural change, 85–87, *86*
    on gay rights, 146
    on same-sex marriage, 120–34, *123*, *125*,
        139, 271*n*-72*n*
Public Religion Research Institute (PRRI), 42,
    80, 85–87, 96, 97, 102, 108, 123, *123*, 124,
    132, 135, 137, 145–46, 153, 157, 159,
    215, 225
    American Values Atlas of, 124, 135

public schools:
    persistence of segregation in, 161–62
    religion in, 66
Pulitzer, Joseph, 6
Putnam, Robert, 53–54, 132, 163, 236

Quakers, 62

race relations:
    resurgence of tension in, 42–43, 236
    unions and, 161
racial injustice, 147–95
    reconciliation and, 172, 175, 189–92, 195, 236
    repentance and, 180, 190, 191, 236
    WCA and, 167–95
    white vs. black perceptions of, 152–55, *153*,
        154, 160
racism, 79–80
Rankin County, Miss., 59
Raphael, Charles, 18
Rauschenbusch, Walter, 176–77, 283*n*
Reagan, Ronald, 22, 90–91, 95, 122
reconciliation, 172, 175, 189–92, 195, 236
Reconstruction, 31, 203
Reed, Ralph, 91, 93
religion:
    positive actions inspired by, 226
    worldview and, 229
religious affiliation:
    age differences in, 48, *49*, 54–55, *54*, 56,
        132–33
    decline in, 1–2, 42, 47, 48–49, 50–51, 55,
        129, 202, 225
    demographics of, 47–49, *47*, *48*
    historical change in, 49–54, *50*, *51*, *53*
    perception of racial injustice and, 154–55, *154*
    same-sex marriage and, 126–31, *130*
religious liberty, anti-gay redefinition of,
    144–45
Religious Roundtable, 90
repentance, 180, 190, 191, 236
Republican Party, Republicans, 46, 65, 70, 72,
    74, 75, 80, 92, 93, 95, 96, 98, 99, 100,
    101–10, 118, 119–20, 121, 131, 209, 210,
    233, 234, 281*n*
    abortion issue and, 67
    Christian Right and, 26, 77, 94, 235
    Hispanics' views of, 102
    Millennials and, 102
    same-sex marriage and, 131
    Southern Strategy of, 88–90, 91
    2012 "autopsy report" of, 101–4, 235
    in 2014 midterm elections, 104

Resident Aliens (Hauerwas and Willimon), 213–14, 247
Reynolds v. United States, 69–70
Riverside Church (New York City), *15*, 19, 246
Robertson, Pat, 82, 91, 120, 204, 247
Rockefeller family, 16, 17
Rockwell, Norman, 38–39, 84
Roland Park, Md., 158
Rolling Stone, 93, 115
Roman Catholic Church, *see* Catholics, Catholicism
Roman Catholic Diocese of Orange County, 28, 30, 247
Rome, Italy, 219
Romney, George, 72, 74
Romney, Mitt, 70, 74–75, 76, 88, 94, 102
   in 2012 election, 98–101, 104, 107, 108–10, *109*
Roosevelt, Theodore, 12
Roozen, David, 287*n*-88*n*
Rove, Karl, 99
Rubin, Jennifer, 103
Ryken, Philip, 68

Sacred Canopy, The (Berger), 228–29
"Sacred Conversation on Race" initiative (2008), 191
St. Andrews, University of, 214
St. Louis, Mo., 147
St. Paul's Chapel (New York City), 6
Salon, 226
Salt Lake City, Utah, 73
Samaritan's Purse, 205
"Same Love" (song), 111–14, 115
same-sex marriage:
   African American Protestants' opposition to, 127
   Catholic opposition to, 68
   courts and, 43, 68, 119, 121–22, 134, 145
   evangelicals' opposition to, 43, 60, 68, 93, 113–14, 115–16, 127, *130*, 138–39, 223
   evangelicals' support for, 135–38, 141–42, 223
   Hispanic Protestants' opposition to, 127
   mainline Protestant support of, 43, 134–35
   Millennials' support of, 102, 124, 129, 131–33, 136, 223
   Mormons' opposition to, 127, 128–31, *130*
   religious affiliation and, 126–31, *130*
   religious liberty and, 144–45
   Republicans and, 131
   rise in public support for, 120–34, *123*, *125*, 139, 271*n*-72*n*
   Tea Party opposition to, 96
   2014 Grammy Awards celebration of, 111–16

"Same-Sex Marriage and the Future" (Moore), 142
San Francisco, Calif., 122
Santelli, Rick, 95
Santorum, Rick, 94
Saturday Evening Post, 84
Save Our Children, 117–18
SBC Life, 73
Scaife foundation, 208
Schaller, Thomas, 224–25
Schlafly, Phyllis, 67
school prayer, 66
Schuller, Robert, 21, 23–29
Schuller, Robert, Jr., 27, 28
Schwarzenegger, Arnold, 121
Schwerner, Micky, 220
Scopes, John, 32, 33
Scopes "Monkey Trial" (1925), 32–33, 203, 246
Secular Coalition for America, 225, 294*n*-95*n*
secularism, secular organizations, 60, 67, 91, 199, 225–26
segregation, 3
   persistence of, 155–58, 161–62
   social, *see* social segregation
   see also desegregation
"segregation academies," 162
Selma, Ala., 85, 183, 195
Selma (film), 183
Senate, U.S., 95, 96, 104, 107, 120
Seneca Falls, N.Y., 85
separation of church and state, 64, 233
September 11, 2001, terrorist attacks, 6, 120, 224
Seventh-Day Adventists, 14, 30
Sexual Revolution, 118, 142
Shattuck, Gardiner H., Jr., 178
Shiloh Metropolitan Baptist Church (Jacksonville), 174, 189
Sierra Club, 207
16th Street Baptist Church (Birmingham), 188
slavery, 3, 79, 166, 171, 176
Smith, Al, 62, 64
Smith, Joseph, 70, 71
Smith Richardson family charities, 208
"social gospel," 176–77
social segregation:
   churches and, 163–66, 194
   persistence of, 156, 159
   WCA and, 159–60, *160*
Social Sources of Denominationalism, The (Niebuhr), 164, 279*n*
Sockman, Ralph, 16
Sojourners, 137

Sojourner's (magazine), 150
South, 39, 58, 59, 62, 88, 89, 91, 118, 156, 166,
    167, 168–71, 175, 176, 187–88, 203, 220,
    224, 225, 232
  Bible bills in, 208–12
  as evangelical Protestant base, 31
  gay rights opposed in, 126, 129
  segregation in, 3, 162–63
South African Council of Churches, 214
South Carolina, 89, 126, 167, 169
Southeastern Baptist Theological Seminary, 55
Southern Baptist Convention (SBC), 43, 52,
    65, 66, 67, 73, 89, 94, 116, 118, 141, 145,
    165, 185, 187, 190, 195, 218, 247
  declining numbers of, 55–56, 56
  desegregation of congregations in, 174
  Ethics and Religious Liberty Commission
    of, 142, 172, 202, 217
  Hispanics in, 202–3
  1995 resolution on racial injustice of,
    171–72, 221
  racial injustice and, 167–75, 219–21
  slavery and, 166, 168, 171
Southern Baptist Theological Seminary, 52,
    173
Southern Strategy, 88–90, 91
Stark, Rodney, 72
Starnes, Todd, 115–16
State of Black America report (Urban League),
    157–58
Stephenson, Edwin, 62
Stephenson, Ruth, 62
Stetzer, Ed, 55–56, 116
Stevens, John Paul, 41
Stonewall riots, 85
Super Bowl, 45–46, 114, 239
Supreme Court, U.S., 11, 41, 62, 63, 71, 89,
    136, 167, 168, 247, 254n
  abortion legalized by, 66
  residential segregation laws struck down
    by, 156
  Reynolds decision of, 69–70
  same-sex marriage legalized by, 43, 68, 122,
    134, 145–46
  school prayer decision of, 66
Syria, 158, 277n

Tassler, Nina, 115
Tea Party, 42, 87, 94–99, 103, 104, 106, 247
temperance movement, 9–10, 11–12, 13–14
Tempting Faith (Kuo), 216
Tennessee, 32, 33, 58, 126, 210
"Terms of Our Surrender, The" (Douthat), 145

Texas, 94, 129, 213, 233
Thanksgiving, 82–84, *83*, 92
"theology of self-esteem," 23, 24
"This Is Wholesome" ad, 239
Thompson, Chuck, 224
Thompson, Eliza Jane, 9–10
Thurmond, Strom, 89, 167
Thy Kingdom Come (Balmer), 281n-82n
Till, Emmett, 168
Time, 34–35, 150, 170, 214
Tooley, Mark, 201
Trinity Church (New York City), 6
Truman, Harry S., 34, 177, 204
Turning Hurts into Halos (Schuller), 27
Twenty-first Amendment, 14
Twitter, 46, 148, 151, 225
"Two Shall Become One Flesh, The"
    (Evangelicals and Catholics Together
    coalition), 68, 140–41, 142

UnChristian (Kinnaman), 131–32
Unification Church (the "Moonies"), 73
Union Theological Seminary, 36, 164, 204
Unitarians, 234, 260n
United Church of Christ, 80, 114, 134, 191
United Methodist Building (Washington,
    D.C.), 7, 8–15, *8*, 16, 21, 178, 234, 246,
    247
United Methodist Church, 14, 29–30, 135, 200,
    201, 246
United Nations, 34, 36
Urban League, 157–58
Utah, 71, 72, 73, 128, 129

"Values Voters" campaign (2004), 93, 120, 247
Vietnam War, 14, 89
Vines, Matthew, 137
Voting Rights Act (1965), 88

Waite, Morrison, 69
Wallis, Jim, 137
Warren, Rick, 151
Washington, D.C., 9, 80, 121, 122, 294n
  National Cathedral in, 165
  United Methodist Building in, 7, 8–15, *8*,
    16, 21, 178, 234, 246, 247
Washington, George, 2, 6, 249n
WASPs (White Anglo-Saxon Protestants),
    30–31, 82
Watergate scandal, 66, 89
Wells, Larry, 210–11
West, Allen, 46
Western Michigan University, 164, 279n-80n

West Virginia, 58, 98, 126
Weyrich, Paul, 171, 281*n*-82*n*
Wheaton College, 68
"When Will They Ever Learn?" (Mohler), 52
Whistling Past Dixie (Schaller), 224–25
White Christian America (WCA):
  ad hoc alliances of, 60–61, 65–69, 77
  anti-Catholic prejudice in, 61–66, 79
  anxiety of, 40, 41–42, 49
  civic integration and, 227–28
  critics of, 223–27, 231, 232–33
  declining numbers of, 1, 39, 47–56, *51, 53,*
    54, 55–56, *56,* 77, 105–10, *106, 107,* 200,
    201–2, 217–18, 255*n,* 256*n*
  defense strategies of, 58–59
  demographic change and, 194–95
  free speech rights of, 233
  future of, 43–44, 227–39
  geographical bases of, 31, 57–59, *57*
  history of, 31–38
  mainline-evangelical feuds in, 40, 52, 60, 68
  Mormons and, 70–77
  Obama presidency and, 40–41, 80–82,
    94–96
  obituary of, 1–3
  political influence of, *see* White Christian
    Strategy
  racial injustice and, 167–79
  racial reconciliation and, 172, 175, 189–92,
    195, 236
  seen as outdated relic, 224
  segregation and, 3
  slavery and, 3, 166
  social and cultural influence of, 2, 38–40,
    227–28
  social segregation and, 159–60, *160*
  use of term, 30–31, 38
  see also evangelical white Protestants; Prot-
    estants, white mainline
White Christian America (WCA), end of:
  celebrators of, 223–27

new social engagement required by, 231–34
sense of loss and dislocation in, 228–31
stages of grief and, 198–223
White Christian Strategy, 79–110, 121, 235
  changing voter demographics and, 104–10,
    106, 107
  cultural change and, 85–87, *86*
  nostalgia and, 82–88, 91–92
  Reagan and, 90–91
  Southern Strategy as forerunner of, 88–90
  Tea Party as continuation of, 97
  2012 election and, 98–101
  see also Christian Right
white flight, 162, 188
White House Office of Faith-Based and
  Community Initiatives, 216
Whiteness of a Different Color (Jacobson), 61
Wilcrest Baptist Church (Houston), 193
Willard, Frances, 10
William III, King of England, 180
Willimon, William, 247
Wilson, Clarence True, 10, 11
Wilson, Darren, 147
women, ordination of, 187
Women's Christian Temperance Union, 10
women's rights, evangelicals and, 26
Woodruff, Wilford, 71
workplace, 116, 160–61
World's Fair (1964), 17
World Trade Center, 5, 120
worldview, religion and, 229
World War I, 157
World War II, 38, 63, 72, 84, 105
Worldwide Church of God, 73
Wright, Jeremiah, 80

YMCA (Young Men's Christian Association),
  2, 35, 38, 237–38
Young, Brigham, 70–71

Zimmerman, George, 172, 179